CH 7/19

JONATHAN CRANSTON is a veterinary surgeon based in the Cotswolds who has treated over a hundred different species across five continents, including giant pandas in China and all variety of wildlife in South Africa.

www.jonathancranston.com

Jonathan Cranston

# The Travelling Vet

ALLEN&UNWIN

First published in Great Britain in 2018 by Allen & Unwin
This paperback edition published in Great Britain in 2019
by Allen & Unwin

Text and photographs (unless otherwise noted) copyright
© Jonathan Cranston, 2018
Illustrations copyright © Sarah Jones, www.sjonesfineart.com

The moral right of Jonathan Cranston to be identified as the author
of this work has been asserted by him in accordance with the
Copyright, Designs and Patents Act of 1988.

All rights reserved. No part of this book may be reproduced or
transmitted in any form or by any means, electronic or mechanical,
including photocopying, recording or by any information storage and
retrieval system, without prior permission in writing from the publisher.
Every effort has been made to trace or contact all copyright holders. The
publishers will be pleased to make good any omissions or rectify any
mistakes brought to their attention at the earliest opportunity.

Allen & Unwin
c/o Atlantic Books
Ormond House
26–27 Boswell Street
London WC1N 3JZ

Phone: 020 7269 1610
Fax: 020 7430 0916
Email: UK@allenandunwin.com
Web: www.allenandunwin.com/uk

A CIP catalogue record for this book is available from the British Library.

Internal design by e-type

Paperback ISBN: 978 1 76063 320 2
E-Book ISBN: 978 1 76063 397 4

Printed and bound in Great Britain by
Clays Ltd, Elcograf S.p.A.

10 9 8 7 6 5 4 3 2 1

*To Max:*

*true friend, companion and teacher*

| LONDON BOROUGH OF SUTTON LIBRARY SERVICE | |
|---|---|
| 30119 028 562 04 1 | |
| **Askews & Holts** | Jul-2019 |
| 636.089 | |
| | |

# CONTENTS

# PREFACE

Animalia. The term incorporates an untold number of eclectic animals that inhabit our planet. Estimates of individual species range from 2 to 50 million. For many people, they are simply the sporadic cohabitants of their world – the spider in their bathtub, the bird in their garden, the rat in their garage, or the monkey that plagues their market stalls. For me, though, they have always been an intrinsic part of my life. I trace my conscious desire to become a vet back to the age of six.

Fast-forward thirty-one years, and now eleven years after qualifying, my passion is if anything stronger than ever. Annual trips to Africa, and the wide range of species I have been fortunate enough to work with, have only served to broaden my horizons as to how spectacular the animal world is. Where my three-year-old self was once content with chickens, lambs and dogs, his thirty-seven-year-old counterpart now deals with giant pandas, giraffes, leopards and rhinos – wonders at them, in exactly the same way. For just as an addict craves his next fix, or a surfer longs for that next big swell, my drug of choice has always been the animal kingdom. I have always been captivated by meeting and treating any new species, so to experience them at first hand in their natural environment, learn about them, and make a positive contribution to their propagation, has been a constant privilege.

What started off as the dream of a six-year-old boy to become a vet has now evolved into a desire to travel the world and encounter the spectacular diversity of animals that share this planet with us. From the prehistoric Nile crocodile to the endearing sugar glider or enigmatic snow leopard, the more variety I encounter, the more it fuels my passion.

Yet this evolution in my interests has not detracted or diminished from the joy and thrill I still get every day as a rural veterinary surgeon in the UK. Eleven years in, and the job is still as fascinating and challenging as ever. No two days have ever, or will ever, be the same, and when I go into work in the morning I never know what the day will hold, or which animals or situations I will encounter. Dog, cow, rabbit, horse, chicken, pig, alpaca or tortoise; death, life, tragedy, triumph, hilarity, solemnity, routine or bizarre – mine is a completely unique profession. Every day is an emotional rollercoaster, where the minute you think you've cracked a problem, something always pops up to remind you of how much you still have to learn.

There's a common misconception that being a vet is all about working with animals. The truth is that it is as much, if not more, about working with people. The best vets in the world will only have a reputation to match their skill if they can communicate well with people. But it's only when this is fully comprehended and embraced that the beauty and power of the human–animal bond can be fully appreciated, as wonderful and unique a relationship as any individual human being on the planet. The Inuit who relies on their pack of sled dogs for transport, or the Nepalese farmer on their ox to plough; the Mongol who requires their eagle to hunt; the farmer who knows every one of their cattle by name; the zookeeper who daily feeds and cares for their collection; the widow whose only companion is her dog; the child with their first pet: whatever the circumstance, veterinary intervention invariably involves understanding and managing this relationship, sharing the joy or sadness, gently correcting or encouraging, asserting or humbling yourself, as the situation demands.

For me, this relationship adds great joy and interest to my job, and although I have witnessed some incomprehensible acts of animal cruelty, the vast majority of my experiences have highlighted the very best in human nature, and I have felt as privileged to meet the people who care for this vast array of animals as I have to treat the animals themselves.

In this book I hope to convey my passion for a job that I love, to give the reader a sense of how weird and wonderful a veterinary surgeon's life can be, as I recount true stories that range from the inspiring to the absurd. Some names and locations have been changed to protect identities. Some of these animals were pets, some livestock, and others were from zoological collections or encounters in the wild. I have also set out to share some facts about these wonderful animals and to highlight the plight that too many of them are facing. There is no chronology to the stories I tell, or the species I mention, nor do the episodes I recount present these animals in alphabetical order or by geographical distribution. The beauty of life – of all life – is its rich and random tapestry, and one of the fascinations and great joys in mine is never knowing what will happen from one day to the next, or who will come through the door.

So do, please, step into my consultation room, for this book is your own consulting list, and each chapter introduces you to a new client: a different animal with its own individual and unique problem.

Jonathan Cranston
March 2018

# INTRODUCTION

*'The greatness of a nation can be judged by the way its animals are treated.'*

Mahatma Gandhi

There can't be many vets who have stitched up a dinosaur. It's not the sort of ambition that would be taken too seriously by a careers teacher. Mine had even advised me against applying to vet school. He felt the course was too competitive and that I might struggle. After thirteen rejections, he might have had a point, but the ambitions of a six-year-old boy were not easily going to be thwarted. And now eleven years after qualifying, not only am I a vet, I have worked in nearly every facet of my profession, across four continents, treated some of the most iconic animals on the planet, and offered veterinary expertize on a multi-million-dollar Hollywood blockbuster. As I reflect on it now, I still can't quite believe it myself.

'There are a million ways to live a life, my friend.'

Bill's words echoed around my head as I gazed out of the car window. It was a mild, wet November morning, the kind that feels more autumnal than bracing winter. Bill, a family friend, and I were winding our way through the pretty villages and valleys of the Brecon Beacons, the low-lying mist creating an eerie wonderland around me. I thought of the people who lived behind the doors we were passing, the farmers who worked the beautiful landscape, the shopkeepers, postmen and bus drivers. They were all living their lives, and within each came a multitude of choices, a host of possibilities, stories, tragedies, wonders, that had led them to the life they were living on this wet November day in 2015.

As for me, my life could easily have turned out so differently. I had wanted to be a veterinary surgeon since the age of six. I mean, I *really* wanted to be one, and nothing could, would or ever did change my mind. Although the clues were probably there when I was even younger. Early pictures show me with chickens or lambs under my arms as soon as I could walk, or falling asleep next to my grandparents' golden retriever. You could say it was what I was born to do, and I never wavered. Yet on Sunday, 13 August 2000, I found myself preparing to study Pathology and Microbiology at Bristol University, having been rejected at least twice from every veterinary school in the UK – and once from University College Dublin. The previous year I had turned down an offer to study Zoology at Liverpool, and taken an enforced gap year in the hope that I would later get a veterinary place somewhere, anywhere. Where would I have been in 2017 if I had chosen a different path? A different city, different friends, a different career – my mind reels at the millions of permutations. And even within the veterinary career I eventually pursued, it could all have been so different.

I remember sitting round the table one evening, with a handful of friends, in my parents' living room, towards the end of my eighteenth birthday party, as the music started to fade and lights to come on, supping on the remnants of my beer. Empty bottles, half-drunk glasses, red wine stains on the table-cloth, half-finished plates of finger food and bowls of crisps and nibbles surrounded us. My parents were busily tidying up around us as we continued chatting, entering that marvellous reflective mood, preparing for the next big step of our lives, and contemplating our hopes, ambitions and dreams. Where would we each be in ten years' time? For me, the answer was quite simple. I would be in the middle of a field at six o'clock on a damp, foggy spring morning, with the sun just starting to break through. My green Land Rover Defender would be parked with its back door open, and two dogs would be running around the field. I would be a few yards away, lying prostrate at the rear end of a recumbent cow, assisting her to calve while the farmer stood over me, offering words of encouragement. All I had ever dreamed of being was a regular, country, mixed-animal vet.

And ten years on, at the age of twenty-eight, that is exactly what I was – though for 'Land Rover Defender' read 'Isuzu Trooper', and make it one dog – Max – rather than two. I had found myself being offered my dream first job out of vet school, working down in rural North Devon. But then fast-forward another seven years: I had worked on four continents, and had treated over a hundred different species – everything from the routine dog, cat, cow, horse, pig and sheep, to the more exotic snow leopard, elephant, rhino and giant panda (to name just a few). And now I am consulting on film sets, including advising on extinct dinosaurs. It certainly was an unusual and unplanned career path that I had taken. But that's life: things happen, opportunities present themselves, and choices get made.

So wise old Bill was right, there truly were a million different ways to live a life, not just as one of the 7.2 billion people on the planet, but as one of 20,000 veterinary surgeons in the UK. Now ten years qualified, though, the rose-tinted spectacles had long been removed. I had battled through the application process, competing for a place on the intense and protracted course, eventually qualifying, relocating far from my support network, starting out in a job where the days were long, lonely, demanding and stressful, as well as being both physically and emotionally draining. And despite the pride I have always taken in those privileged initials MRCVS (Member of the Royal College of Veterinary Surgeons), it is sobering to reflect that my chosen profession consistently ranks among those with the highest suicide rates, and which, contrary to public perception, generally pays its employees less than the minimum wage when calculated against hours worked. I had a plethora of scars and injuries having been bitten, kicked, scratched, stabbed, cut, stitched up, stood on, squashed, stamped and charged. I'd been covered in every possible bodily fluid: blood, pus, urine, diarrhoea, amniotic fluid, rumen contents, anal gland secretion, decomposing tissue. I had accidentally jumped into a silage pit, driven into two ditches, fallen into a pond and had even been hospitalized with a two-litre pleural effusion after contracting bovine tuberculosis and then having to undergo a year of treatment.

So if I had my time over again, would I change anything? Would I go back and tell my six-year-old self that the game wasn't worth the candle, and to set his ambitions on something else? Gazing out the window on that November morning, and reflecting on what I had done over those ten long years, the people I had met, both colleagues and clients, the animals I had worked with and treated, the experiences I had gained, and the places I had visited, I knew without a moment's hesitation that the answer was an emphatic 'No'.

In fact, it now struck me, I was only just getting started.

# 1

# ARMADILLO

'*Armadillos make affectionate pets, if you need affection that much.*'

Will Cuppy

The animal kingdom is vast and incredible. I personally think it's impossible not to watch nature documentaries without being filled with awe and amazement at the array of different types of animals with whom we are privileged to share this planet.

It is a common assumption that, as a veterinary surgeon, I will automatically know about, and be able to treat, any animal that finds itself on the consulting-room table, or behind a stable door. So it often comes as a shock and disappointment to others when I confess that I don't immediately know, say, the common ailments of *Triturus cristatus* (the great crested newt). That said, I still love that assumption, and I have tried my hardest to fulfil it, but sadly, even over a five-year degree course, there are several species that just don't make the cut. The maned wolf, the giant panda, the snow leopard and the pufferfish, to name but a few.

So how does the veterinary curriculum work? Well, there are six main species we study in great depth at veterinary school, and they are all mammals: the horse, the cow, the pig, the sheep, the dog and the cat. A few weeks' teaching is given over to 'small furries' (rabbits, hamsters, guinea pigs and the like), with a couple of days allocated to reptiles and birds, and maybe the odd hour to amphibians and fish. This may seem woefully inadequate, particularly if you are a lover of one of the many species that doesn't feature prominently in the veterinary curriculum, but let's think about this for a minute and do some maths. At a conservative estimate there are 8.7 million different species on the planet, so in a typical degree course we would have precisely 18 seconds per species to learn everything there is to know about their anatomy, physiology, behaviour, therapeutic pharmacology, medicine, surgery, dentistry, endocrinology, oncology, and reproduction. Oh, and that would be studying twenty-four hours a day, seven days a week, for the entire five years, and with no time to prepare for the biggest part of the job, namely the three Cs of human interactions: care, compassion and counselling. So unfortunately, but I hope understandably, there have to be one or two omissions.

For some, gaining an MRCVS qualification is just the first step in a lifetime's journey of studying these more exotic animals, and for the rest of us these specialists become the go-to-gurus. For those in general practice there are several skills we have to learn to mitigate this knowledge deficit. Firstly there is the principle of animal comparisons. For example, to most intents and purposes, you can treat a rabbit as if it were a miniature horse: they are both hindgut fermenters, doing most of their digestion in their caecum, and have hypsodont teeth meaning that their teeth continually grow. Alpacas and llamas are both ruminants like cattle and sheep, and ferrets share many characteristics with dogs. Then there is the idea of lateral thinking. If I am treating a dog with diarrhoea, who has involuntarily redecorated his owner's sitting room, I am faced with a series of questions. What has caused it? What body systems are involved? What are the animal's immediate and long-term requirements? Is it dehydrated, requiring fluid therapy? Does it have a bacterial infection, necessitating antibiotics? Does it have a parasitic burden and require deworming? Or has he just gorged on the family's Sunday lunch? If I can solve the puzzle for a dog, why can't I solve it for a meerkat, reindeer or wallaby? And, of course, if all this fails, there's always Google . . .

Yes, I confess that in my ten-year career I may have referred to Google one or two or several hundred times. I remember the first occasion. I was a couple of months qualified and my boss, Simon, asked me to do a home visit to inject a client's private collection of green tree pythons. Several of them had gone down with a respiratory infection caused by mycoplasma and, given the value of such a collection, Simon had suggested treating them all. I was game and eager for anything. Besides, it was my boss's request, so I did not feel I could refuse. The only problem as I saw it was that I had never even heard of a green tree python before, let alone known anything about them. And as the 'newbie', I would need to gain the client's trust as well as fending off a barrage of questions over the hour it would take to treat every one of his ten snakes. I did not want to appear a complete ignoramus, of course, and so knowing that attack is often the best form of defence, I thought if I could drop in a few useful facts early on, I might just gain his confidence and respect enough to transform this daunting visit into a more manageable and interesting experience. So to Google I went. I discovered that *Morelia viridis* is found in or near the rainforests of New Guinea, the Indonesian Islands and Cape York Peninsula in Australia, thus requiring a hot humid environment. As its name suggests, it lives mainly in trees, and feeds on small rodents and reptiles. They require a certain expertize to keep in captivity, but if conditions are right then they'll thrive. Armed with this knowledge and feeling a bit more confident, I set off.

The owner greeted me suspiciously, clearly assessing my credentials as a veterinary surgeon to the herpetoculture community. I smiled warmly as I introduced myself, trying to disguise my trepidation. I was going to have to work hard to earn his trust, I could see, but I wasn't surprised: a collection as extensive as his was worth several thousand pounds, so this was a serious hobby. He took me through the house to a purpose-built reptile house in the garden. It was an impressive set-up. The heat and humidity hit me instantly and I felt like I had just stepped into the Amazon Jungle. There were half a dozen vivariums in a 'U' shape against the three walls, all just a mass of green arboreal foliage camouflaging the occupants within. Next to each glass tank was a digital monitor displaying its temperature and humidity. I'd only ever seen such a professional set-up in a public reptile house before, and I realized this guy definitely knew what he was doing. I felt way out of my depth, but tried to compose myself. After all, all I had to do was inject them, and I had done that before. But this was someone from whom I could learn a lot, so I had to pitch it just right. He had to feel confident and comfortable with my professional ability, and able to relax enough to start talking about his passion, rather than being guarded and protective over his babies. I knew I had a limited window of opportunity to make an impression, and this was it.

'The humidity really hits you when you walk in,' I began, 'we could actually be in a New Guinea or Indonesian rainforest.' It wasn't my best one-liner ever. It was a start, but I needed to follow it up.

'They can be pretty difficult to keep in captivity, replicating their natural arboreal environment, but I have to say this is the most impressive set-up I've ever seen.' The compliment paid off; I could sense him start to relax. Maybe one more would do it. I wandered over to one of the vivariums and peered in. The camouflage was incredible and it took me a moment to see the occupant. Saddling one of the branches in three coiled loops, her head resting in the middle, was a stunning lime-green snake with flecks of white across the whole of its body. I'd seen pictures on Google, but in real life they were truly incredible.

'I love the unique way they saddle a branch . . . They really are so beautiful.'

That final comment was enough to engage him, and his guard went down. It was as though I knew the secret handshake to the club. I was in! As we proceeded with the task in hand, he started telling me about each snake individually as I injected it. The job was quickly done, but with plenty more serpentine knowledge to share, and a captive audience to share it with, he offered me a cup of tea. Fascinated with what I was learning and relieved that the visit had gone so well, I happily accepted. An hour later I finally left and the warmth with which he bid me farewell felt like a lifelong friendship. As I walked down the drive to my car, I allowed myself a smile of satisfaction. From then on, whenever he rang the practice he always requested 'the veterinary herpetologist'.

Google paid off on that occasion, but I'd had a leisurely half-hour lunchbreak in which to do my research and preparation. The next occasion it came to my rescue I was not afforded the same luxury.

I've often been asked what the strangest animal I've ever seen in the consulting room would be. There are a few contenders – a Cuban tree frog, a sugar glider and a skunk would probably make the top ten – but there was one consultation that will forever stick in my memory: the armadillo.

It had been a regular Friday in March. I'd started my day at 6 a.m. on the middle of Exmoor reading a tuberculin test for a herd of sixty cattle. It was a cold morning and we were working in a small dilapidated farmyard miles from any other human habitation. The single intradermal comparative cervical tuberculin test (SICCT) is the standard TB test for cattle. Dating back a hundred years, it involves injecting the skin on the animal's neck with avian and bovine tuberculin, then returning seventy-two hours later to inspect the injection site: if the bovine site has swollen more than the avian site it is highly suggestive that the animal has the disease. This was my return visit, and I knew that the second part of the test was not going to be completely straightforward; it never was with the Exmoor cattle. This was an eclectic herd of year-old animals, which had been bought from market as calves and barely known any human interaction from the day they stepped off the lorry. All were hybrid breeds, mostly from a Friesian–Hereford mother crossed with a beef bull such as a Charolais, Aberdeen Angus, Belgian Blue, Simmental or Limousin. It was the Limousin crosses that always caused the problem. Wild and liable to spook, it only required one of those in a herd to set the rest of the group off. I had spent enough time chasing flighty cattle across fields, marshes and moorland to know that it was always them leading the charge. While my Tuesday visit had gone smoothly enough, the cattle were now primed, wary of the cattle crush – and of us.

As we let them out of the barn into the orchard, the leading steer told me all I needed to know. Head up, eyes alert, snorting as he trotted at a fast pace, he was wild and agitated. In that moment I knew this job, which could have been over and done with in half an hour, was going to take several hours, and require Land Rovers and quad bikes to chase the herd over the moor. Sure enough, the steer immediately led the charge, jumping and circling in the orchard, looking for any weakness in the gate, wall or hedge. After a few moments he found it, and headed for the 4-foot gate separating the orchard from the field and moorland beyond. Making a poor attempt to jump the gate, his back quarters landed on the gate, buckling it, but his momentum was enough to snap the bail twine that had fixed it to a rotten post, and so the gate was dragged 10 metres into the field before the steer finally cast it off as he bolted for freedom. With no gate, and the field and freedom so inviting, the rest of the herd didn't waste any time following their comrade, leaving the four of us standing in the orchard looking on at the mud being churned up behind them as they disappeared into the distance.

Three hours later I left the farm, job done, but now running late for my next visits.

The rest of the day's visits passed less energetically: a calf with pneumonia, a few calf castrations, a lame horse with a foot abscess, and then a lambing which turned out to be a caesarean. Since my days as a vet student I had always loved lambing time, and to bring two little lambs into the world and then see them up and suckling Mum, their tails wiggling like crazy, was such a happy sight. Sadly, though, the economics didn't always stack up, and so we were rarely called upon to assist, but this was a good ewe, and the farmer had been keen, so I had done the caesarean and the two healthy lambs justified the decision.

With my large-animal visits completed, I raced back to the surgery to start my small-animal consultations at 4 p.m. It had been a non-stop day, shovelling a sandwich into my mouth as I drove between my visits, and only giving my dog Max a quick few minutes' exercise down a farm track. When he gave me a look of disgust I promised him a walk on the beach after work as I coaxed him back into the car.

Arriving back at the surgery, I saw it was 3.45 p.m.: only enough time to clean myself up, grab a cup of tea and my white coat, and then head into my consulting room. I looked over my list of bookings to mentally prepare myself and see if there were any ongoing cases that needed more attention. I was fully booked with consultations running from 4 to 6.30 p.m. Each slot was ten minutes long, so there were fifteen in all. An initial glance told me it was a fairly routine list: half a dozen vaccinations, a lame dog, a couple of vomiting/diarrhoea cases, a cat with a skin irritation . . . I scanned the list more closely, to see if there were any clients or animals I recognized. The 5.10 p.m. appointment caught my attention; according to the computer, the client was called Mr Smith and the patient was called 'Armadillo'.

I'd come across some odd animal names in my time. In fact, we used to play a game at vet school, in our final year on rotations, to see if we could identify the animal breed by the name its owner had given it. 'Charlie' was going to be a black Labrador, destined for the orthopaedics department; 'Rocky' would be a boxer coming in to see the cardiologist; and 'Tiny' was obviously a dachshund, off to see the neurologist. 'Armadillo' was a new one for me. I clicked on his client card to bring it up. Was this a dog or a cat, I thought? Looking through the information, it seemed that this was a new client with a new animal, and all it told me was that Mr Smith was bringing Armadillo in to be microchipped.

The first half of my session proceeded uneventfully. As I bid farewell to my 5 p.m. appointment, I couldn't help but notice the client who sat clutching a blue cat box; he had taken up the corner seat, which happened to be in my direct line of sight. He must have been in his mid-fifties, with a mat of white hair and a slightly unkempt bushy beard. He was hunched over the cat box, holding it in a most circumspect manner. I'd seen all sorts of human behaviours within the waiting room – the relaxed, the nervous, the reluctant, the protective – but there was something slightly different about this gentleman which I couldn't quite put my finger on.

When I looked at my computer screen, my 5.10 p.m. appointment – 'Armadillo Smith' – was highlighted to signal their arrival, and of course Mr Smith turned out to be the gentleman in the corner. Standing up with his precious cargo, I was surprised at how heavy it seemed. My logical assumption was that the cat box contained a cat, so if it was coming in to be microchipped, the chances were it was a kitten, and should therefore weigh less than a kilo. The way he appeared to be struggling with the box, however, suggested it was closer to ten times that weight. Maybe it was a rescue cat that he had adopted? But that didn't compute, because in that case it should have already been chipped. I sketched a scenario in my mind: a morbidly obese cat that was being killed with kindness as the sole companion of an elderly person who had just died. Maybe this was the son who had now taken charge of the cat, and his first duty was to get it chipped. No wonder he was precious about it: the last link to a deceased parent. If my assumption was correct, this might well be more complicated than a simple microchip. I played through the range of health issues that may have inadvertently gone by the board: fleas, worms, skin issues, dental disease, diabetes, arthritis were all possibilities.

I shut the door behind Mr Smith and introduced myself. He placed the cat box carefully on my consulting-room table, then shook my hand with a broad smile.

'Pleasure to meet you.'

I turned my attention to my computer as he started unclipping the lid.

'I bet you don't see many of these!' he said.

His words took several seconds to register. Microchipping a cat was a simple job, whatever other health issues it might have, so I'd allowed my mind to wander. If I got through this consultation quickly, I might just have time to make a cup of tea before my next one. Still focused on my computer screen, I turned to fully engage with my new patient.

It was not an obese cat. The creature before me had a rodent-like face with large pointed ears, a domed body and a long, segmented tail. Covering his body was what looked like a medieval knight's suit of armour, and his head seemed protected by a perfectly fitted moulded helmet. The shock and surprise on my face must have been evident, to judge by the wry smile that appeared on Mr Smith's face, but I tried to cover it up and maintain my professional composure.

'You're right, I certainly don't see many armadillos here. This is definitely a first for me!' I said with an attempted casual air.

'This is a nine-banded armadillo,' he replied. 'They originate in the Americas, but I'm sure a clever chap like yourself knew that.'

This had completely thrown me, and I had to face up to the fact that I didn't really know the first thing about armadillos. With no useful facts up my sleeve, I couldn't even engage in an educated conversation about the creature before me. Worse than that, as I surveyed it, the realization dawned that this mammal was completed covered in about a centimetre of armoured plating. Where on earth was I going to shove a very large needle to implant the microchip? I racked my brain, thinking of how best to handle this.

'So how does someone end up with a pet armadillo in North Devon?' I asked, to buy me some more time.

'*I've never seen a Jaguar, Nor yet an Armadill- O dilloing in his armour, And I s'pose I never will,*' he recited, before noticing the bemused look on my face and continuing: '*O Best Beloved, no one on the banks of the turbid Amazon has ever called Stickly-Prickly and Slow-Solid anything except Armadillo.'* Clearly my expression didn't change, because he snapped out of his reverie to address me more directly. 'Where's your education, my dear boy? Did you never read Rudyard Kipling's *Just So Stories*?'

'Gosh, yes!' I replied. 'But a long time ago.'

'So you don't remember "The Beginning of the Armadillos"? It was my favourite story as a child and ever since then I always wanted an armadillo as a pet. It's only taken forty-five years!'

'I see,' I said in acknowledgement, but in truth I was utterly baffled.

I was quickly brought back to reality as he started telling me about how he had come to acquire his pet.

'Do you need a Dangerous Wild Animal licence for . . . it?' I asked, realizing as I spoke that I didn't know if it was male or female.

'No,' he said. 'You only need one for the giant armadillo, *Priodontes maximus*. The banded, fairy and screaming armadillos are thankfully all exempt from a DWA licence.'

I'd never heard of fairy or screaming armadillos before. I was learning so much already, while at the same time I was painfully aware of how completely clueless I was as to how I was going to microchip this creature. I knew I had to take the lead before he asked me about it.

'So . . . we're microchipping it today, is that right?'

'Yes, please,' he said. 'But "it" is actually a "he", and his name is Arnie.'

'Of course it is,' I said sharing his wry smile. 'I'll just pop out and get the things I need, I won't be a moment.'

Before he could enquire any further about the procedure I left the consulting room. All the equipment I needed to microchip a dog or a cat was actually just outside the back of the consulting room in our pharmacy, but that wasn't the main reason for excusing myself. I headed straight through the pharmacy into the prep room, and straight to the computer. I clicked on the browser, brought up the Google homepage and typed, 'How do you microchip an armadillo?' The initial results were unhelpful: something about the Armadillo-43/T Embedded Computer Display Module (which my brothers would probably know about, but was no help to me). I tried a different tack. I typed in 'microchipping exotic animals', but that too proved unsuccessful. I was keenly aware of the limited window of time in which I could reasonably absent myself without raising suspicion. *Think, boy, think!*

I tried again: 'microchipping locations in animals'. Wikipedia came up with 'Microchip implant (animal)', but this just mentioned dogs, cats, horses and birds. I scrolled further down the page. 'Microchip identification guidelines WSAVA' (the World Small Animal Veterinary Association): that looked hopeful. I clicked on the link. Scrolling through the article I found a section titled 'Microchip implantation sites for small (companion) animals'. I thought Mr Smith might be pleased to view Arnie as a 'companion animal', but I didn't think the WSAVA would consider an armadillo in quite those terms. I read on, frantically. 'Recommended implantation sites in other species'. Now that seemed more helpful. Unsurprisingly, there was no mention of armadillos. But the implantation site it specified for 'other mammals' was between the shoulder blades, if the adult length was less than 17 cm from spine to shoulder. Arnie was the right size, all right, but that would mean implanting through his armour plating!

I read on. Agricultural animals, elephants, hyrax, loris, alpacas, amphibians, avians, emus, penguins, vultures, fish, chelonians, crocodilians, snakes, lizards . . . and that was where the list ended. It was time for some lateral thinking. Of all the animals on the list, the closest had to be a chelonian –

a turtle, terrapin or tortoise – with a hard shell covering most of its body. I scrolled back up to the 'chelonians' section. *'The left hind limb socket, subcutaneously in small species and intramuscularly in larger species ... then the implantation site is sealed with tissue glue.'* Jackpot! I closed the window on the computer and grabbed some tissue glue from the prep-room cupboard, and then with a renewed air of confidence strolled back through the pharmacy, picking up the micro-chip and microchip reader as I went, before re-entering the consulting room.

'Right, I think I've got all I need. It's quite a simple proced-ure,' I said, with an assured authority that suggested I knew what I was doing. 'The microchip goes into the muscle of the left thigh. I need you to hold Arnie on the table while I first clean the leg and then insert the chip. After that I'll glue the skin closed to prevent the microchip coming out. Armadillos don't have elastic skin,' I added, 'so there'll be a hole left from the needle insertion if we don't glue it closed.'

'Oh, OK, that does sound pretty simple,' he said, a note of relief in his voice. 'I wasn't sure if he would need an anaesthetic or something.' He picked Arnie out of his box and placed him on the table.

Arnie was fairly cooperative at first, but having a twelve-gauge 1.5-inch needle thrust into his upper thigh did not appear to be his idea of a fun day out, so when I tried to expose his limb from beneath the armour plating I soon discovered how immensely powerful his legs were, even with Mr Smith helping to hold him down. It took all my strength and both hands to extend the leg into the position I needed for injecting the micro-chip, but this of course left me with no hands free to prep, inject or glue the wound. A third pair of hands would be required!

'He's a strong little fella,' I commented, as casually as I could. 'I think I might need some assistance.' I left the room in search of a nurse, and found Louise, our head nurse, seeing to one of the in-patients.

'Any chance of a hand microchipping an ... animal?' I asked, deliberately omitting to identify the exact species I was referring to. I had to keep the element of surprise – the look on her face would be priceless, I thought.

'Sure,' she said. 'I'll just be a moment, when I've finished with Poppy.'

'Thanks, I'm in the end consulting room.'

It was only a few moments before Louise knocked on the door and came in. Her reaction was better than I could have wished. When she laid eyes on Arnie her whole body immediately convulsed backwards in fear, shock and disbelief. I think she would have yelled out an expletive, but her professionalism converted it into 'Oh goodness, not quite what I was expecting.'

'Louise,' I said, allowing her a moment to regain her composure. 'This is Mr Smith, and this is Arnie, a nine-banded armadillo. The microchip goes in his left thigh, and so I need some help extending his leg out from underneath his armour. He's pretty strong, so can you hold the leg while Mr Smith holds Arnie's body, so I can prep it and then implant the microchip?'

Stepping over to the table, she tentatively reached out to touch Arnie on the back. As her tactile senses adjusted from the fur she was accustomed to handling, to the unusual texture of leathery shell, and her emotions to the lack of any affectionate response from her human-to-animal contact, she relaxed into the situation and her professionalism took over.

The procedure was quickly and effectively performed, and after assuring myself that the skin glue had set, and scanning the left hind thigh to ensure the chip was in place, Mr Smith returned Arnie to the cat box, thanked us both gratefully and headed out of the door.

As the door closed behind him, Louise caught my eye.

'In ten years, that is definitely the weirdest animal I have ever seen in here,' she said. 'Thanks for the warning!'

'I was a bit surprised too,' I admitted. 'I thought it was going to be a cat.'

'I have one question, though. North Devon isn't exactly overrun with armadillos, so if it goes missing, it's not exactly going to be hard to track down, is it? So why go to all the trouble of getting it microchipped?'

Although I knew there were good reasons, I had to admit Louise had a point.

'Anyway,' she continued. 'How did you know to put the microchip into the back left thigh?'

'You call yourself a veterinary nurse and you didn't know that?' I replied with a grin, taking advantage that I'd closed the window on the computer, hiding the evidence of my Google search. 'I thought it was common knowledge.'

# Armadillos: fast facts

*Dasypus novemcinctus*: The nine-banded armadillo

**Distribution:** North, Central and South America.

**Description:** Nocturnal mammal. Twenty different species.

**Names:** The young are called 'pups'; a group of armadillos is called a 'fez'.

**Life span:** Up to 20 years.

**Habitat:** Armadillos live in burrows, ideally suited to a warm, rainy environment such as rainforest, but they adapt to scrubland, open prairies or grassland. They have a poor amount of fat so can't cope in cold or dry environments, where they lose heat and water easily.

**Diet:** Armadillos are insectivores, feeding chiefly on ants, termites and worms, which they lap up with their sticky tongue.

**Gestation:** 122 days, but implantation is delayed for between 3 and 4 months after mating.

**Weight:** 85 g at birth, reaching 2.5–6.5 kg as adults.

**Growth:** They wean at 3 months, are sexually mature at 1 year, and breed annually.

**Anatomy:** Covering the back, sides, head, tail, and outside surfaces of the legs is an armoured shell composed of bony dermal scutes, covered by non-overlapping, keratinized scales connected by flexible bands of skin.

**Body temperature:** 30–35 °C.

**Interesting fact:** If sufficiently frightened, armadillos can jump 4 feet straight in the air. They can also cross rivers by either floating across them by inflating their intestines, or else by diving to the bottom of the river bed, and running across, because they can hold their breath for up to 6 minutes.

**Predators:** Many, including alligators, raptors and bears, but the cougar is the most common.

**Conservation:** The nine-banded armadillo is classified by the International Union for Conservation of Nature (IUCN) as being of least concern. Its bigger cousin, the giant armadillo, however, which inhabits the grasslands, forest and wetlands of South America, is classified as vulnerable. On the critical role being discovered about this previously mysterious species, as an ecosystem engineer and advocate of biodiversity through the continual production and abandonment of their burrows, see: **www.rzss.org.uk/conservation/our-projects/project-search/ field-work/giant-armadillo-conservation-project.**

# 2

# GIRAFFE

*'Wildlife is something which man cannot construct. Once
it is gone, it is gone forever. Man can rebuild a pyramid,
but he can't rebuild ecology, or a giraffe.'*

Joy Adamson

I stepped out of my lodge into the darkness of a brisk African morning. It was 5.30 a.m. on Saturday 9 August; sunrise wasn't for another hour. The chill of the morning embraced me and with that, the last memory of my cosy handcrafted African bed evaporated. Eight days before I would have been about to wake for work as a vet in the Cotswold town of Cheltenham, but for August my home was the Ngonigoni game reserve just outside Nelspruit in the South African province of Mpumalanga. I was assisting Dr Cobus Raath and his team at Wildlife Vets, a practice specializing in the capture, relocation, clinical treatment, research and education of African wildlife, for a month.

Unlike many African countries, South Africa has established a vibrant game farming industry. Wildlife is not just government property, restricted to the National Parks, but can be traded by private game reserve owners. Integral to this industry is the ability to safely catch, load, transport and release these animals. Every step requires veterinary supervision, so life is busy for Cobus's team at Wildlife Vets.

I headed down for breakfast. It was too early to enjoy the daily spectacle of the farm's giraffes, zebras, wildebeest, blesboks and impalas all grazing on the feeding ground a mere 100 metres from where we dined. The early start was mandatory due to the 8 a.m. rendezvous at a game reserve two hours north of us in Hoedspruit, a town on the Western border of Kruger National Park. There was a buzz around the breakfast table: today we had three adult male giraffes to catch and transport. Such are the perils of giraffe capture that there are only a few companies in the whole of South Africa with the experience, knowledge and expertize to do it. The hypertensive effect of the drugs used in immobilization can pose a life-threatening risk to an animal whose unique anatomical adaptations already require a vastly higher blood pressure than any other mammal. The complications of the respiratory depressive effect of the drugs used are enhanced by the fact that there is a large volume of dead space created by a giraffe's immensely long trachea. As well as this, their height can result in serious injury if allowed to fall to the ground unguided.

As I sipped my coffee the clatter of the convoy could be heard leaving from the workshop at the top of the farm: one HGV lorry, a truck with the giraffe trailer in tow, and Derik's pickup. That was our prompt; we piled into the minibus and set off to join the procession. The logistics of every single capture are astonishing; permits, five vehicles, one helicopter and a fifteen-strong team were today's requirement.

As the crimson glow of the penetrating African sun broke over the horizon, we watched the scenes of everyday life play out before us: the orange and avocado sellers by the side of the road, the men in torn blue overalls walking beside the road on their way to work, the burning sugar cane fields in the first process of harvesting. Then there were the community towns – dusty dirt roads lined with an odd assortment of tin shacks, multiple small square concrete buildings variously advertising a hair salon, funeral parlour, grocery shop or bar. All of these were interspersed with several Coca-Cola adverts, the only link to the Western world I had left behind.

After two hours we pulled into the designated rendezvous point, a small petrol station just a few miles from the reserve we were heading to. There was time for a coffee while we waited for the HGV and truck to catch up. It was then that the call came through: the helicopter pilot had had to divert to help attend to a white rhino, and he would be delayed by several hours. In a cruel, callous world where rhinos are brutally poached for a commodity no different to our fingernails, they must always come first. So, with no helicopter, all we could do was sit and wait. 'Hurry up and wait' is a popular mantra in wildlife circles and this was certainly one of those occasions.

With coffee, and the prospect of a hearty breakfast, our spirits were lifted and conversation started to flow. What were the pros and cons of legalizing the trade of rhino horn? Does vegetarianism extend to one's holiday and when travelling? What animals would play which positions in an African wildlife rugby team? These were just a few of the discussions that arose as we surveyed the comings and goings of the petrol station forecourt: mostly 'bakkies' (pickup-trucks) and retired German tourists, dressed in the obligatory khaki and heavily laden bum bag, arriving in their hired safari van piled high with enough gear to equip a small army.

By 12.30 p.m. the table was awash with the remnants of an eclectic mix of fodder, including hartebeest biltong, cashew nuts dowsed in peri-peri sauce, and Mrs Balls's pickle-flavoured crisps. Bjorn the capture specialist and vet Derik were just finishing their twelfth cigarette, and Bjorn his eighth cup of coffee.

Into this chaotic scene, order was abruptly restored when Bjorn's phone rang. Even before the conversation had finished he was heading for his truck and signalling us to head for the minibus. The helicopter was ten minutes away – giraffe capture was go!

We set off for the short 3-mile drive down a dusty dirt road. Just off the main road were two dilapidated, 5-metre-high wire-meshed gates, held shut by a chain and padlock. The bakkie parked up beside them was the only clue that we had reached our destination. The driver – the reserve's owner – jumped out, unlocked and threw open the gates, and we followed him through. We had barely stepped from the bus when the distant whirr of the propellers reached our ears. We looked skywards at the growing yellow speck of the helicopter as it raced towards us. It circled once, just above the treeline, and then landed amid the plume of dust generated from the downdraught.

The farm was 8,000 hectares of scrubland and rocky mountainous terrain. To the human eye, this desiccated environment appeared hostile, offering little shelter from the scorching African sun, with every plant armed and ready to impale, poison or lacerate. Yet this was home to a vast range of African animals.

Giraffe usually live in relative harmony, sometimes in fairly loose herds led by a single adult male, or else in bachelor herds, while others live as solitary individuals. Generally, fights only break out between males competing for a mate, though on this reserve, males now considerably outnumbered females, and fights were becoming a frequent occurrence, to the extent that an old male bull had been found dead a few weeks previously.

It is a beautiful concept to just let nature be and do, but the reality of conservation is that when man builds a fence to contain animals, however big the area, those animals need to be managed. So some of the young males had to go, and today we were after three such solitary individuals.

Having now seen the size of the terrain we would be dealing with, the requirement of the helicopter was becoming clear. The local contingent, minus Derik, briefly busied themselves unloading the spare fuel canisters and detaching the doors from the helicopter before the now all too familiar habitual ritual played out: reaching for the cigarette packet from the left shirt pocket, tapping out a solitary smoke and embracing it with pursed lips then lighting and relaxing into it, as though they had been working for hours. Derik was oblivious to them all as they leant against the helicopter deep in conversation, smoking away. His exclusive attention was on the large spinal needle in his left hand. It was attached to a 3-ml syringe that was decanting the mixed concoction of Thiofentanal, Etorphine and Hyaluronidase into a small dart in preparation for the job ahead of anaesthetizing the giraffe. Potent opioids Etorphine and Thiofentanyl have become the drugs of choice for in-field anaesthesia of giraffes because they work rapidly, an effect enhanced by the Hyaluronidase, which further accelerates absorption.

The smoking party disbanded as the pilot jumped into the helicopter and started the engine. As Derik walked towards the chopper into the plume of dust created by the downdraught, dart gun over his right shoulder and carrying his dart box in his left hand, the scene resembled something from an American Vietnam movie.

Within moments the helicopter was a mere speck in the skyline heading into the mountainous terrain in search of our first giraffe. Loading up the two trucks, we headed out in the direction of the helicopter, down one of the main arterial tracks that bisected the reserve. The giraffe trailer brought up the rear. Even this stage was technically complicated – we needed to position ourselves so that we could respond and intercept the giraffe within two minutes of it being darted. The mounting tension was palpable, and conversation minimal as we each reflected on the questions playing through our racing minds. Would we be able to catch any of the giraffe? Would we get to them in time once they were darted? Would they survive the anaesthetic? The sight of a solitary white rhino, grazing 20 metres from where we passed it, briefly distracted us.

Then the crackly sound of Derik's voice could be heard from the portable radio as he updated us on their progress. They had spotted a solitary male and were in pursuit, trying to guide him to a safe area for darting. The convoy pulled into a clearing to wait for the follow-up instructions. It shouldn't be long now. The helicopter appeared in the distance coming over the ridge, about a mile away.

This stage, too, was extremely technical. To our untrained eyes and from our vantage point on the ground, the helicopter was just hovering towards us, turning right, then left, now dropping to tree level, now rising high into the clear blue African sky, demonstrating the pilot's full range of skills. Communication between vet and pilot had to be intuitive, anticipating the giraffe's every move, gently and skilfully forcing him in a direction that avoided any potential hazards while also controlling the pace of his escape so as not to overexert him and thus induce a fatal 'capture myopathy'.

Stress, overexertion and dehydration, combined with the increased blood pressure induced by the drugs that are used to immobilize any wild animal, can be a fatal combination, and the risk is multiplied several fold when capturing under the baking African sun. Capture myopathy is invariably fatal. Degeneration of the muscles induced by hyperthermia, together with an excessive build-up of lactic acid, causes an extreme release of potassium from muscle cells which, in acute cases, results in heart failure. If the animal survives the first stage, then muscle rupture invariably means the animal is recumbent and a fatal acidosis leads to destruction of the muscle and kidney cells, kidney failure and death within a few days. So the stakes were high.

It was another ten minutes before Derik's voice came across the radio.

'We have a hit and confirmation the dart has discharged. We're hovering in pursuit, so you have two minutes from now!'

Instinctively Bjorn started his stopwatch, knowing the exact time from impact could prove crucial.

After hours of leisurely inactivity, we were suddenly catapulted into a frenzy of action. The hugely experienced capture team who, moments before, had been laughing and joking without a care in the world, were now focused and determined, but discernibly anxious. No two captures were ever the same and so much could go wrong in the space of seconds. Everyone knew that the slightest mistake could be fatal to the giraffe or result in serious injury to one of the team. I could feel my heart pounding in my chest. I had never felt an adrenaline surge like it.

The bakkie's engine kicked into life without warning and we accelerated off towards the helicopter, trailing a cloud of dusty African soil. Perched on the back, we instinctively knew we had to hold on for dear life. There were no niceties now: engage your brain, anticipate, or one way or another get hurt!

We did one final check to make sure that we had the required drugs – the reversal, Diprenorophine, was the most essential and several of us carried it, so whoever reached the giraffe first could immediately inject it into his jugular vein. Once the animal was down, we only had seconds before the respiratory depressive effects of the Etorphine and Thiofentanyl could prove fatal. There was also an antibiotic injection for the dart wound, anti-inflammatories and a multivitamin injection to help prevent any muscle damage.

The capture team readied themselves with the ropes, blindfolds, earplugs, gaffer tape and the halter. At the first sign of the animal's unsteadiness on his feet, two of the team would jump from the bakkie in pursuit. It was their job to intercept the giraffe, throw a rope around his chest and then use this to stall the giraffe and control his fall. All this was usually done while the giraffe was still in full flight, albeit in a slightly drunken state. The theory was great, but in practice, if the leap and chase from the bakkie was timed too soon, they could be chasing the giraffe for a mile, and if too late, the giraffe might crash to the ground unassisted and severely injure himself. And even if they successfully roped the giraffe's chest, attempting to break a 1,500-kg giraffe travelling at 30 mph through the African bush was obviously fraught with danger, to both man and beast.

We came to a clearing, the helicopter hovering 400 metres ahead of us. It was then that we got our first sighting. Our quarry was still moving at a fair pace, but there were unmistakable signs that the drug was taking effect. Two minutes and ten seconds had passed. Bjorn shouted for his men to disembark, but they hadn't needed telling. By the time the order came through they were already a good 10 metres clear of the bakkie and in full pursuit, having bailed out while we were still travelling at speed across the unforgiving terrain. The rest of the team were throwing themselves from the truck as Bjorn brought it to an abrupt stop. Seconds later, it stood abandoned, the engine still running and its doors open. We were focused on one thing, and one thing only: the swaying animal skyscraper a few hundred metres ahead of us.

With the Thiofentanyl rapidly taking effect, the giraffe was now unaware of the direction he was heading. Stumbling and swaying, he was travelling at reduced speed, but nevertheless he still easily outpaced us as we struggled to negotiate the hostile terrain. With a sudden change in the giraffe's direction, the urgency to catch him escalated: he was now heading straight for the perimeter fence, which, at 6 metres high, and with copious amounts of barbed wire, would spell complete disaster.

Less than 100 metres from the fence, the capture team were now rapidly gaining on the giraffe, but were still too far away to secure him. Bjorn, still sprinting, was frantically gesticulating to his team to try to influence his direction of travel, but the giraffe wasn't able to process the human deterrents and his course persisted unaltered, despite the best attempts of the helicopter pilot overhead. The impending impact with the fence seemed inevitable. I could see the panic on Bjorn's face, helpless despite all his best efforts to control the uncontrollable. In the wildlife-capture business, skill and expertise are vital, but luck counts for a hell of a lot, too.

With 60 metres to go, we suddenly got our luck. As the giraffe broke through the bush onto one of the dusty tracks, he lost his footing, slipped and fell, and within seconds the capture team were on him. Working slickly and efficiently, they had already fixed a blindfold, earplug and head collar on him by the time we arrived only moments later. Three of the team saddled his neck to prevent any attempt by the giraffe to stand. For any animal lying on their side, the neck is the point of leverage to sitting up and then standing; immobilize the neck and the animal is effectively immobilized. By now the effects of the Thiofentanyl had been fully realized and he was unable to struggle against the hive of activity that surrounded him. His breathing and heart rate were stable at this initial stage, but until he had been given the partial reversal, the Diprenorphine, his life was on a knife edge: he could stop breathing at any moment.

The ability to be able to reverse any of the anaesthetic drugs used when dealing with wild animals is crucial. Partial reversal not only stabilizes the cardiorespiratory effects of the drug, but also enables an animal to be moved, manipulated, loaded and transported with minimal stress. A full reversal is essential before release into the natural environment, since a sedated animal wouldn't survive an hour in such a fiercely competitive environment, where rivals or predators would ruthlessly seize any opportunity to take advantage of their weakness.

It was actually Derik who, having jumped from the hovering helicopter as soon as the giraffe had gone down, was first on hand to administer the reversal. With the giraffe secured, stabilized, and with no obvious injuries, I could briefly relax, leaving it to others to variously remove the dart, inject a long-acting antibiotic into the associated wound, administer a multivitamin shot and anti-inflammatory injection, and monitor the animal's heart rate and breathing. Meanwhile, the transport trailer was brought within 20 metres of the patient, the ramp lowered and preparations made for loading him.

With all necessary procedures completed, Bjorn took the lead rope, and the rest of the capture team assigned themselves to the array of other ropes that to my untrained eye resembled a tangled mess on the floor. The three team-members holding down the neck now removed themselves in a single, swift movement and within moments the giraffe was once again towering above us. As the assembly of rope holders took up their positions, the previously confusing tangle of rope unfurled into an organized arrangement, with two ropes looped round the giraffe's neck and passed behind each forelimb. Bjorn had the lead rope and a final rope passed high up behind the back legs. With this set-up, even the most stubborn giraffe could be encouraged to move forward, one step at a time, as the team worked together, first pulling on the left foreleg, then the right, while the two on the rear rope goaded from behind. Fortunately, this giraffe was very amenable, and within minutes he had been safely led onto the trailer, where another flurry of activity secured his position with a series of metal bars that were fed along the two sides to form a wedge. The tailgate was lifted – and there was a palpable release of tension in the air, as backslaps, high-fives and general congratulations were exchanged. We had safely caught one giraffe. Only two more to go, then . . .

As Moses, a member of the capture team, was making his final adjustments to a metal bar on the truck, we were all given a stark reminder of the power of this animal. Objecting to his temporary incarceration, the giraffe lashed out with a hind leg in the direction of the noise and Moses suddenly found himself eyeballing the splintered remains of one of the truck's wooden panels, now complete with a hoof-shaped hole in it. My mind went back to my first trip to Africa. We had come across a male lion on a game drive whose lower jaw no longer occluded with his upper jaw and one canine tooth protruded at an obtuse angle through his cheek. Our guide informed us that a female giraffe had inflicted the injury with a kick in defence of her calf. Giraffes are generally perceived as graceful, elegant and gentle animals, but that day had reminded me of the danger they can pose. In fact, these wooden panels were deliberately designed to minimize injury to the giraffe – better that they splinter than the giraffe's leg – and it wasn't unusual to find several such hoofprints after a relocation exercise. The vital thing to remember was that the safety zone was not the trailer itself, but the giraffe's extended kicking range.

We spent a few moments gathering together the strewn ropes and other remaining debris, and then Derik returned to the helicopter and we climbed into the bakkie we had abandoned barely twenty minutes before. As the chopper once again disappeared into the cerulean African sky, the ground crew reassembled in a clearing that gave us a good vantage point to observe the pilot's progress. While preparations were made for the second giraffe's capture, the air was thick with feverish accounts of the first. Then Derik's voice crackled across on the radio.

'We've located a small bachelor herd, we're attempting to separate them and decide on which one to dart.'

Even this decision was complicated. Judging the size, age and health of a giraffe from 50 metres above it, and when travelling at 30 mph, took immense experience, and though the dart gun would be preloaded with a standard dose, it was up to Derik to decide which animal in the group was most suitable for it.

There were four in the herd, and as they made their bid to escape from the chopper, one giraffe was soon lagging behind the others. He might have seemed the obvious choice for darting, but in fact he was probably ailing and therefore a poor candidate. Attention turned to the remaining three. One was noticeably smaller than the other two; a standard adult dose might be excessive for him, so he too was ruled out. That left two suitable animals so now the choice was based on which would make the easiest shot. Prompted by a mixture of intuition and experience, Derik made his decision, then stuck to the cardinal rule: Never change your mind. He pointed out his quarry to the pilot, who immediately manouevred the aircraft to the optimum position, and moments later Derik pulled the trigger – a perfect shot with the dart embedding into the left gluteal muscles. The giraffe responded by breaking left, away from the rest of the group. The pilot managed to broaden the split and it wasn't long before the other three were distant spots among the acacia trees far behind the helicopter. All this had happened within seconds of the herd being located.

Once again the confirmation of a successful darting was immediately relayed to the ground crew and we set off in the direction of the hovering chopper. Luck seemed to be on our side.

The preliminary gallop with which he took off after being darted slowed into a trot and then an amble as the Thiofentanyl dispersed through his body, reaching the opioid receptors in the brain and central nervous system where its effect was realized. Having initially been immersed in dense bush, his drug-induced disorientation fortuitously brought him to a halt in a clearing, close to one of the primary tracks through the reserve. So a mere two minutes and forty-five seconds after Derik had pulled the trigger on his specialist darting rifle, we had disembarked from the trucks and were just reaching the giraffe. In his confused state he stood his ground as we entered the clearing, trying to focus on what was unfolding around him, and this was the ideal scenario for the capture team, who quickly immobilized him with their ropes and successfully brought him to the ground.

Following the standard protocol, blindfolds, ear plugs, halter and ropes were all applied. This time Bjorn administered the reversal and I found myself monitoring his breathing. Things had gone well, I reflected, as I stood there watching the chest wall gently and rhythmically move up and out, and down and in, about eight times a minute. After the first animal, this one had been a piece of cake. He seemed perfectly stable, and the Diprenorphine would soon partially displace the Thiofentanyl, and the respiratory and cardiovascular effects would ease. 'They can stop breathing at any moment,' Bjorn had warned. *Not this boy, though*, I thought. *He's stable.*

I turned to talk to Bjorn and for a split second was distracted by two of the capture team who were busily trying to untangle one of the ropes that had been caught in a bush as the giraffe had gone down. Turning back to the giraffe, it took me a moment to refocus on his breathing. As I stared at his chest time seemed to slow down – but there was no movement. I must have missed it, I thought. I carried on staring – nothing. On reflection, I suppose it must have been shock and disbelief, but for some bizarre reason the words just wouldn't come out. And as familiar as I was with cardiopulmonary resuscitation in dogs and cats, I was suddenly acutely aware that I was way out of my depth here. Theory was great, but this was no drill – the giraffe had stopped breathing and every second counted.

People do often experience slow motion perception when caught up in extreme and unexpected events. I remember clearly feeling it when I was involved in a car crash at the age of eighteen. Despite braking frantically, the car wasn't going to stop in time and that instant before impact felt like a lifetime. And now here I was once again, experiencing the same phenomenon. I stood up, mute, and turned to Bjorn. The confused alarm on my face immediately alerted him that all was not as it should be. He sharply asked me the respiratory rate, but all I could muster was a shake of the head. For Bjorn that was enough. In an instant he pushed me aside and, using one of the capture team for support, started repeatedly jumping up and down on the giraffe's chest with as much force as he could manage. I had once attempted resuscitation on a cow by repeatedly and forcefully kneeling on it, but even to me this was a new approach. After five or six sizeable chest compressions, Bjorn stopped and evaluated progress. Nothing. He repeated the procedure, but still to no avail. My heart sank. Bjorn started up again, jumping up and down with such vigour that at one point he lost balance and came crashing down on the giraffe's chest. Unfazed, he was back up immediately, continuing with his unconventional resuscitation technique.

After the fourth cycle, the giraffe finally took a short shallow breath – just one, but a breath nonetheless. We all stood around, our eyes fixed on the animal's chest, praying and hoping. Another breath came, and then another, a bit deeper this time; and then another . . . He was breathing again, and the relief on everyone's faces was clear to see. His respiratory rate soon returned to a healthy 8 breaths a minute.

With this drama now behind us, everyone once again busied themselves in preparing to stand and load the giraffe. The trailer was backed into the clearing, and slowly but surely he was led towards the trailer. This time the giraffe was quite clumsy on his feet and so every step had to be slowly and methodically controlled. Things progressed well until he reached the ramp to the trailer, where the concept of having to lift his feet high enough to follow the inclined gradient was simply too much. Attempting his first step onto the ramp, he buckled, lost balance and fell sideways off the trailer. Immediately Bjorn and the rest of the capture team were on hand, pulling the giraffe away from the trailer, giving him the space to stand again. Once up, he was led away from the trailer, turned round and a second attempt was made to load him. This time he made it halfway up the ramp, only to lose his balance again, now falling backwards into a sitting position. The force of the impact alarmed the first giraffe, who kicked out in disgust, inserting several more holes in the trailer's side panels. Taking hold of the lead rope, one of the capture team climbed up to the front of the trailer to pull on the giraffe's head while Bjorn and Derik pushed him from behind – a very dangerous tactic, because just as the giraffe found his feet, he lashed them out in remonstration. Fortunately, both Bjorn and Derik had anticipated the reaction, and just managed to retreat from the firing line in time. With that, the giraffe then stepped up and into the trailer and the tailgate was quickly closed behind him. We had now caught two giraffes.

By comparison, the third giraffe proved to be a very straightforward and uneventful affair. Returning to the skies, the helicopter pilot quickly relocated the bachelor herd and Derik darted another one of them with ease. As luck would have it, the capture team was able to bring him down on one of the tracks so we were all quickly on hand to administer the Diprenorphine, and soon had him loaded onto another trailer.

'That's how easy they can be,' Bjorn commented as we strolled back to the trailer, jubilant with our success. 'But they seldom are. We've been lucky today, very lucky. But a successful day is still a great day. It's time to celebrate, time for a beer!'

As I sat there quaffing my Black Label, I reflected on the day's events. It had gone well; incredibly well, in fact and, despite the odd tricky moment, we had all got through it unscathed. I cast my eyes across the Afrikaner contingent. I could see the delight and relief on the team's faces as they gulped down their liquid reward. What was this life that they had signed up to? The barometer of success was gauged by the human and animal participants having survived the ordeal; completing the job was an added bonus. If everyone was safe, then 'Eat drink and be merry, for tomorrow you may die!' If not . . . well, you just had to hope for a better day tomorrow. Fearless positivity was the formula.

I silently gazed into my beer speculating on the experiences that made up their portfolio of capture tales, suddenly envious of their adventurous lives, where the conservation and protection of a species was top of the agenda, far away from selfishly climbing the ladder of self-importance. There is a beauty to working with animals that humbles even the most arrogant of men and nowhere is this truer than when dealing with wildlife. These were Afrikaner men in every sense of the stereotype, and yet there was a gentleness, a compassion, a real humility to them. They were passionate about their Africa and their animals, but they knew that the very animals they strove to protect could tomorrow bring about their downfall. Their life might seem glamorous for a month or two, but the reality was a tough, tiring, unpredictable and physically demanding existence that very few were cut out for.

I felt privileged to have briefly shared that life, but I knew I couldn't sustain it for very long, and my respect for them grew all the stronger for it.

# Giraffes: fast facts

*Giraffa camelopardalis*: The giraffe

**Distribution:** Scattered across Africa, from Chad in the north, South Africa to the south, Niger in the west and Somalia to the east.

**Description:** Tallest terrestrial mammal and largest ruminant. One species with nine different sub-species.

**Names:** The male is called a 'bull', the female a 'cow', and their young a 'calf'. A group of giraffes is called a 'tower'.

**Life span:** About 25 years.

**Habitat:** Savannahs and woodland.

**Diet:** Giraffes are browsers, eating the leaves, fruits and flowers of woody plants, primarily acacia species, at heights that most other herbivores cannot reach.

**Gestation:** 400–460 days.

**Height:** 1.7–2 metres at birth, growing up to 5.7 metres as adults.

**Weight:** 65 kg at birth, reaching 800–1,200 kg as adults.

**Growth:** Mothers raise calves in groups called 'calving pools'. They are weaned at about 1 year, and reach sexual maturity at 4–5 years old.

**Anatomy:** Giraffes have the longest nerve in the world: the left recurrent laryngeal nerve, which innervates the left side of the larynx, is about 2 metres long. To enable them to pump blood up their 2.5-metre-long neck, their heart weighs up to 11 kg, measuring about 60 cm long with a muscle wall 7.5 cm thick. Their network of blood vessels at the base of the skull, the so-called 'rete mirabile' system, regulates blood flow to the brain, restricting it when they lower their head, and facilitating it when they raise it. The skin in their lower legs is abnormally thick and tight to prevent blood pooling in the limbs. As ruminants, they must regurgitate their food to aid digestion, which means the oesophageal muscle has to be incredibly strong to allow food to travel 3.5 metres from rumen to mouth. A giraffe's intestines are more than 70 metres long.

**Body temperature:** 38–39 °C.

**Predators:** Adults are rarely preyed on because of their size and dangerously powerful kick, but they are still vulnerable to lions, leopards and wild dogs, and to crocodiles when they drink.

**Conservation:** Giraffe numbers have dropped by 40 per cent in the last thirty years, with only about 97,500 now left in the wild. For this reason, in 2016 the IUCN categorized giraffes as 'vulnerable', and the West African and Rothschild sub-species as 'endangered'. This has been mainly due to habitat loss or degradation as well as poaching. For more information on how you can help protect this beautiful animal visit **www.giraffe-conservation.org**.

# 3

# SWAN

'His own image: no longer a dark, grey bird, ugly and disagreeable to look at, but a graceful and beautiful swan. To be born in a duck's nest, in a farmyard, is of no consequence to a bird, if it hatched from a swan's egg.'

Hans Christian Andersen

It was my first weekend on call since qualifying. I had been one of the lucky ones compared with many of my peer group, and I had been well nurtured as a new graduate by my practice. Not wanting to throw me in the deep end until they felt I was ready, I had been kept off the night and weekend on-call rota. Now two months qualified, my time had come.

'Jon, we're going to put you on call this weekend,' Martin had said on Wednesday. 'I'll back you up so if you have any problems, concerns or queries, call me, but you should be fine.'

It was reassuring to have a safety net, I'd heard horror stories from some of my friends who had been put on call the very first night of their first job, only to find that, when they needed assistance, their boss had gone out for the evening and switched off their phone. Nevertheless, it was a daunting prospect. The usual filtering out of the more challenging calls that occurred during weekdays would be removed so I could end up with anything, from a horse with severe colic to a cow caesarean. Being pushed beyond my comfort zone was certainly not a new experience for me. It had happened every step of the way through vet school, and now as a new graduate I hoped it would continue through my career, since that is the only true way to learn, grow and improve. However, coping with being on call was the final hurdle in the transition from student to professional, so as Thursday came and went, and then Friday progressed, I felt the nervous anticipation of what was to come in the sixty-two hours between 6.30 p.m. on Friday and 8.30 a.m. on Monday.

The weekend turned out to be a busy one, kicking off at 7.30 on Friday night. A client had come home to find her horse with a large gaping wound on the inside of his upper right leg after getting caught in a barbed-wire fence. She had managed to bring the horse into his dilapidated stable next to her house, but she was convinced that the wound needed stitching. It certainly did. In fact, I was so daunted by the size of it that I decided I required Martin's assistance, only to discover, deep in this valley on the edge of Exmoor, that there was no phone reception. There was nothing for it: I would have to stitch it on my own. Three hours later, cold, tired and achy after a protracted period bent over between the horse's front legs, having painstakingly sewn over a hundred stitches by the light of a very dim torch as a howling gale tore through the gaping holes in the rustic wooden shed, the job was completed. The owner was incredibly patient, kind and grateful, and so, on leaving the farm, I had felt a triumphant sense of satisfaction at having dealt with the situation on my own.

That feeling was short-lived, however, since, as soon as I found myself back in phone reception, a rush of missed calls and messages pinged up on my phone. Kate, the duty nurse, had been trying to reach me for two hours because she had an emergency calving that was likely to be a caesarean section. Her messages started with repeated requests for me to call her as soon as I received them, progressed to frustrated annoyance and ended with a deep concern that I had been unreachable for so long. With nervous trepidation I at last returned Kate's call, despairing that I had to go straight on to another appointment when I was so tired, cold and hungry, and dreading the tirade I would get from the farmer, presumably angry at having been kept waiting, or – worse – furious that the calf or cow had died. To my great relief, however, Kate greeted my call with the news that Martin had gone on the visit. She was gratified to discover I was OK and that my visit had been a success, and, sensing my exhaustion, urged me to go home and get some dinner and some sleep while I still had the opportunity. I didn't need telling twice.

Fortunately, the rest of the night was quiet, but the long weekend continued at six the following morning. A cow with milk fever, a calf with pneumonia, a horse with a sore eye, a check on the injured horse from the night before, a calving, a cow with mastitis . . . and so it went on. I always seemed to have at least one call booked ahead of me, and just when I thought I was catching up, Corrina would ring me with a new one. It was relentless, but they were all visits that I felt able to handle and so as I successfully dealt with each one, my confidence grew. By 2 p.m., though, I was flagging, famished from lack of food and weary from the unyielding busyness of the day. Having at last finished my final visit, I warily rang the practice, grateful to hear Heather inform me that there no new calls, and that I finally had the chance to get home and have some lunch.

Thirty minutes later, the simple pleasure of being able to collapse onto my sofa and tuck into some leftover spaghetti bolognese was such an amplified luxury that when the phone rang ten minutes into the experience I almost cried.

'Jon, I'm afraid I've got another call for you . . .' It was Corrina. 'And I'm afraid it's an unusual one. In fact I'm not really sure it's our responsibility, but I don't quite know what else to do. A member of the public has called me several times in the last couple of hours. I've encouraged them to contact the RSPCA, but for some reason they aren't responding. Anyway, I'm sorry to ask, but there is a swan in the fields behind Braunton that seems to be unwell. They aren't sure if it's trapped or injured, and no one can get near enough to be able to tell exactly what the problem is because apparently it's being quite aggressive. So you may not be able to catch it, but maybe you could at least go and have a look at it. Would you mind?'

It was a splurge of information to receive all at once, so it took me a moment to calm my emotions, regain a sense of professionalism, process what I had just been told and respond.

'OK, I see the predicament, but yeah, of course I can go, I'll just finish my lunch and then head over there. Do you know where exactly the swan is?'

'I've got the contact details of the lady who called me, a Mrs Lovell. She said if you call her, she'll be able to direct you to the field and you should be able to drive quite near to where the swan is.'

'OK, great,' I replied as Corrina read off the number.

'Oh, and Jon? Apparently it's attracted quite a crowd, so good luck.'

I felt a mixture of intrigue and trepidation. I had never handled a swan before. As a child the fear had been instilled into us of how dangerous they could be – never anger them, never get between them and their cygnets, they can break a man's arm et cetera. It was obviously one of those common occurrences when a caring member of the public had seen an animal in distress and, wanting to help, but feeling out of her depth, had called the nearest veterinary practice, certain they would know what to do.

Indeed we do: a quick call to the RSPCA, RSPB or a local wild-life sanctuary was the usual modus operandi. However, in this case those avenues had proved fruitless. What she didn't know, though, was that the person responding – i.e. me – would have about as much idea about what to do as any of the onlookers. I desperately hoped I wouldn't disappoint them. And so, energized by my lunch, my brief respite and the novelty of the call ahead, I called Mrs Lovell to inform her that I was on my way.

As I drove, I contemplated my tactics. The element of surprise always had the greatest degree of success with animals, but it required a full, 100 per cent commitment. If there was any hesitation, someone would get hurt. That was fine in theory, but it also required overcoming my customary fear, anxiety and self-doubt. Of course, it might well not even be possible to get close enough without endangering myself, in which case another solution would need to be found . . . I concluded that I had to at least assume I was going to catch the swan. Suddenly a realization struck me: if I caught it, then what? Where would I put the swan? How would I transport it? I made a quick stop at the practice to pick up a small dog crate, some towels and some gauntlets. Maybe I could throw a towel over its head, or the gauntlets would protect my hands from being pecked. I had no idea how vicious their peck was, but equally I didn't want to find out. Now feeling relatively confident about the task ahead, I began to drive towards Braunton.

A short, middle-aged lady in wellies, blue jeans and a mac was patiently waiting for me as I came to the end of a long dirt track. I slowed and wound down my passenger window.

'Mrs Lovell? I'm Jon the vet.'

'Yes, thank you so much for coming. The field entrance is just at the end of this track. My husband's there on the gate, and the swan is in the far corner, beyond where the crowd is. I'll meet you there.'

I turned down the bumpy dirt track. Arriving at a gate, a tall gentleman pointed down the hedge line. I followed his gaze expecting to see the swan in the distance, but instead my eyes fell upon a crowd of about twenty spectators, gathered 50 feet into the field. Hearing the sound of a car engine, they all turned in my direction, forming an eager welcoming committee to the climax of their unscripted Saturday afternoon entertainment. Driving through the field and circumventing the awaiting crowd, I was able to get my first sighting of the swan. It was sitting a few metres from the corner of the field, head raised, alert and attentive to its surroundings. I was some distance away from it, so I couldn't see for sure, but at first glance there didn't appear to be anything too obviously wrong with it.

Stepping out of the car I was haled with a barrage of whispered questions, enquiries, praise, thanks and encouragement. It was all a bit intimidating, so I was grateful when Mrs Lovell arrived with her husband in tow and took control of the situation.

'I think we should stand back and allow the vet an opportunity to assess the swan,' she decisively announced.

Murmurs of agreement followed, and then someone piped up: 'Have you warned him how aggressive it is?'

Prompted by this reminder, Mrs Lovell turned to me, 'Yes . . . he does seem somewhat vicious. He doesn't seem able to walk or fly, so I guess it's his only way of defending himself, but he certainly warns us off. So no one has dared go near him, but I'm sure you know what you are doing.' Then addressing the source of the comment, she added, 'I'm sure the vet knows exactly what to do.'

*If only I did*, I thought. I briefly imagined that the next phone call Mrs Lovell made would be a request for an ambulance for the vet who had been savaged by a swan. To my giddy mind, it almost sounded like the basis of a nursery rhyme: 'There was an old lady that called an ambulance, she called the ambulance to rescue the vet, she called the vet to rescue the swan . . .'

'Is there anything you need, Jon?' Mrs Lovell enquired, bringing me back to reality.

'I've brought a small dog cage, which I'll put it in, if I can catch it, so if you could be on standby with that it would be a great help.'

'Of course,' she said eagerly, pleased to have a role in the adventure. 'And what do you mean, *if* you catch him? I have every faith in you, I bet you've done this sort of thing hundreds of times!'

I decided not to respond to her statement. Sensing the anticipation in the crowd, only a successful capture, ideally following a dramatic stand-off, would do – and though they would probably settle for me sustaining a dinner-party-anecdote-worthy injury, I felt they were basically willing me to succeed.

As I neared the swan, it fixated on me and immediately started a tirade of aggressive hissing in an attempt to intimidate the perceived threat I presented. It worked. I stopped at an exaggerated distance from my patient, nervous that he might suddenly lunge at me, before turning to the expectant crowd and squeezing out a smile to suggest that everything was going to plan.

I considered my tools. If I threw a towel over the swan's head, it could give me a brief window in which to pounce, but then again, if I missed, I would probably just prime it even more for my additional offensive manoeuvre. Trying on the gauntlets, I found they actually inhibited my sense of touch, which seemed important in not inadvertently crushing the bird, and more so than any need to protect my hands. So that meant it was just me versus the swan, and I suddenly felt very exposed. In order to successfully restrain the bird, I would need one hand on the top of its neck, and the other wrapped around its body, holding it close to my chest to secure the wings. If I could manage that, then ideally I would grab the swan's feet as well with the hand that was wrapped around the body. What felt most natural was to hold the neck with my left hand and the body with my right, which fortunately corresponded with the way the bird was positioned. This was all good theory, but as I stood there eyeballing the swan, I had no idea how much resistance it would put up or whether I would be able to restrain it. There could be all number of possible outcomes, most of which, as I saw it, would leave me with some sort of injury.

I inched closer to the bird, as slowly, steadily and subtly as I could, gradually getting within pouncing distance, but my movements didn't go unnoticed and were met by an increased fervour of hissing. Nevertheless I prepared my assault, rehearsing the plan over and over in my mind to reassure and convince myself of its efficacy, gradually positioning my hands and my body. I could feel twenty pairs of eyes glaring into the back of my head. I took a deep breath . . . and sprang at the swan.

My sudden change of speed afforded me a momentary upper hand, and years of rugby had given me a muscle memory of the tackle, which now came to my aid. And so seconds later, as much to my surprise as the swan's, I found myself in secure possession of it, and although it tried to put up a fight, it was actually too weak to really present me with a problem. I clambered to my feet, in a very ungainly fashion for fear of releasing my hold, and wandered over to where Mrs Lovell was standing with the cage.

Murmurs of awe and wonderment broke out among the crowd, with an undercurrent of quiet disappointment that the stand-off had been so short-lived. However, with the bird secured in the cage a ripple of applause broke out in my honour, before the crowd started dispersing, the spectacle now over. Mr Lovell retrieved my towels and gauntlets as I loaded the cage onto my passenger seat, and a few spectators wandered over to enquire what imminent fate the swan could expect. I told them I'd be taking it back to the practice for a medical assessment and hospitalization, until either it was well enough to be released or we could otherwise send it on to a wildlife sanctuary for rehabilitation, which is in fact what happened. Content with this answer, they encouraged me on my way for the plan to be implemented without delay.

I climbed into my car to a barrage of hissing from the passenger seat, reminding me, in case I had forgotten, of my unusual passenger, whose cage I now surreptitiously covered with a towel to shut him up. Then amid waves of polite farewell, I set off, at once relieved and relaxed with how the visit had turned out.

Driving back to the practice, I reflected that my first weekend on call had been something of a baptism of fire. Then, looking at the clock on the dashboard, I realized I was only halfway through it.

# Swans: fast facts

*Cygnus olor*: The mute swan

**Distribution:** Native to most of Europe and Asia. Introduced to North America, Australasia and Southern Africa.

**Description:** One of the heaviest flying birds in the world. The mute swan is the largest of the six swan species.

**Names:** The male is called a 'cob', the female a 'pen', and their young a 'cygnet'. A group of swans is called a 'bevy'.

**Life span:** About 15 years in the wild.

**Habitat:** Temperate areas, shallow lakes and slow-flowing rivers. (Incidentally, a lake is distinguished from a pond by a swan's ability to take off and land on it.)

**Diet:** Aquatic vegetation, cropped grass, molluscs, small fish, frogs and worms.

**Incubation:** 36 days. The female lays 4–10 eggs, which both sexes incubate.

**Wingspan:** 208–238 cm.

**Weight:** 225 grams at birth, reaching 8.5–11.8 kg as adults.

**Growth:** Cygnets stay with their parents until 4–5 months, when they are able to fly and will join a large flock. Breeding won't begin until 2 years.

**Body temperature:** 39–40 °C.

**The 'Royal connection':** Historically, swans were domesticated for food, and ownership was determined by a mark on their webs or beak, which were then registered with the Crown; any bird not marked automatically became Crown property. Today the British Monarch retains the technical right to ownership of all unmarked mute swans in open water, but the Queen only exercises her ownership over certain stretches of the Thames and its tributaries, which is shared with the Worshipful Company of Vintners and the Worshipful Company of Dyers, who together take part in an annual 'swan-upping', where all mute swans are rounded up, ringed and released.

**Predators:** Adults are rarely preyed on because of their aggression in defence, but foxes, coyotes, lynxes and bears pose a potential threat.

**Conservation:** Swans were nearly hunted to extinction between the thirteenth and nineteenth centuries, but protection measures led to a dramatic increase in numbers. Another peril arose during the 1960s–1980s because of lead poisoning from ingestion of fishing sinkers. Their numbers have since recovered, but they are still categorized as of 'amber' concern by the Royal Society for the Protection of Birds. There are currently around 6,400 breeding pairs in the UK, with 74,000 wintering here. There are about 500,000 birds worldwide, 350,000 of which are in the former Soviet Union. For more information on the mute swan, or to help support and protect them, visit **www.rspb.org.uk**.

# 4

# SNOW LEOPARD

*'They call the snow leopard the ghost cat. Never lets itself be seen... Beautiful things don't ask for attention.'*

Sean O'Connell, *The Secret Life of Walter Mitty*

I t had been a great weekend, celebrating my brother's birthday, in the midst of the manic final few months of vet school – squeezing in the last few weeks of 'seeing practice', spending every spare moment reading through one of the twelve ring-bound files of notes accumulated over the last five years, or practising any one of a number of 'Day One skills' on the stuffed animals in the practical lab. Long days, late nights, and I was feeling the strain. So to have an opportunity for a brotherly get-together was just the thing to help me unwind. Beer and curry while watching *Where Eagles Dare* was our usual preference – invariably accompanied, much to my sister-in-law's irritation, by our word-perfect chorus of almost every line. On this occasion, however, the unanimous decision was to watch an episode of David Attenborough's *Planet Earth* series, the one that featured the first intimate images of a snow leopard ever filmed in the wild. We all sat mesmerized by the extraordinary footage of this beautiful and rare cat, hunting with such stealth and agility along the sheer cliff-faces of the Himalayas.

Fast-forward a year, and I was working in a mixed practice in rural Devon, with the vast majority of my work taken up with TB testing, farm visits, small-animal consulting and routine operations. It was proving a steep learning curve, at once exhilarating and exhausting, but I loved it and rapidly found myself energized by the variety of patients I was fortunate to work with and help. The fact that one of our clients was a wildlife park, where I was occasionally asked to go and see a sea lion, lemur, capuchin monkey or raccoon was a real privilege.

Over the course of the nine months since I had qualified, I had been to the wildlife park a handful of times, so I knew the layout fairly well, but somehow I had failed to clock that their collection of animals included two snow leopards. That was until my colleague, Dave, called me one morning from our other surgery.

'What have you got on today? Can you come and help me at the wildlife park? I've got to operate on their fifteen-year-old snow leopard Amira. She's got a wound in her front left armpit.'

I was immediately transported back to that footage in the Himalayas, to the mystery and majesty of this beautiful animal. Of course, this was not the wild – a far cry from it – but to be presented with an opportunity to work with and care for such a beautiful creature was momentarily stunning.

'. . . Absolutely,' I replied eventually. 'When do you need me?'

'I'm consulting this morning till twelve, so the plan is to do it at about one. Can you bring the portable anaesthetic machine? Will it fit in your car? I can bring the rest of what we need.'

The portable anaesthetic machine comprised a trolley carrying an oxygen cylinder with a set of pipes that fed the gas through a vaporizer to allow an anaesthetic combination to be delivered to the patient. It was quite a bulky and heavy piece of kit, but with a bit of rearranging of my car, it wouldn't be a problem.

'I've got a couple of visits this morning,' I said, 'but I'll come back and pick it up before I head over to meet you.'

'Perfect, thanks. See you at one. I'll call if there's any change.'

My two morning visits were to a pet pig that needed stitching up after a disagreement with the barbed-wire fence she was trying to crawl under, and then to a bull whose hooves needed a trim. The pig required a couple of sutures; the bull required a dose of sedatives, the recruitment of all available manpower to rope him down, and an uncomfortable time lying at a very awkward angle in dung-soaked straw as I administered his strenuously unwanted manicure. By the time these two visits were done, it was midday, and I headed straight back to the practice, loaded the anaesthetic machine onto the back seat of my car, and drove to meet Dave at the wildlife park.

We arrived at virtually the same time, and had a brief chat about our plan before heading to reception to find Tony, the head keeper, who told us Amira was suffering from a burst abscess in the armpit on her front left leg.

'I'm not sure what's caused it,' he said, 'but she's quite lame with it.'

'Could we take a look at her first,' Dave asked, 'and then decide whether we need to anaesthetize her for a closer examination? Where is she?'

'She's still in her outdoor enclosure. There's a run from that into her house, with a cage we can trap her in. She's trained to go through it, so we can administer any injections she might need.'

'Great! So we shouldn't need to dart her. That makes life a lot easier.'

Following Tony through the staff room, and out the back of the main building, we found ourselves among the melee of punters who were just beginning their exploration of the park. In contrast to their meanderings, Tony was very purposeful in his direction. We passed the macaws and giant tortoises, wallabies and lemurs, through a beautiful oriental garden, and then reached a large chain-linked enclosure that was about 25 feet high. A 3-foot-high fence in front of it kept the public at a distance, and signs warned people against climbing them. A plaque mounted on the fence indicated the enclosure's inhabitants: two snow leopards named Amira and Sasha. Looking into the enclosure, it was at first difficult to identify any occupants at all among the thick foliage, logs and boulders. Tony, however, spotted Sasha immediately, perched on a wooden platform 15 feet up, in the far corner. After a further few seconds he found Amira, who was hiding between two boulders in the other corner of the enclosure. As we stood there watching them, Jason, the keeper in charge of the snow leopards, came over.

'Can you call Amira over?' Tony said after making the introductions. 'We just want to observe her first before we do anything.'

The four of us climbed over the fence and Jason softly started calling Amira over. Alert to the sound of his voice, which was usually associated with food, Sasha silently and effortlessly jumped off her platform and headed straight over to us. Amira was more cautious, initially just focusing her attention in our direction, but after some gentle encouragement from Jason, she stood and gingerly walked over to us, clearly uncomfortable on her front left leg.

'She's pretty sore, isn't she?' Tony commented.

'How long has she been lame?' I asked Jason.

'In hindsight probably two days. She's not quite been herself, and she's been spending most of her time in one spot, which is unusual for her, but it was most noticeable this morning.'

As she came closer, we could see some streaks of dried blood that had run down the inside of her leg. Dave and I crouched down to get a better view of her underside, but her immensely dense, thick fur obstructed our view of the injury.

'Looking at the colour of those bloody streaks down her leg,' said Dave, 'I agree it's probably an abscess, but she's clearly quite sore on it, so I think it's best if we knock her out to look at it properly.'

'I agree,' said Jason. 'I'd like to know what's going on with her and I don't want it to progress to something worse.'

'Where's the run with the cage?' asked Dave. 'Will you be able to get her in without Sasha?'

'It's just over there.' Jason pointed to the left front corner. We could see a wire-mesh cuboid, 2 by 2 by 15 feet in size, connecting to a small whitewashed building on the other side of the enclosure. 'It shouldn't be too much of a problem.'

'Great. Well, Jon and I need to get our equipment, so if you could coax Amira into the cage, we'll go and get what we need.'

As we turned to head back to the car we realized a crowd was gathering, obviously aware that something unusual was happening. Accustomed to such a scenario, Tony was quick to address them as we slipped away.

'One of the snow leopards has got a problem with her leg, so the vets are here to examine her, but I'm afraid I need to ask you all to move away so we don't unduly stress her.'

Disappointed but understanding murmurs followed his announcement. Since it was in the animal's best interest, they would be happy to oblige. A few parents simplified the explanation to their inquisitive and disappointed children as they slowly moved away.

'What's the plan?' I asked Dave as we headed back to the car.

'We'll inject her with Ketamine and Medetomidine in the cage, and then get her to walk into the house before they take effect and she goes to sleep. That way we'll be away from Sasha and out of view. We'll intubate her and then you can do the anaesthetic while I have a thorough look at her leg. We'll take some blood, too, while we've got the chance, so we can check her general health status.'

'Sure.' I said. Then, 'Do I just treat her as I would a big cat?'

'Yeah. Jaw-tone, eye-position to gauge how asleep she is, just like you would any other cat.'

Dave had pre-packed a box with everything he thought we'd need. Opening it now, and rechecking the items, we talked through the procedure step by step, happy we hadn't forgotten anything. I then lugged out the anaesthetic machine from the back seat, and we headed back to the snow leopard enclosure.

We had been gone maybe ten minutes. In that time, Tony had cordoned off the area from the public and Jason was just coaxing a protesting Amira down the walkway into the built-in trap. We carried the equipment round the corner of the enclosure to the door of the housed enclosure, which Tony now confirmed would be where we'd be carrying out the procedure. Dave then drew up the drug combination, after estimating her weight. We walked over to the trap where Amira was now caged. Threatened by our presence, she growled, hissed and swiped at us from her confinement with an intimidating ferocity.

'Are you ready to inject her?' Jason asked Dave.

'Yeah, all set.'

'Can you help me pull these handles, Jon? That way, we can pin her against the side of the cage for Dave to safely inject her.'

There were two handles, one at the front of the cage and one at the back, and these were connected to a sheet of wire mesh. Pulling on them temporarily constricted the area where

Amira was contained, allowing Dave enough time to safely inject into her rump before she could deploy her immense strength against us.

As soon as the injection was done, we released the handles, and Jason then opened the front shutter of the cage, allowing Amira access to her indoor pen. A combination of displeasure and fear made her rapidly vanish down the run and into her house, where Jason then shut her in. The first phase of the procedure had been successfully achieved. We now had to let the drugs take effect, trusting that Dave's calculations had been correct.

'How long should it take for her to go to sleep, Dave?' Tony whispered, conscious of the need for quiet.

'About five to ten minutes.'

A small window ran along the top wall of the building. It was fairly opaque with dust, but through it we were just able to make out Amira within her barred pen. Initially she prowled around the enclosure, growling as she went, but gradually as the drugs took effect, she lay down, head swaying from side to side. Eight minutes after the injection she slumped onto her side, completely unconscious. We sprang into action, opening the door into the housed area and carrying in our equipment.

Before opening Amira's cage, Jason gently prodded her with a stick to confirm she was asleep. She didn't flinch. The cage door swung inwards and so it gently pushed Amira out of the way – another good test of how asleep she was. Loading her onto the stretcher, we then carried her into the alleyway, her head towards the door. Dave gently opened her mouth to check her jaw-tone: the action stimulated her tongue to unfurl and then curl up, a normal reflex, but no less intimidating. Her inch-long canines gleamed at us.

'We need to intubate her, but I've brought a gag to use. If she inadvertently closes her mouth, those teeth will crush through a human hand effortlessly,' Dave warned me. It was an alarming thought. 'Can you see the gag in the box with the endotracheal tubes?'

I located a small block of wood covered in Vetrap, then found an endotracheal (ET) tube and the laryngoscope. Tying a strip of the bandage material around her upper jaw, Dave held up her head and opened her mouth. I gently placed the gag between her upper and lower molars until it caught, and then, happy I wouldn't lose any fingers if she clamped down, pulled out her tongue and used the laryngoscope to visualize the vocal folds, between which I gently inserted the ET tube. Removing the laryngoscope, we used the Vetrap to secure the ET tube to Amira's upper jaw, before, with an airway now secured, connecting up the anaesthetic machine. While Dave and Jason then positioned Amira on her back so they could examine her wound, I used my stethoscope to assess her heart rate (108), then her respiratory rate (26). The values felt right for her size, but it was the pattern that was important. Dave had packed an anaesthetic chart, which I started filling in, monitoring her parameters every five minutes. If everything stayed roughly the same, then all was good; any sudden changes and I would need to respond. Next, I put some lubricating gel on her eyes to keep them moist, thus compensating for the lack of tear production during her anaesthesia.

'How does she seem?' Dave said, turning to me.

I gave him the figures. 'She seems pretty stable.'

'Good. What flow rate have you got her on?' The flow rate is the concentration of vaporized anaesthetic agent that is added to the oxygen and delivered to the patient.

'Two and a half per cent.'

'Fine. Well, just keep a close eye on her, particularly when I start examining her wound. It's a bit cramped in here, so if she suddenly wakes up, we're in trouble.'

With four of us in the alleyway, plus Amira and all the equipment, there was indeed very little room to move. Furthermore, the door only opened inwards and the anaesthetic machine and I were blocking that escape route. As I looked at her curled lips, and those large gleaming canines, and her dinner-plate-sized paws with inch-long claws, I suddenly felt very exposed and vulnerable. She certainly seemed to be asleep, but any sudden pain stimulus and she might react. Nervously I checked her jaw-tone and blink-reflex, and decided to turn the vaporizer flow rate up to 3 per cent.

'Are you happy with her, Jon? I'm going to start examining this wound. I'm not sure how painful this could be, so be prepared.'

'She seems very stable,' I confirmed.

Dave abducted her left front leg away from her body, revealing a mat of bloody dried fur surrounding a large puncture wound. The wound was still weeping and the exposed flesh was purulent and inflamed.

'It's pretty nasty. I wonder how she did it. Let's clip and clean it, and go from there.' He started clipping away at the dense matted fur around the wound. Amira didn't flinch. I rechecked her parameters: heart rate 120, respiration 24. She was reacting slightly to the stimulation, but there was still no blink-reflex or jaw-tone. I was happy with that. Dave continued slowly and methodically around the area, then took a litre bag of sterile saline, inserted a needle, and then used this to flush and clean the wound. As he continued his work, I found myself mesmerized by the beauty of the creature before me. I took in the soft, thick, dense, smoky-grey and straw-yellow fur of her coat, dotted with the black open rosettes across her body and the smaller black spots across her face and legs. Her velvety smooth tail, as long as her body, the large supple paws with their springy pads that allowed for such silent movement yet contained such deadly razor sharp claws. Her small ears that minimized heat loss, but nonetheless allowed for such acute hearing; the thirty-two teeth that could crush through bone, or tear through flesh, with such effortless ease; and the usually alert, attentive eyes that now lay concealed, behind her third eyelids.

Dave had by now finished flushing the wound; Amira remained motionless, save for her rhythmical breathing. Removing the purulent material had revealed healthy granulation tissue underneath, but Dave's attention was now drawn to what appeared to be a track in the wound. Using a pair of 15-cm crocodile forceps, he gently probed the wound, inserting them down the track which seemed to lead to the front of her shoulder. To our shock, the forceps disappeared up to their handle.

'This looks like a migrating foreign body,' Dave said in surprise. 'Can you find anything on the front of her shoulder?'

I immediately turned my attention to the area Dave indicated, parting the thick fur and methodically feeling all over her shoulder. Moments later I found what I was looking for: a scab, just inside and in front of the shoulder blade. It was a healed entry wound.

'There's a scab here.'

'Hold your finger over it, and I'll reinsert the crocodile forceps and let's see if they match up.'

They did. As I pressed against the scab, I could just feel the tip of the forceps.

'Well, that's your answer,' said Dave, turning to Jason. 'Something's gone in at the front of her shoulder and migrated through, and then burst out in her armpit. It probably happened a couple of weeks ago. Does that square with anything you've noticed?'

'Come to think of it, there were a couple of days around that time frame when she seemed to be obsessing with that front leg and licking it more than normal. I guess that was why. What sort of thing could it have been?'

'We see this sort of thing a lot. It's often caused by grass seeds in dogs. They get them caught in their thick fur and then they gradually progress, penetrating the skin and then migrating. Usually they don't travel too far before the owner notices and we remove them, but they can sometimes move deep into the body.'

'We had a case when I was at vet school,' I piped up. 'The dog unknowingly aspirated one. It had a cough for months that wouldn't clear. Six months later it developed an abscess on its flank, and when we cut into it, we found the grass seed.'

'Yeah, I've seen something similar with a grass seed,' agreed Dave. 'But a thorn or splinter could also cause it.'

'Poor Amira . . . So what's the plan?' asked Tony.

'We'll flush the track and wound again, then give her a course of antibiotics and pain relief, and then we should probably re-examine her in a week or two, depending on how things are going. You'll be able to administer medication to her in her food, won't you?'

'Yeah, no problem. If we bury the tablets in some meat, she should take it without a problem.'

'Great.'

After flushing the wound again, Dave gently dried it with sterile swabs and then applied a wound cream before laying her leg down. We repositioned her on her side.

'Before I turn her off, did you want to take some blood?' I asked Dave.

'Good, yes. Probably from her cephalic vein?' The cephalic vein ran down the front of the leg below the elbow. Along with the jugular vein, it was generally the most accessible.

Taking off his gloves, Dave handed me the clippers, some vacuum blood tubes and a needle. I clipped a small patch of fur on the front of her leg, below the elbow and Dave then raised the vein for me. Filling the two vacuum tubes, the job was quickly done.

'Anything else we need to do?' Dave asked.

Unlike with our usual patients, whom we could recheck regularly, this was our one opportunity to ensure we had done everything we needed to. Once we woke her up, there'd be no second chance today.

'I don't think so.'

'Good. Let's turn off the anaesthetic and move her back into her cage. Then we can reverse her and wake her up.'

I turned off the machine and disconnected the ET tube, then we manoeuvred her back into her cage and lifted her onto the floor. I untied the bandage that held the ET tube secure while Dave drew up the anaesthetic reversal agent. Happy that she was still stable, I removed the ET tube and pulled out her tongue to open her airway, Dave injected into her muscle, and we both evacuated the cage, closing and securing the door behind us.

After about ten minutes, Amira started to stir, slowly lifting her head in an attempt to orientate herself, but with it came a rhythmic head sway she was at first unable to control, so after a few seconds she collapsed down again. For a further few minutes a gently swishing tail was the only indication that she was rousing, but then she rocked onto her chest and powered herself to her feet. Her head continued to sway, and she was very unsteady on her feet as she circled the cage, but her tail eventually maintained her balance. As time elapsed, she slowly settled and assumed a more natural lying position, attentive to our presence as her ability to focus grew.

'Best to leave her now, but I'd keep her shut in for the next hour or two until she's fully awake,' Dave advised Jason as we headed out.

'Will do,' Jason assured us, and we said our goodbyes. 'And about the medication?'

'She's had all she needs for today. I'll get it put up at the practice, for someone to pick up.'

That night I sat down and re-watched that second *Planet Earth* episode. As the snow leopard agilely navigated the cliff-face in pursuit of a markhor kid, the sequence came to life in an entirely new way as I now profoundly understood almost every detail, from the pad of her paws to the tip of her tail, of the animal's unique anatomy, which allows it to thrive in such a hostile environment – where snow leopards dare.

# Snow leopards: fast facts

*Panthera uncia*: The snow leopard

**Distribution:** The mountain ranges of Central and South Asia.

**Description:** The least aggressive, most secretive and camouflaged of the big cats, snow leopards are crepuscular, being most active at dawn and dusk. There is one species of snow leopard with two recognized sub-species.

**Names:** The male is called a 'leopard', the female a 'leopardess', and their young a 'cub'. A group of snow leopards is called a 'leap'.

**Life span:** About 15–18 years in the wild.

**Habitat:** Rocky regions or mountainous meadows, between 9,800 and 19,700 feet in the summer, coming down to forest areas between 3,900 and 6,600 feet in the winter.

**Diet:** Snow leopards are opportunistic carnivores, eating whatever meat they can find, including carrion and domestic livestock. They can kill animals up to four times their own weight, but readily take hares and birds, and are capable of killing most animals in their range except for an adult male yak. They can survive on a single bharal (or Himalayan blue sheep) for two weeks, consuming all edible parts of the carcass.

**Gestation:** 90–100 days. Cubs are born between April and June, with litter sizes of between 1 and 5.

**Size:** Up to 150 cm long, from nose to the base of the tail, their tail being nearly the same length again.

**Weight:** 320 grams at birth, reaching 27–55 kg as adults.

**Growth:** Leaving the den at about 4 months, cubs remain with their mother until independence at 18–22 months, and sexual maturity at 2–3 years.

**Body temperature:** 37.4–38.8 °C.

**Adaptations for cold climate:** A long, soft dense fur gives powerful insulation, short rounded ears reduce heat loss, large furry paws lend grip on rocky terrain and prevent sinking into snow, a long thick tail assists balance and stores fat and can therefore serve as a blanket for extra warmth, and a large nasal cavity helps the animal breathe the thin, cold air.

**Conservation:** Snow leopards have no natural predators, but like so many creatures around the world, humanity is their biggest threat. The IUCN has classified them as 'vulnerable', with estimates ranging from 4,500 to 8,745 adults left in the wild. Poachers kill them for their thick fur or bones, which are used in traditional Asian medicines; global warming is reducing their habitat; and the overgrazing of domestic animals has led to a reduction in their natural prey, and therefore an increased contact and conflict with humans, who kill them to defend their livelihood. Unlike other big cats, however, snow leopards have never been known to attack humans and can be easily chased away. For more information on how you can help protect this magical creature, visit **www.snowleopard.org**.

# 5

# GOAT

*'The lust of the goat is the bounty of God.'*

William Blake

Martin headed into the practice with a spring in his step. The surfboard on the roof of his car was reason enough to explain it.

'Morning Martin,' I said. 'Catch any good waves?' It was 8.30 a.m. and I had only just arrived myself.

'It's always so great. No better way to start the day. You got the bug yet?'

'I need to get a wetsuit and a board first,' I mumbled. Being a surfing nut was obviously one of the most important prerequisites to joining a vet practice so close to Woolacombe Beach in North Devon. So to confess I hadn't even ventured in after six weeks at the practice was almost criminal.

'You need to head to Second Skin in Braunton! Andy will sort you out with a suit and a second-hand board and then you'll be away. Trust me, you'll love it. Make sure you get a 5/3mm suit, then you can venture out in December without freezing.'

'Thanks,' I said, making a mental note to do just that. It wasn't that I had been avoiding surfing – far from it. It was just that, with all the changes I had undergone since graduating, moving down to Devon and starting my career as a veterinary surgeon, I simply hadn't got round to exploring any new hobbies, but I was still keen to do so. Next time I was in Braunton I would get my wetsuit.

With that we both headed into the practice to see what the day had in store. Looking through the diary, I saw I had a couple of lame cows to see, a cow with mastitis, and then, as luck would have it I had a visit, booked for midday, to see Mr Giles at Home Farm to castrate a dozen of his bullocks. Home Farm was just outside Braunton, so if all went to plan and no emergencies came in I could grab my lunch and take a look at some wetsuits.

And sure enough, at a quarter to two on that Thursday afternoon I found myself heading back to my car with a brand-new 5/3mm Second Skin wetsuit and with Andy on the look-out for a second-hand Bic 7ft9 Mini Mal surfboard – a good beginners' board, apparently. Clearly, I would soon be just another North Devon vet driving around with my surfboard on the car roof ready for a pre- or post-work dip.

As I sat in the car enjoying my lunch, I resolved to try out my new purchase at the weekend, and maybe even book a surfing lesson. I wasn't on call and didn't have any plans for Saturday. The holiday season was over, so what better way to pass the day? My phone rang, breaking my train of thought. It was Jackie, the practice's farm and equine receptionist.

'Jonny, you done all your castrations? Can you go to Mr Watts at Upper Hill Farm in Umberleigh? He's got a calving that he's struggling with.'

'Sure, I'm just in Braunton now . . . Where is Umberleigh?' Six weeks in, and I was still getting to know my way around.

I had naïvely purchased a sat nav before I moved down, only to discover that farms located on either side of a valley could both have the same postcode; it might be a good device for London, but it wasn't much use in rural Devon. Fortunately, Jackie knew every postbox, streetlight, pub and phone box in a 30-mile radius and could direct me with pinpoint accuracy.

'South of Barnstaple, head out on the A377 through Bishop's Tawton, and just keep going on that road until you reach Umberleigh, turn left over the bridge at the Rising Sun . . .' I was furiously writing down her directions on a crumpled scrap of paper I found in the passenger footwell. '. . . and the farm is 100 metres down that road on the right.'

'Great, thanks.'

'It should take you about half an hour, depending on traffic. I'll let Mr Watts know you're on your way. It's marked on the map so it should be quite easy to find . . . Oh, and he said the cow's down in the field and he can't get her in.'

'I'm on my way.'

'Thanks Jonny. Martin or Neil will be around if you think it's a caesarean.' And with that she hung up.

I pulled out my Ordnance Survey map from the driver's door pocket, opening it over the steering wheel, then folded it down to centre on Umberleigh, before spreading it on the passenger seat and setting off.

Forty minutes later I pulled into the farmyard, having exhausted myself on the journey trying to play through every possible permutation of what I might find with the calving and how I would handle it. Every day of the last six weeks had felt like a cross between *The Crystal Maze* and *Mastermind*. Book knowledge and some basic practical skills had got me through finals, but I was now having to rapidly expand the repertoire of my practical skills and problem-solving capabilities to bring theory into practice. It's that transition that makes the first-year post qualification far more stressful than anything at university. Having good supportive bosses and colleagues was the key and in that regard I had been very lucky.

Mr Watts greeted me in that characteristic Devonian smile I was becoming accustomed too.

'Good afternoon, young man. I don't believe we've met, but Jackie says you're all right!'

'Nice to meet you, Mr Watts. You've got calving trouble I believe?'

'It's Arthur, call me Arthur – I can't be doing with any of this formal talk, I'm just a man of the fields . . . Yes, indeed, she's a fourth-calver, never given me trouble before, but she's gone down in the fields . . . Tail is up and she's pushing, but nothing is happening. I tried to have a feel and, well, it's pretty tight, I can barely get my hand in, I've no idea what's going on. So I thought this is one for the professionals.'

'How long has she been calving for?' I asked.

'Oh, about two or three hours, I would think. I noticed her down this morning. Probably a spot of milk fever, I thought, so I gave her a bottle of calcium under the skin about eleven. She wasn't calving then. When I checked her again at one she was still down, but straining – that's when I had a feel and then called you. I mean, she might not even be calving, but she *is* due . . . It's an odd one for sure, got me flummoxed.'

'Well, let's go and have a look.'

He cast a disparaging glance at my Ford Focus estate. 'Don't think your car will make it in the field, so best grab what you need and come with me.' *One day I'll get a Defender*, I thought, as I tried to collect every possible item I might conceivably require.

'You planning on camping?' he asked as I loaded my two boxes of equipment onto the back of his Land Rover.

'Is that all right?' I bantered back. 'Have you got a calving jack?'

'Yeah, it's in the field next to her.'

'Great. Then we're set.'

We set off through the farmyard and down an old cobbled track with a high broom and gorse hedgerow on either side. The farm collie rushed out from one of the buildings and started in pursuit behind us, and Arthur slowed down.

'Come on then, Fly,' he cried, looking in his wing mirror. 'They never like to be left out.'

The dog effortlessly jumped into the back and then we continued on down the track. After about 200 metres he swung left, stopping at the gate entrance, which I hopped out to open. I could see the cow sitting up in the field, about 20 metres away: a Holstein Friesian. She seemed bright enough. I could see a large bucket of water and a pile of hay just in front of her and the calving jack discarded a couple of metres behind where she lay. Arthur drove through and I shut the gate behind him. As I strolled over to join him where he was parking up by the cow, I noticed the other cattle at the far end of the field grazing. There were probably thirty; this was the field of 'dry' cows – the ones that were no longer being milked because they were due to calve in the next two months.

Arriving at the Land Rover I grabbed my box of rectal sleeves and lube, and approached the cow's back end. Glove on, lube applied, I inserted my hand. I could immediately feel what Arthur had told me: everything did indeed feel abnormally tight. For a moment I too was confused, and then as I examined her further I realized my arm was having to twist like a corkscrew as I explored. And suddenly I knew exactly what was wrong.

'What do you think?' Arthur said.

'She's got a uterine torsion – that's why you can't get your hand in very far.'

'A *what*?'

'A uterine torsion. It tends to happen right at the end of pregnancy when the calf is so big, the cow slips or rolls, and the uterus ends up twisting over on itself so that it prevents the calf from being born. We either need to untwist it or we'll have to do a caesarean.'

'Well, there it is!' he said, removing his flat cap and scratching his forehead. 'I've been calving cows for forty years and never to my knowledge come across this. Can we *un*twist it?'

'We can have a go – but is there anyone who can give us a hand? This will be a three-person job. We need to roll the cow, but I need to keep my hand inside her to keep the uterus and calf in one place, then we rotate the cow around her and hopefully it will untwist.'

'Well I never. I'm sure Mrs Watts is about, I'll go and find her.' He jumped in the Land Rover and headed back to the gate.

My heart was pumping. Of course I knew the theory behind the technique of correcting a uterine torsion – it was a classic exam question – but actually executing the procedure was a whole new ball game. Unlike some vet students, though, I had been lucky enough to have witnessed it at first hand, when I was seconded to a practice in Fermoy in Ireland. I remembered Ian, the vet, stripped to the waist on a bitterly cold night, demonstrating how important it was to work out which way the uterus had twisted so that you unroll it properly.

With Arthur gone, I kept checking and double-checking the direction of the twist; it was going anticlockwise, which meant the uterus had to be rotated clockwise to untwist it, or else rotating the cow anticlockwise if the uterus was held in place . . . Was that right? It seemed counter-intuitive to be rolling the cow in the direction of the twist. I went through it again in my mind, step by step. Yes . . . that *was* right, I was certain. Or if I was wrong, I suppose I'd be calling Martin or Neil to help me with my first caesarean!

Arthur soon returned with his wife, a small, round lady with red rosy cheeks and a friendly smile. It looked as if Arthur had dragged her away from doing something in the kitchen; probably baking some delicious cake, I thought. Her floral dress and apron were visible under her threadbare, fern green quilted jacket, which she had obviously just thrown on when Arthur called for her, along with her wellies and beige bucket hat.

'Well, you must be the new vet. I'm Mary, Arthur's wife, very nice to meet you,' she said. 'Arthur tells me this is a tricky one, and something about rolling the cow?'

I set about explaining the situation to her and the object of the manoeuvre.

'Well, what a job!' she replied.

'Is that OK? Will you and Arthur be able to roll her?' I asked.

'Oh, don't you worry about us. We've been farming since long before you were born, and we've rolled a cow or two in that time. Haven't we, Arthur? But never for this, mind.'

'Indeed we have,' Arthur agreed.

'Great. Well, we need to roll her onto her left and then all the way over,' I said, miming the action as I mentally checked I was right.

'Right you are.'

Lying fully stretched out on the grass behind the cow, I gently reinserted my right arm. I felt the taut band and, following it in an anticlockwise direction as far as I could, I could just feel a hoof of the calf. It was tight, but I gently managed to insert my arm far enough to grab the leg. That was a good sign. If I was able to get my arm in that far, it meant the twist was probably only 180 degrees and we had a better chance of untwisting it.

'OK,' I said, 'I'm ready for you to roll her.' They gently rocked her onto her left flank. With the cow's legs now exposed, I had to be careful not to be kicked. Arthur took some ropes and looped them around the front and back legs separately, then took hold of the front legs and head, while Mary took the back legs, and together they pulled on them, gradually rolling her onto her back and then onto her right side. Bending both hind and front legs up, they were then able to rock her back up into a sitting position.

The effect was miraculous: the taut band was gone, and I could now insert my arm much further and more easily I could feel the calf's legs and the head, so it was presenting normally, and its mother was obviously feeling more comfortable. I felt a contraction, then another. On the third one, her waters broke. With my arm still inside her up to my shoulder, my head just inches away and my whole body stretched out behind me, I was on the receiving end of the entirety of her amniotic and allantoic fluid. About 12 litres of warm, slimy, pungent foetal fluid drenched my head, flooded down my back into my pants, and down my legs, filling the bottom couple of inches of my wellingtons. It was as though someone had just thrown a bathtub full of the stuff all over me. I could not have been any wetter. I realized why, on that wild and windy night in Ireland, Ian had taken his top off. Why hadn't I thought that through? The result was, quite simply, disgusting.

'Oh my! Well, I never!' commented Mary. 'I think you might be a little wet young man. But should I deduce from this that rolling her has worked?'

I desperately attempted to maintain my composure and professionalism and sound in complete control.

'Yes, yes indeed, Mrs Watts. It worked perfectly. We . . . we should be able to calve her without too much difficulty now.'

I hadn't moved at all since being drenched. There was no need for me to stay in that position now the uterus had untwisted; besides, the next job was to get the calf out. But I knew any movement I made would just reinforce how disgustingly drenched I was. There was nothing for it though, so taking a deep breath, while at the same time trying not to inhale, I got up and squelched over to the back of the Land Rover to retrieved my calving ropes.

Placing one of these around each of the calf's forelegs, we then connected them up to the jack and slowly ratcheted him out: a large, healthy bull calf. All was well. It was a great result; the torsion must have been a recent event for it to have caused so little trauma to either the uterus or calf. I was delighted with the outcome – though couldn't help being somewhat distracted by the warm, slimy fluid that was rapidly cooling and congealing against my body and, as it did so, becoming more viscose, sticking my hairs to my clothing. The result was that every movement I now made involved a painful plucking of my body hair. I tried to maintain a cool air of professionalism, but my movements must have resembled that of a possessed robot. Fortunately, Arthur and Mary were too delighted with the calf to notice me.

'That 'ere Jackie was right – you *are* all right! Well done, Mr Vet, that there I think was a most impressive job.' Arthur slapped me on the back. I tried to appear grateful – I was genuinely thrilled – but his slap had sent a jet of cold fluid down into my pants, reawakening that cold and slimy sensation that my body was desperately trying to forget.

Happy that the mother was attending her calf and all seemed well, Mary now turned her attention to me.

'I think it's time we got you a shower. Have you got a change of clothes?'

Still new to this way of life, I felt slightly uncomfortable taking a shower in a stranger's house. Besides, I didn't have anything else to change into so the thought of putting my cold, wet, slimy and pungent clothes back on after a warm shower did not appeal.

'That's very kind, Mrs Watts, but unfortunately I don't have a change of clothes so I'll probably just head home to clean up.'

'You mean you won't even stay for some tea and cake?' she said, crestfallen. 'I baked one specially . . . I'm sure we could find some old flannel trousers of Arthur's for you to change into.'

I stole a subtle glance at Arthur. He was 6 foot tall, with at least a 36-inch waist. A pair of his trousers would drown me, I thought, but then it would be the height of rudeness to decline tea and cake.

'You are so extremely kind,' I stammered, 'but I think it best to get off home to shower and change, and I wouldn't want to come into you house like this, so maybe I could just have a cup of tea and cake outside . . .'

'Oh don't you worry about our house, dear, it's seen far worse than the likes of you in that state, believe you me.'

And so, fifteen minutes later, against every instinct for normal manners, decorum and etiquette, I found myself pre-cariously perched on a kitchen chair, a drenched, sticky, smelly mess, opposite a very relaxed Arthur, while Mary busied herself cutting into a delightful-looking sponge cake and then seeing to the kettle boiling away on the Rayburn behind me. The tea was quenching and the cake delicious so I made the best of my unpleasant state by having seconds of both. My external predicament was not improved, however, despite the satisfying tea break. Having exchanged thanks with them, I carefully lowered myself behind the steering wheel, started the engine and drove out of the farm.

Retracing my journey I passed the church, headed down the hill to cross the bridge over the river, but then pulled into the car park of the Rising Sun to call the practice to inform them of the successful calving and that I wouldn't be needing any assistance.

It was Hazel who answered. 'Hi, Jonathan. How are you getting on?'

'Yeah, all done, I managed to calve her – a lovely healthy bull calf.' Before I could add anything else, Hazel cut back in.

'Well done, well done indeed. Now before you head back in, there's a goat visit for you. It's in Harracott, so not far from where you are now. A Mrs Parker, at Oak Tree Cottage, she has a billy-goat that's gone lame, so if you could pop in there on your way back, that would be great.'

What I should have said was: 'I'm covered in 12 litres of unbelievable disgustingness, a lame goat isn't an emergency, so I'll go tomorrow because I'm not in any sort of state to see someone on a professional basis.'

Instead, doubtless because of my new graduate eagerness to please, the words I heard coming out of my mouth were: 'Sure! Do you have an address? I'm afraid I have no idea where that is in relation to where I am, but I can certainly head there now.'

'Great,' she replied. 'Harracott is about ten minutes away from Umberleigh . . .'

I jotted down the grid reference.

'Tell her I'm on my way.'

'Will do. Thanks, Jonathan.'

*You idiot*, I thought to myself. *What on earth were you thinking? You can't go to see a client like this!* I adjusted the rear-view mirror so I could survey the damage. I had globules of afterbirth stuck in my hair; my face had a tainted sheen to it from the dried foetal fluid; and I was still soaking wet. I thought through my options. They were limited: to go as I was, or to ring Hazel back and cancel. Neither seemed particularly appealing.

Then, in a flash of inspiration, I remembered the wetsuit I'd bought that morning, and which was still lying in its packaging in the back of the car. I remembered how snugly it had fitted when I'd tried it on, and imagined how warm it would keep me.

I could put that on, with clean waterproof trousers and top over it so it would be invisible, and what's more, I'd be dry, which would feel a hundred times better. It seemed like a perfect plan.

If anyone passing the Rising Sun on that late Thursday afternoon in September had glanced into the car park, they may have seen a green Ford Focus estate in the far corner, parked at an odd angle in an attempt to hide the dishevelled semi-naked figure behind it. After extracting myself from my sodden, odorous clothes, I made a moderate success of patting myself dry and cleaning my face with the roll of blue paper towel I always carried in the boot.

The first flaw in my plan came when I attempted to squeeze into the wetsuit. Forcing my bare left leg through the appropriate aperture, the unforgiving neoprene exfoliated most of my leg hairs, causing me to howl in pain. The dried amniotic fluid had stuck the hairs together in clumps, so any friction caused them to be ripped from their follicles. Knowing now what torture lay ahead for my right leg, I gritted my teeth and thrust it down as quickly and bravely as I could. The pain was so acute and intense I nearly collapsed.

With my legs in, I pulled the suit up to my waist, before realizing I now had to go through the whole ordeal again with both my arms. It was starting to dawn on me that maybe this wasn't the most robust and foolproof plan in the world. Nevertheless I continued with a stubborn defiance drawn from the conviction that this was now my only option: Hazel would by now have called Mrs Parker, and she would be expecting me.

Wetsuit now on, I blanched at zipping it up, so instead hauled a clean pair of waterproofs over the top and slipped my bare feet into my saturated wellies. I looked at my reflection in the passenger window. The collar of my waterproof top did a good job of hiding the wetsuit at the neck, but the long sheaths of its rubberized arms could not be disguised, poking out weirdly from the short sleeves of the waterproof. It would have to do. Was it such a ludicrous idea, after all, that a professional vet would attire themselves in a wetsuit? And in any case, British politeness would surely save the day.

Ten minutes later, I was speeding towards Harracott to attend to Mrs Parker's lame billy-goat. And it was now that I discovered the insulating benefits of the 5/3mm wetsuit that Martin had recommended. Within minutes I was sweating profusely and, despite turning the air-conditioning on full blast, I felt there was a distinct possibility that I could evaporate before making it to my destination. The chinks in this plan were rapidly turning into gapping chasms; perhaps I needed to re-evaluate my method of decision-making as a matter of priority.

Oak Tree Cottage was a quaint, whitewashed, nineteenth-century cottage, with black timber-framed windows and a slated tiled roof, and I easily found it. Parking outside, I wiped the sweat from my brow as I reviewed my appearance in the rear-view mirror. My face was flushed, my hair was a mess, and the combined aroma of sweat and foetal waters was overwhelmingly unpleasant. *Poor Mrs Parker*, I thought. I threw together a box of basic equipment that I might require: hoof knives, thermometer, gloves, stethoscope, needles, syringes and a choice selection of drugs. *Here goes*, I thought, as I shut the boot, headed for the front door and rang the doorbell.

Moments later the door was opened by a middle-aged lady in socks, jeans and a jumper, with a toddler crooked in her left arm.

'Hi! I'm Jonathan the vet. I've come to see a lame goat I believe?' She studied me for a moment. The initial and familiar facial expression of a client grateful at a vet's arrival to sort out their ailing animal quickly turned to confusion as she tried to process the figure before her: a supposedly respectable professional with a very peculiar dress sense.

'Are you . . . wearing a wetsuit underneath your water-proofs?' she enquired after a moment. I couldn't believe it. My attempt to disguise it hadn't even survived ten seconds. Maybe in Camden it could have passed as a type of self-expression, but in Devon it was just pure weird.

'It's a long story,' I began.

'Interrupting your afternoon surfing?' she guessed.

'Not exactly.' I could see I wasn't going to get away with this lightly. 'I got a bit wet from my last visit and this was all I had to wear . . .'

She laughed. 'Well, I suppose I have to admire your dedication to the cause, but it wasn't an urgent call. It could have waited till tomorrow.'

I was an idiot. Why hadn't I asked Hazel to postpone the visit till tomorrow?

'Well we can't let pride get in the way of doing our job,' I said, rather primly, as much to convince her of my professionalism as to justify the humiliation I felt.

'Very admirable,' she said, moving away from the door and beckoning me in. 'I suppose you'd best come this way.'

'Er . . . my boots are very wet. Could I go around the side of the house?'

'Sure. Just head round there,' she said, pointing. 'I'll just put on my boots and meet you around the back.'

As I sashayed round the side of the house, the constricting wetsuit lending my movements an oddly stilted gait, I was grateful for the few seconds to myself. There was a large garden behind the house, littered with children's toys and paraphernalia, and beyond that was a small paddock containing three goats. Mrs Parker joined me, toddler still on her arm; in addition a little boy of around five was now accompanying her, wearing bright blue wellies and an oversized coat. He eyed me suspiciously.

'Mummy, who's that?' he asked, pointing at me.

'That's the vet, Jamie. He's come to look at Bertie. Remember I said Bertie had a sore leg? The vet has come to make him better.' The answer seemed to satisfy him, but he continued to assess me warily.

'They're over this way, in the paddock,' Mrs Parker said leading the way. 'We have three. Two girls and a boy.'

The little boy followed close behind, and then, tugging on his mother's jacket, piped up again.

'Mummy, Mummy! Why is he wearing a wetsuit?'

Mrs Parker burst out laughing. Then, in a brave attempt to salvage my dignity from her five-year-old son, said, 'Sometimes vets do jobs where they get wet or mucky so it's useful to have something to stop their clothes getting wet.' It was an admirable effort and I was grateful, but Jamie wasn't so easily bought.

'But a wetsuit is for going in the water and we are on land. It seems silly to me.'

'You're right, darling,' Mrs Parker conceded, and with this confirmation that his logic had been faultless, Jamie proceeded to start repeatedly chanting, 'Silly wetsuit man, silly wetsuit man, silly, silly wetsuit man!' all the while oblivious to his mother's whispered commands of 'Jamie that's enough.'

'Bertie is that one over there,' she said, pointing at the obvious male of the group as we reached the gate. 'I put him on his chain earlier so he'd be easier to catch, but I'm afraid I can't really hold him for you with this one on my arm –' gesturing at the baby she was holding. 'Can you manage on your own? They're pretty tame, but you could always wait for my husband to get back if not.'

It wasn't ideal, but I was keen to get the visit over and done with as quickly as possible, and with Jamie insisting on being such an angelic child, I preferred not to have the humiliation of meeting Mr Parker as well.

'No problem,' I said, and opened the gate to head into the paddock. Mrs Parker and Jamie stayed in the garden, Mrs Parker leaning against the fence, Jamie peering through it.

'Don't worry, Bertie,' he shouted. 'Silly wetsuit man is going to make you better.'

Wetsuits and vets would probably now be synonymous for Jamie, seared into his consciousness forever.

The paddock was about an acre. An open-fronted shed was situated in the corner to the left of the gate, straw-bedding spilling out onto the grass. To the right of that, a large metal peg, connected to a 5-metre chain, was imbedded in the ground. At the end of the chain was a large white billy-goat, who after grazing contentedly moments before, now eyed me balefully as I approached. I could immediately see from his tentative movements that the problem was located in his left hind leg. Bertie's initial suspicion did not develop into attempted flight. Instead he clearly assumed that my vet's box bore some delicious delicacy, and he limped over to greet me. His interest in the box, which swiftly became an obsession, meant it would be impossible to put it down without him attempting to devour its contents. But it gave me an idea.

'Do you have any feed you give them that I could use as a distraction?' I asked Mrs Parker

'I've got some hay, but otherwise they just graze the grass.'

'Hay will do. Could you put some in a bucket?'

'Sure.' She disappeared off to the garden shed, returning moments later with a bucket of hay, full to overflowing.

'Perfect, thanks,' I said, taking it off her. Bertie was still intrigued by my box, and followed it as far as his chain would allow. I carefully left it by the fence, extracting a hoof knife, and returned to Bertie with the bucket of hay. He immediately descended on it, tucking into the hay with gusto. The distraction allowed me the chance to examine his foot. I bent down to pick it up – and immediately felt the embarrassing restriction of my ridiculous attire. *I had voluntarily decided to wear this?* I thought. *What was I thinking?* Examining Bertie's foot, it was quite clear what the problem was (and I was grateful for the distraction). There was an ulcerated sore in between its two claws. I examined the rest of the leg, but there were no other problems, so some painkillers and a burst of Terramycin spray should do the trick. I put the foot down and wandered back to my box, Bertie remaining engrossed in his bucket of hay.

'What do you think the problem is?' Mrs Parker asked.

'He's got scald,' I told her. 'It's very common, don't worry. It's an ulcerative sore between the claws caused by environmental bacteria. Very easy to treat . . .'

Back at my box, I drew up some Finadyne, an anti-inflammatory, grabbed the Terramycin spray, and returned to the goat.

'I'll give him some pain relief as well,' I said, injecting into his muscle. Bertie didn't flinch, his head still in the bucket. *Goats really are food-obsessed*, I thought. I picked up his foot and sprayed between the claws.

'That should do it,' I said, releasing his foot to the ground and heading back to my box.

'Thank you,' said Mrs Parker. 'He'll be happy finishing off his bucket of hay. You must be a little hot in your outfit,' she added with a chuckle. I became conscious of the beads of sweat now dripping from my forehead.

Then Jamie joined in. 'Did you make Bertie better, Mr Silly Wetsuit Man?'

'I hope so,' I said, making my way through the gate back into the garden.

'Poor Bertie,' he sighed.

'He's your favourite, isn't he, Jamie?' said Mrs Parker as we headed back to the house. Then, turning to me, she added,

'Would you like a cup of tea? I completely understand if you want to just get home, but the offer's there.'

'That's very kind of you, but . . . yes, I think I will just head off.'

'I thought you might.'

As we reached the front of the house, a car pulled into the drive.

'Daddy's home, Daddy's home!' Jamie shouted in excitement, rushing to the driver's door of the now parked car.

My heart sank as Mr Parker stepped out of the car and gathered Jamie into his arms.

'Have you been a good boy for Mummy?' he enquired, but Jamie completely ignored the question.

'Daddy, Daddy, this man is wearing a wetsuit on land, silly man, he came to make Bertie better.'

Mr Parker, having only half listened to his son, turned to his wife.

'Hi, darling,' she said. 'This is Jonathan, the vet. He came to have a look at Bertie.' Her husband stuck out his hand to shake mine, only then gaining a full appreciation of what Jamie had been saying.

'Oh, I see . . . You are indeed wearing a wetsuit. Have you been treating seals today or something?'

'It's a . . . long story?' I replied feebly, noticing the exchange of glances between Mr and Mrs Parker. 'Anyway, I'd best be getting off. Bertie should be fine now, but any further problems, then give me a call.'

And with that I made a dash for the car, quickly loading my box into the boot, before slumping behind my steering wheel, starting the engine and speeding away, praying that Bertie would not actually need a revisit in the next few days.

# Goats: fast facts

*Capra aegagrus hircus*: The domestic goat

**Distribution:** Global, following domestication of the wild goat of south-west Asia and eastern Europe.

**Description:** The domestic goat is a sub-species of the wild goat, *Capra aegagrus*, with over 300 distinct breeds.

**Names:** The male is called a 'buck' or 'billy', the female a 'doe' or 'nanny', and their young a 'kid'. A group of goats is called a 'tribe'.

**Life span:** About 15–18 years.

**Husbandry:** In much of the world they are usually free to wander hills and other grazing areas tended by goatherds, who are frequently children. Elsewhere, they are usually stabled, tethered or contained in small paddocks.

**Diet:** Goats are ruminants, like cattle and sheep, but are browsers rather than grazers. They will often chew on anything, but prefer vines, shrubs and weeds to grasses. They are used in Chinese tea plantations, to eat the weeds and fertilize the plants while avoiding the tea leaves themselves because of their bitter taste.

**Gestation:** 150 days. The breeding season depends on their global location, the female's 21-day cycle either commencing when day-length shortens or lasting all year round in equatorial regions.

Aged 2 with my grandparents' dog Ben on holiday in the New Forest; we were inseparable.

Helping out with lambing in North Devon, aged 8.

Proud of my chicken-wrangling skills, aged 3.

IMAGE COURTESY ALL THINGS WILD

A Brazilian three-banded armadillo – the nine-banded armadillo's little cousin.

The Wildlife Vet's capture team walking a giraffe to the trailer.

The head collar allows for some control as we drive the giraffe out of the bush to the waiting trailer and with a blindfold on and ear plugs in, he is much calmer, but I still had to be careful that he didn't knock me off the platform with an effortless swipe of his neck.

IMAGE COURTESY OF PRIYA BAPODRA-VILLAVERDE

Bjorn demonstrating successful cardiopulmonary resuscitation on a giraffe.

Leopards are very cuddly when they are asleep! This was a young female leopard we worked on out in Africa.

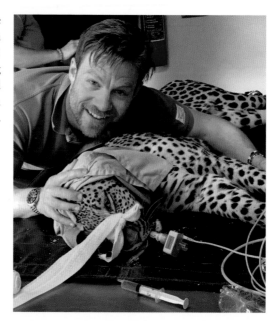

I had to get a quick photo with her before she was woken up.

IMAGE COURTESY ALL THINGS WILD

No surprise that these Boer goats were more interested in their food than posing for a photo with me!

Job done! Elephants successfully sedated for relocation, there's just time for a quick photo with Derek, Wayne and Lotter before they wake up.

Standing on the trailer with Lotter at our final destination, just before we unloaded and woke him and his fellow elephants.

The first elephant I ever worked on (a 30-year-old bull elephant), having just finished replacing his tracking collar.

Two beautiful, fully-horned rhinos. I took this in Kruger National Park in 2013. On my last two trips to Kruger I have not seen a single rhino; their absence a tragic reality and proof of how hard the park has been hit by poaching in the last decade.

A successful humane dehorning; a good team can carry out the procedure in about twenty minutes with minimal stress to the rhino, but sadly even dehorned rhinos are now being targeted by poachers.

**Weight:** Anything from 20 kg for pygmy breeds to 140 kg for Boers.

**Size and growth:** Sexual maturity is reached anywhere between 3 and 15 months, and full size at 2–3 years.

**Body temperature:** 38.8–39.4 °C.

**Conservation:** The domestic goat is one of the most wildly distributed agricultural animals in the world, due to its multiplicity of uses to humanity. More humans consume goat's milk globally than cow's milk; their meat is popular to consume, their manure can be used as a fertilizer, their fibre and hide for clothing or leather products, and they are useful for clearing land of unwanted vegetation and carrying light loads. It is estimated that there are around 924 million domestic goats worldwide, so happily they are not a threatened species, like some others in this book. Why not celebrate the huge benefit this animal has been to humanity by sending a goat to someone in the developing world, by visiting: **www. musthavegifts.org/a-goat.html?**.

# 6

# ELEPHANT

*'There is no creature among all the Beasts of the world
which hath so great and ample demonstration of the
power and wisdom of Almighty God as the Elephant.'*

Edward Topsell

I was sitting in the driving seat of the Ford Ranger, seat reclined, feet resting on the frame of my open door, watching the interactions of two lilac-breasted rollers in the mimosa trees on the other side of the sandy track, lost in my thoughts. My two sleeping passengers were oblivious to this, as they were to the little duiker that moments before had darted across the track just feet in front of me, disappearing as quickly as it had come. For the moment, it was a waiting game. The two-way radio that lay next to the gearstick had been silent since Ben, Andres and Lyle had left three hours before.

We were in thick bush at the base of a mountain region just outside the South African town of Hoedspruit. Our objective was to find, dart and radio-collar one of three young bull elephants that had broken out of a game reserve several months previously. They had migrated 40 km from their home and had now settled in this region, hiding in thick bush during the day and then feasting on a local farmer's mango and orange crops at night. Understandably, the farmer felt that the elephants had outstayed their welcome and was keen to have them removed from the farm before they destroyed his livelihood.

Over the previous two months various attempts had been made by helicopter, initially to herd them back towards the reserve, and then, when they had migrated too far, to move them away from areas where they would cause destruction, but both had failed. Now they had a taste for oranges and mangos, and seemed to have settled into their daily routine, making this area their new home, and only two options remained: to shoot them, or to relocate them. Fortunately, the farmer was keen on the latter if possible, and the charity, Elephants Alive, had stepped in to organize and fund the operation.

The logistics of relocating three bull elephants weighing in the region of 3 tonnes each, from a relatively inaccessible mountainous area, were colossal, so it was decided to break the operation down into two components. Fortunately, the elephants were sticking together, running as a small bachelor herd. So Phase One was to dart and collar one of the three elephants so that their movements could be monitored and they could easily be located for Phase Two, which would be the actual relocation. Phase One would also give the time for a proper understanding of what would be required for Phase Two. This was our second attempt at Phase One, the first having ended in failure a few days earlier, when darkness had fallen before we were able to locate the elephants. So today we had set off from Nelspruit at 4.30 a.m., in order to arrive at the farm for 7 a.m., to give us a full day to try to find the group, and collar one.

These elephants were completely wild, which not only meant that they were easily spooked, but also that they were potentially very dangerous, a danger enhanced by the fact that they were only accessible by foot. For these reasons, the plan was for a skeleton team to go in first to locate and dart one, and then the rest of the team would drive as close as possible, bringing in the equipment for the procedure, once the elephant was down and the area secure. This skeleton team consisted of Andres, the tracker, who was key to finding the elephants; Ben, who would dart the elephant; and Lyle, the third member of the team, who, armed with a rifle, would act as their body-guard, in case the worst happened and one of the elephants charged them.

After an hour of trying to pick up a good lead on the elephants' movements from the night before, we had got the two trucks as close as we could, and then Andres, Ben and Lyle had left on foot. It had been an extraordinary experience to watch Andres work. His vision for things that seemed undetectable to the rest of us was incredible. Water droplets on a sandy track 50 metres from a dam told him that they had drunk from there a few hours previously: walking away from the dam with their trunks down, the water drips out of them in a character-istic fashion. Dry sap from broken branches indicated when the branches were broken. Dung could be aged to the nearest few hours, and then footprints and trunk prints indicated the direction, time and speed of their movement. It was a com-pletely invisible language to me, but for Andres it was as clear and as easy as reading a book.

It was now 11 a.m.; the team had been gone for three hours. It was impossible to know how long the wait would be; a call could come at any moment, or else not for another five hours. Looking in my rear-view mirror I could see the Elephant Alive team passing the time playing cards. This was not an unfamiliar scenario to them. Anyone with any experience of wildlife work quickly learns how to pass endless hours of waiting. It could infuriate some, but for me there was something magical and wonderful about just being out in the African bush and waiting for that call to action: the job you had come to do, and an experience that would become a treasured memory for the rest of your life.

The perfect peace and tranquillity was suddenly lost as a whispering voice crackled across the radio. It was Lyle.

'We've located them, 100 metres in front of us. Ben and Andres are making an approach to get close enough to dart. I will send through our GPS location. Stand by.'

'Roger that,' I replied.

My two passengers were instantly roused and ready to go. I climbed out of the truck to relay the news to the others. From the GPS coordinates we could plan how best to access them and how close we could get in with the vehicles. But there was no guarantee that this would be their final location. The elephants might spook, leading to several more hours of tracking, and even if darted, they could still travel about 2 km in the eight minutes it took for the dart to take effect. We had to be ready to respond instantly.

A further half an hour passed before we heard anything, but then Lyle came back on the radio.

'They've just darted one. He hasn't fled, but is moving off. Ben and Andres are following him – but come to the location I sent you.' The relief in his voice was evident. It was difficult to speculate what exactly had happened, but it had obviously been a very tense time.

I passed on the information, and then jumped behind the driver's seat. As we set off I pulled over to let Jess, who was driving the Elephants Alive team vehicle, take the lead. They had been patrolling the area for over a month now and had an intimate knowledge of the arterial network of tracks in this thick maze of bush and rocks – though to call them 'tracks' was a generous description. They were more like an area in this thick bush where there was slightly less flora and a few more rocks.

Within moments the truck in front was invisible amid the haze of dust it generated. Jess wasn't hanging about, and with large boulders partially blocking the route in places, it took all my concentration to navigate these obstacles at speed to stay on her tail.

Ten minutes later we arrived at the GPS location. Lyle was standing by the side of the road, gun at the ready.

'He's gone down over there.' He pointed off into the thick bush to our right. 'Fortunately, he only travelled about 200 metres after he was darted, so he's just a few minutes away by foot. The two others seem to have fled, but I'll escort you just in case they decide to come back for their mate.' It was a matter-of-fact comment, but the way he left it hanging conjured images in my mind of what that would be like, and I knew it would be utterly terrifying.

Even the ostensibly simple job of placing a radio collar on an elephant required a fair amount of equipment. For starters, the collar itself was about 6 inches wide, half an inch thick and 10 feet long. Then there was the counterweight, weighing in at about 15 kg, which would be attached to the collar on the underside of the elephant's neck to stop it slipping when the elephant moved. Not to mention the portable angle grinder, an electric drill, and lengths of metal cable and cable ties that were all essential for making the job as quick and efficient as possible. The danger was extreme – not because the anaesthetic might fail, but because every passing moment that this bull elephant was separated from his fellows increased the risk of their returning to find him.

We headed into the bush lugging the boxes of equipment, with Lyle directing us from the rear, gun at the ready, as he carefully and systematically studied every direction for signs of imminent danger. Fortunately none came, and after five minutes of negotiating trees, bushes, a ditch and thick undergrowth, we arrived at the darted elephant. At about twenty-five years of age, he was a sub-adult, but at such close quarters his size was still formidable. Lying on his right side, trunk fully extended, he had gone down perfectly in a small clearing and was sleeping soundly. With every breath came a booming snore that reverberated through his trunk and filled our otherwise silent surroundings. Ben and Andres had already covered his upper eye with his large leafy ear to minimize external stimulation, and placed a carefully constructed twig in the end of his trunk to keep it unobstructed and to ease his breathing.

Once we had absorbed the initial beauty and majesty of the animal sleeping in front of us, we set about fixing the collar. First, the metal cable was fed under his neck, using cable ties to secure it to the collar itself, which we were then able to pull back through, under his neck. Next, we measured it for size, ensuring the transmitter would sit on the top of his neck, and allowing a gap of two hand-breadths between the collar and his neck so that it wasn't too tight. The counterweight was then fitted and bolted to the collar, the excess length of the bolts and the collar were removed with the angle grinder, and the job was done. It took no more than ten minutes in total. While Ben, Jess and I had been fixing the collar, the others had been gathering various data on the animal for Elephants Alive's records and database, our safety all the while guaranteed by Lyle's careful patrol of the area.

The equipment was finally gathered up and people started heading back to the trucks. Drawing up the reversal drug into a 2-ml syringe, Ben handed it to me.

'You can wake him up now.'

'OK,' I replied. I waited till everyone was a safe distance away, then found one of the large ear veins and injected the Naltrexone into it, before heading back in the direction of the truck to join Ben by a tree 100 metres away, from where we could safely monitor the elephant's recovery. Within a minute he was attempting to lift his head and gain some purchase on the ground with his feet. He had a few failed attempts at lifting his head, rocking himself onto his chest, but within a further minute he had done so and from there he was soon on his feet. Happy that he was alive and well, and with the collar secured, we scurried back to the truck, and rapidly withdrew.

Once back at the farm, Jess got out her iPad to show us a map of the area, on which could now be seen the route the elephant had taken since waking up and wandering off. The tracking collar was working. Phase One was complete.

The following Friday we returned to the farm for Phase Two: relocation. The logistics of this operation were truly massive, including two helicopters, three flatbed trailers, a crane, a JCB, the capture team, the veterinary team, the Elephants Alive team, and a television crew. The local highways authorities had also been informed, and a road escort arranged.

When we arrived at the farm at 6.30 a.m. there was already a fleet of vehicles and a crowd of people milling around. It was such an exciting and rare event that the Elephant Alive volunteers, some veterinary students and friends of those involved in the procedure, had all come along to witness it. There must have been thirty people there already, and that was without the capture team, helicopter pilots and many of the other essential participants.

We headed over to greet Michelle, the senior member of the Elephants Alive team and key coordinator of the operation. We had met her at the first collaring attempt, but she hadn't been at the second, successful one because she was attending the funeral of Wayne Derek Lotter, the great wildlife and elephant conservationist who had been tragically murdered two weeks before. Amazingly bravely, his wife and two daughters had decided to participate in this relocation as a way of honouring Wayne's memory, and Michelle had asked them if they would allow the three elephants to be named after him. It was a wonderful gesture for a man who had worked tirelessly for twenty-seven years and ultimately given his life to protect Africa's wildlife, and elephants in particular.

The news was frustrating: the team had been feeding the elephants all week to encourage them into a more accessible area, but the night before they had migrated back into the thick bush in the mountains. They were totally inaccessible by road so we would be completely reliant on the skill of the helicopter pilots to locate them and then drive them out of the mountains to a more approachable area where we could bring in the crane and flatbed trailers to load them. The fear was that because the elephants had already been exposed to helicopters several times they might just ignore them, staying hidden and inaccessible. If that happened the whole operation would have to be abandoned and rearranged at vast extra expense with further coordination headaches. No wonder Michelle looked tense.

As if on cue, a gentle humming suddenly caught our ear, growing slowly louder as its source became visible. Both helicopters came into view flying in tandem, one in front of the other, first Gerry in his little R22, followed by Jacques in his bigger R44.

Produced by the Robinson Helicopter Company, these were the two models of choice in wildlife work, and I had seen them both in action. The R44, designed in 1992, was a four-seater helicopter, more stable and sturdy, but less manoeuvrable than its older brother, the two-seater R22, designed nearly twenty years earlier. The R22 was great for herding animals – it could come in very low, and keep up with the jinking, weaving and direction change of even the quickest antelope – but the R44 was the better craft for darting. The vet could sit behind the pilot and follow his line of sight as they came upon the animal, and the R44 would hold more steadily against the wind for the shot.

They circled several times looking for a safe landing spot, but with electricity cables running above us and trees surrounding the area there didn't seem an obvious location. Jacques settled for somewhere on the other side of the farm buildings, but Gerry opted for a small clearing among a collection of macadamia trees, 20 metres from us. It was a tiny spot that in no way seemed large enough for a helicopter to fit through, but with pinpoint precision, propeller blades only a foot or two away from the branches, Gerry brought his R22 down. Johan and his capture team arrived shortly after the helicopters. They had parked the flatbed trailers and crane at the entrance to the farm.

With the whole team assembled, the plan was discussed. The GPS coordinates of the elephants' current location were given to Gerry and Jacques, who discussed their plan of approach while Ben, Silke and I sorted through our equipment. Ben would be darting them from Jacques's helicopter, Silke and I would then monitor them until Ben joined us, and once loaded onto their respective trailers we would each travel with an elephant, to monitor and maintain its anaesthetic for the three-hour journey. We would be using a drug called Etorphine

as the main anaesthetic, a highly potent and extremely dangerous opioid and the most feared drug in veterinary medicine.
A few drops injected into a human, in an open wound, in the
eye or in the mouth, would be fatal without administering the
reversal agent. Depending on the depth of anaesthesia and the
size of the animal, a mere 0.2 or 0.3 ml injected into an ear
vein every twenty minutes was all that was required to keep a
3-tonne elephant asleep.

I had worked with Etorphine before, but never quite like
this; I would be riding on a flatbed trailer across bumpy,
bouncy tracks trying to maintain my balance by wedging
myself between the elephant's tusks while attempting to draw
up a dose of Etorphine that would easily kill me if I accidentally
injected myself. The thought alone made me perspire nervously.
It was going to require all my concentration and focus to keep
the elephant asleep and not myself. It was probably best to lay
off the coffee; I didn't want to risk a case of the shakes.

With their equipment checked and a plan in place, Ben
and Jacques headed to the R44, while Gerry returned to
his R22. Moments later the two helicopters were airborne,
mere specks in the sky as they ventured to the mountains in
search of the three elephants. The rest of us loaded into our
respective vehicles and made for the edge of the dense bush
that surrounded the base of this mountain region. The plan
was to bring the elephants down to this area to dart them, but
even if it worked, we would still have to use a JCB to clear a
path through the bush for the trailers. Once loaded, the trailers
would be exiting across three fields to join the main track out
of the farm. These were each about 100 acres, one of tobacco,
one of potatoes and the third a recently ploughed fallow field.
With each trailer laden with an elephant, getting stuck was a
real possibility. Once out of the farm, the journey would take us
onto the main road to Hoedspruit, 10 miles away, through the

town, and then onto the arterial road (speed limit 70 mph) for 12 miles, before turning off to the game reserve where we would have another fifteen-minute journey to the airfield, where they would then be unloaded and woken up. There were going to be challenges every step of the way, and to list the whole host of things that could potentially go wrong would be paralysing.

Once we were all in place, it became another waiting game, only this time we could gauge some of what was going on by watching the helicopters in the distance scouring the forest below them. Despite the GPS coordinates that Michelle had given them, the elephants seemed elusive among the dense flora. Back and forth the two helicopters went, working together like a pair of collie dogs combing the Welsh hills for sheep, but after half an hour they still hadn't located them. It dawned on me how difficult the task would have been without one of them being collared: a needle in a haystack, utterly impossible.

Gerry landed briefly to recheck Michelle's map and confirm their current location and then was gone again, but this time they had more success. Reporting back, Gerry informed us that they were at the bottom of a ravine by a stream that ran down from the mountain. As we watched from a distance the R22 disappeared as Gerry took it down into the ravine in an attempt to get this small bachelor herd moving. From our vantage point a mile away it was impossible to know how dangerous the manoeuvre was, but Jacques said afterwards that there wasn't enough room for the R44 to do it. Just another day in the office for a wildlife helicopter pilot.

The manoeuvre worked and word came back that the elephants were on the move following the stream down the mountain. Gerry said afterwards that the animals were clearly familiar with the route, and so he knew his best chance of keeping them moving was to let them travel this path at their own pace, only occasionally intervening with gentle encouragement. His technique worked well and with Jacques now flanking him on the right, the elephants maintained a steady pace down the mountain in our direction. Most of the fears for the job had centred on this first part of the operation: getting the elephants to an area where they could be darted and accessed relatively easily. It had gone incredibly well. Now it was time for the relocation.

'The first one's darted,' Jacques's voice crackled across the radio. 'Stand by, we're trying to keep the group together.'

Even without hearing that message, an onlooker would have known something had changed. A frenzy descended around the helicopters as their course changed. No longer travelling at a slow, steady directional pace, they were now nipping back and forth circling an area no bigger than a couple of hundred metres in diameter. Meanwhile Johan signalled to his team to get ready, as we jumped onto the back of the truck. I would take the first elephant.

'OK, he's going down, we need a team in.'

Johan didn't need telling twice. Starting up his truck, he bulldozed his own path through the trees and bushes, oblivious to the hazards he was creating for his passengers on the back as we dodged the thorny branches that threatened to whip or impale us. Time was of the essence: if the elephant came down on his trunk, he could suffocate. We headed in the direction of where Jacques's R44 was hovering, but seemingly through ever thicker bush. Then suddenly we found ourselves in a clearing and there in front of us was the elephant, lying on his side against some small trees, his trunk safely coiled out in front of him. Seeing our arrival, Ben gave us the thumbs-up from the helicopter hovering 50 metres above us and with that they left in pursuit of the next two.

The initial sight of the elephant was momentarily paralysing, but I quickly regained my composure, conscious that

I now had to step up to my role. I assessed my patient. He seemed stable, and very asleep. His thunderous snores would have been intimidating if I hadn't experienced them the week before, and I felt grateful for that experience.

Happy that he was positioned well and safely asleep, Johan gathered the rest of his team together to head back to wait for the other two to be darted. He turned to me.

'You happy with him? First top-up is usually after forty minutes – he was darted ten minutes ago so in thirty minutes. Dumisum will stay with you, he knows what he's doing, but if the other two bulls come back for their friend, then hide behind this one, and keep quiet and still. The eyes in the sky should protect you.'

His words highlighted the potential danger of the situation, and my mind was racing with scenarios as Johan and the rest of his team jumped back into the truck and disappeared out of sight. I suddenly felt very alone and vulnerable. Dumisum's reaction was very different. Sitting by the elephant's head, relaxing and enjoying himself, he pulled out his phone and started taking selfies with the animal, then handed me the phone and asked me to take one of him with it. As I stood back on the path to get all the elephant into the picture I felt very exposed.

'Have you ever been charged by an elephant?' I asked.

He laughed. 'Yeah, a couple of times. The first time, he came out of nowhere, a full-on charge. I sprinted for the nearest rock, but I didn't think I'd make it, then suddenly the helicopter came in low and scared him off. I needed to change my clothes afterwards . . .' He laughed again at the memory.

Logic told me we were pretty safe with two helicopters in the air so I tried to put stray thoughts out of my mind and concentrate on monitoring my patient, but there was a base level of fear that proved somewhat distracting; my senses were on full alert.

The helicopters seemed to be getting closer now. I looked down the track towards where the noise was coming from. I could see the R44 and . . . was that an elephant in the thicket below it? My whole body tensed nervously, crouching next to the rump of my patient. Surely this track would be the obvious route for his escape. Any moment now I might see him emerge, heading straight for us. I tried to maintain my composure in front of Dumisum as I focused on the elephant-like object 200 metres away. I was looking for any movement to allow me to positively identify it before I sounded the alarm. As the seconds passed and the helicopters moved away, I realized it had just been my mind playing tricks on me.

Panic over, I found myself relaxing into the role. I recorded his breathing: 4 breaths a minute. I found a pulse from an artery in his ear: 44 beats a minute. No trunk movement. I lifted up his ear to check his eye position and palpebral reflex. I jumped in shock to find the eye staring straight back at me. In most species the eye looks down when an animal reaches a good plane of anaesthesia. All my other tests told me he was stable and in a deep sleep, but his eye position was unnerving. This had to be normal for elephants, I thought, as I replaced the flap of his ear to cover the eye, mentally resolving not to scare myself with it again. I looked at my watch. It was 9.20 a.m. He had been darted at nine, so it would be another twenty minutes before his first top-up was due. I just had to wait and watch, but for the time being I had nothing to do. Somehow that didn't seem quite right, so I did my checks again. Breaths: 4. Pulse: 44. Unsurprisingly, they hadn't changed in the last two minutes. I reached for my radio to check it was on. It was; I hadn't missed anything, no one had been trying to get hold of me.

Pull yourself together, I told myself. Your patient is stable; the other two will be darted shortly, and then the crowds will descend. Enjoy this moment while you can; being out here on your own in the African bush, with an anaesthetized elephant. This was something I could have only dreamt of as a fresh-faced eager nineteen-year-old veterinary student; seventeen years on, I was living that dream. As the realization sunk in of where I was and what I was doing, I smiled to myself and gently ran my hands over the elephant's thick, leathery hide down to his feet, just letting all my senses soak up this experience.

Absorbed in the moment, I was unaware of when exactly it happened, but slowly it dawned on me that silence had descended. The helicopters had landed, which could only mean one thing: the other two elephants had been darted and the teams were with them. I knew it would only be a matter of time before our relative tranquillity was interrupted. I checked the elephant's parameters again. Respiratory rate was now 5, and pulse was 48 beats per minute. Then Dumisum pointed out a slight curling of his trunk. I checked my watch: 9.40 a.m. He was obviously just getting slightly lighter, which corresponded with Johan's time frame. I drew up my first dose of Etorphine – 0.3 ml – found the vein and injected it. I was grateful to be giving the first dose in this calm, quiet environment. I could focus fully on what I was doing, undistracted, but I knew the next time would be different. The elephant took a deeper breath, and then nothing for what seemed like an age. He was already responding to the Etorphine; his respiratory rate dropped to 3 breaths a minute and his heart rate down to 40 beats. This was the normal effect of the drug, and it was reassuring to see it. If the anaesthetic followed this pattern, my job would be a lot easier and less stressful.

The engine of a JCB suddenly broke the silence, followed by the cracking of trees as it ploughed a path towards us. Silke's voice came through on the radio.

'Jonathan, how are you doing? Is he still asleep? Is he still alive?' The air of humour was evident in her tone.

'All good,' I replied. 'Still asleep, he hasn't walked off yet.'

'Good. Have you topped him up yet? I'm on my way over to you, I need to swap elephants.'

'Yeah, he had his first top-up a couple of minutes ago. He's stable for you to take over.' The rationale for the swap eluded me, but I wasn't going to question it.

Moments later Silke joined me. I briefed her on the anaesthetic, and after she had pointed me in the direction of the other elephants, which had been darted together, I headed off to find them.

The scene that greeted me there couldn't have been more different from the quiet serenity I had just left. There were people everywhere, maybe fifty in all, some with chainsaws, some with ropes, some moving rocks and branches, some gathered round the fallen elephants with clipboards watching every breath or furiously taking notes, others just spectating. It was organized chaos.

Incredibly, these two elephants had gone down virtually simultaneously, facing each other like two drunken buddies commiserating with each other on how ill they felt before passing out. This was obviously down to the skill with which Gerry and Jacques had managed to keep them together, but it also highlighted the bond between the two elephants. Concerningly, though, one of them had gone down on his chest and was wedged between some small trees. In this position, all the abdominal organs were being pushed against his diaphragm, inhibiting his ability to breath, and if it wasn't corrected quickly it could prove fatal. The chainsaws were being used in a desperate attempt to clear the area around him so he could be pulled onto his side. Ben and Johan were actively involved in that operation, so it was the other elephant that I needed to oversee. Laura had temporarily taken charge of him. With a respiratory rate of 4 and heart rate of 40, the same as the elephant I had just left, this one too was stable and sleeping soundly. I imagined the mayhem that would ensue if one of them woke up with all these people around. I checked the pouch round my waist containing the needles, syringes and drugs.

With the other elephant now freed, lying on his side, and stable, Ben came over to touch base with me.

'Good job,' I said. 'So far, so good!'

'Gerry was insane going into that ravine, but he knows what he's doing and it did the job. How was that other elephant?'

'Sleeping like a baby. Silke's with him now.'

'Great. OK, so they'll get the JCB to clear a path for the trailers and then we can load them up and head out. Oh, and I darted this one at about twenty past nine so he should need his first top-up at ten, in about fifteen minutes.'

'Perfect,' I replied.

All went well, and in less than an hour the JCB had cleared a wide enough path through the thick brush of trees, shrubs and bushes for the first trailer to navigate a way through with the crane. By around 10.30 the first elephant's legs had been roped together, and he was slowly hoisted into the air, with two people supporting his trunk, and a team of others helping to direct his body into the right position so that he could be carefully lowered onto the trailer. Car tyres were placed under his head and hind legs to offer some cushioning, and once everyone was happy with his position he was strapped down. The straps were more to prevent him slipping during the journey than to hold him down; if he woke up, he would have little trouble freeing himself from them.

With the first elephant successfully loaded, it was now the turn for our one. The first trailer was positioned so its crane could be used for loading him onto the second trailer. The timing was perfect: it was 10.45 a.m., and I had just given him his next top-up, which meant the stimulation of the move would be less likely to rouse him. The procedure was repeated, and within ten minutes Lotter (as he had been named) was safely loaded. I made sure his ears and trunk were positioned well, while others busied themselves securing him into position. The move had brought his respiratory rate up to 5 and his heart rate to 44, but this would soon settle down. I was joined by Andrew and Laura, Andrew noting the readings, and supervising the timing and dosage of the Etorphine, and Laura to monitor the animal's breathing – and to inject me with Naltrexone if I accidentally injected myself. We settled ourselves down for the three-hour journey ahead.

Slowly we set off, the driver carefully negotiating his way along the newly created path. He drove hesitantly, constantly looking in his rear-view mirror to catch my eye to ensure that everything was going smoothly. He was clearly more used to transporting a cargo that didn't run the risk of either suddenly getting off the trailer or deciding to join him in the cab if it woke up. After ten minutes we came out of the bush to a large clearing where we were shortly joined by the other two trucks. All three elephants had been safely loaded. The operation so far seemed to be going very smoothly, but the most dangerous stage was yet to come: taking them onto the open road.

Once again, people busied themselves around the trailers, with final checks on each elephant to ensure they were secure for the journey. Others took the opportunity to pour buckets of water over them in an attempt to keep them cool in the ever-increasing midday heat. Silke, Ben and I exchanged updates on our patients. Meanwhile Jacques had once again taken to the sky, this time with the camera crew to get some aerial footage. With everything set and everyone happy it was time to set off. Lyle would be at the front of the convoy with the escort vehicle, and now went round the three trailers in turn to give his final instructions: essentially that if we had any problems we should wave hysterically and get on the radio.

Then we were off, with our trailer taking the lead, but almost instantly disaster nearly struck. A hundred metres or so from the clearing, we had to negotiate a gateway that took us into the first of the three fields. As the trailer bounced over the ruts and potholes that marked the entranceway one of the elephant's feet slipped forward, hanging off the edge of the trailer, as we approached the gate. The gap was so tight between the edge of the trailer and the gatepost that the leg was now in imminent danger of getting wedged between the two, with catastrophic consequences. Fortunately, we spotted the problem seconds before impact and frantically hammered on the driver's back window. His response was instantaneous, and the danger avoided. My heart was pounding; I had imagined all manner of things that could go wrong, but something as simple as negotiating a gatepost was not one of them. I felt my whole body tense. It was exhilarating to be so actively involved in the operation, but everything had to go smoothly, and to plan, for me to enjoy the experience rather than endure the strain that I was now feeling.

With the legs safely repositioned we continued at a crawl. The other two vehicles, cautious after our close encounter, successfully negotiated the gateway. As we made it into the open fields, I became aware of the true beauty of our surroundings, as though seeing it for the first time: the majestic mountain range in the background starkly highlighted against the pastel blue sky, the dense African bush with the acacia trees forming its canopy, and in the foreground our convoy of vehicles negotiating their way across the copper red soil through the tobacco plantation. As I stood wedged between the tusks of this 3.5-tonne elephant, his rhythmic snores audible above the grumble of the truck's engine, I once again contemplated this incredible experience.

The trucks trundled on, but we soon noticed that we had pulled ahead of the second truck, and it became apparent something was amiss. Lyle brought the convoy to a halt and went back to see the cause of the hold-up. The truck's back right wheel had slipped into the furrow bordering the edge of the muddy road, causing the trailer to tilt at a dangerous angle. If the elephant should slide, he would topple the trailer and potentially take the truck with it. I couldn't help remembering the final scene in *The Italian Job*: things were just as precariously balanced when Lyle arrived. Fortunately, the elephant remained securely positioned and with all the passengers moving to the left side of the truck to counterbalance the weight, the driver was able to correct the error and another disaster was safely averted.

The remaining journey through the fields, onto the farm track and to the farm entrance went to plan. We paused to recheck the elephants' positions and the strapping. It was also now time to top up the elephants with Azaperone, a drug that counteracts the hypertensive effects of Etorphine. The drug had been part of the original cocktail Ben had used to dart them, but after a couple of hours, the network of blood vessels in the elephants' ears were all much more prominent: a sure sign that their blood pressure had increased because the Azaperone was wearing off.

This done, we pulled out onto the main road, a convoy of about ten vehicles in total. From here on, we would be on public highways until we reached the game reserve in about an hour's time. Any problems now would become harder to correct and potentially catastrophic. The change in speed was noticeable and with nothing but the elephant to hold on to, I found myself taking up a fairly undignified position around the trunk and tusks to secure myself, but it did at least free up my hands to monitor his pulse rate and administer the Etorphine when required.

With the elephants lying on the trailers, we were each wider than a normal load, which meant that our escort at the head of the convoy had to warn oncoming vehicles of the danger ahead and get them to pull off the road to avoid us. Mindful of the crazy accidents that occur on African roads, it was unnerving to have to rely on the common sense of other drivers for our own safety, but the journey proceeded safely. As we slowly approached the roadside stalls, the proprietors and customers looked on in bewilderment, but this rapidly turned to a feverish excitement when they identified our cargo. Whoops, claps and waves of approval were showered in our direction, creating a ripple effect as they passed down the line of stalls and then died away as our surroundings turned to forests, fields or game reserves. The reactions were even more exaggerated as we passed through Hoedspruit. Even for a town in a central game reserve region, this was clearly an unusual sight. The delighted surprise was replicated on the faces of the drivers that pulled up next to us at traffic lights, the pedestrians walking the streets, restaurant diners enjoying a quiet lunch, the shoppers leaving the supermarket or those filling up with petrol at the garage. It was all a weird if temporary form of eminence that once again brought home how privileged I was to be a part of it.

Leaving Hoedspruit, we turned onto the R40 for the final leg of the journey before arriving at the reserve. This wide, open road is the main artery from north to south on the west side of Kruger, but fortunately we were travelling on it at a quiet time and despite the occasional car whistling past us at 70 mph, the road was fairly deserted. And so at last, at 12.30 p.m., after six hours of hard and dangerous work, we turned off the R40 into the Balule Nature Reserve, immensely relieved that the journey had nearly reached its conclusion and we were off the highways. An expectant crowd had gathered at the park's entrance to cheer us in. These three escapee elephants were very popular within the reserve and had been sorely missed, and as the weeks had turned into months, concern was growing that they might never be safely returned.

Silke's voice came across the radio. 'All OK with your elephant?' she asked. 'Apparently it's fifteen minutes to the airstrip where we unload them.'

'Great, thanks, and yes he's all fine.'

'Good job.'

A long, straight, undulating, dusty road lay ahead, flanked by the perimeter fence on our right and the bush to our left. The sun, now high in the sky, gave the road a golden colour, and with the full entourage stretched out in front and behind us, we looked like an important military convoy on the move. However intimidating we might have looked to human eyes, a female lioness basking by the side of the road barely acknowledged our presence. Up and down we went – this final stretch of road seemed interminable – but then suddenly Lyle turned onto the airstrip, a large expanse that opened to our right and the journey was complete: all three elephants, Wayne, Derek and Lotter, had safely arrived, still asleep and completely oblivious to the epic journey they had been on. One by one the crane unloaded them. The crowd probably numbered a hundred now. Admiring their size and beauty, people feverishly bustled around them for a last picture, a final touch of a tusk, or a feel of their skin, and then it was time to wake them up.

Lyle, Johan and Michelle took charge to evacuate people and vehicles to a safe distance, about 100 metres behind us, with the elephants facing the opposite direction. It was more than likely they would just wake up and head into the bush, but the possibility that one might turn and charge could not be overlooked.

Laura, Silke, Ben and myself were all who remained to wake them up. Determining the total amount of Etorphine our elephants had received allowed us to calculate the amount of Naltrexone we each needed to administer. This drug begins to take full effect within about a minute, so it was critical that we injected our respective elephants at exactly the same time to ensure that none of our patients woke up before we had all safely vacated the area.

'Everyone ready?' Silke enquired as the three of us stood poised over our elephants, loaded syringe at the ready.

'Yup,' Ben and I replied in unison.

'OK, find your vein.'

'I'm in,' Ben replied moments later.

'So am I,' I followed.

'OK, inject.'

I depressed the plunger and 12 ml of Naltrexone entered Lotter's ear vein to flood his system. Each molecule of the drug would start displacing Etorphine molecules that occupied the opioid receptors throughout the brain and spinal cord and with that he would regain full consciousness. It was time to head to the safety of the vehicles.

Moments later they started to stir. Wayne was the first to raise his head, and quickly rocked himself onto his chest and then his feet; Derek and Lotter were slightly slower, taking several attempts to sit up. Concerned for his friends, Wayne wandered over to Lotter to help him up, and in the mean-time Derek staggered up. The three of them took a moment to steady themselves, and then nonchalantly headed into the bush and out of sight as though the last four hours had never happened. As we turned to congratulate each other, I felt a tear roll down my cheek. That moving interaction between those three elephants as they woke up had been a special finale to what had been an astounding and unforgettable experience.

# Elephants: fast facts

## *Loxodonta africana*: The African elephant

**Distribution:** The largest of the three extant species, it is scattered across sub-Saharan Africa, with the greatest populations in the south and east of the continent. The other two species are the African forest elephant (found in the Congo Basin) and the Asian elephant (found in South and South-East Asia).

**Names:** The male is called a 'bull', the female a 'cow', and their young a 'calf'. A group of elephants is called a 'parade' or 'memory'.

**Life span:** About 60–70 years.

**Habitat:** Elephants live in a diversity of habitats, from dry savannahs, deserts, marshes and lake shores, to mountain areas above the snowline.

**Diet:** As predominantly browsing herbivores, they eat leaves, twigs, fruit and bark, but will also eat grass and roots, consuming as much as 150 kg of food and 40 litres of water a day.

**Gestation:** 22 months, with a calf being born every 3–5 years. Sexually mature males up to 25 years old enter 'musth', a state of increased testosterone around mating, which can last up to 4 months at a time, when a fluid is secreted from their temporal glands down their face and they become noticeably aggressive. The female's cycle lasts 16 weeks, during which time a male will follow and guard her until she is in oestrus. A female reaches sexual maturity at 12–16 years, her fertility decreasing from aged 45 years.

**Size and weight:** A calf is about 120 kg at birth, growing to about 6,000 kg as an adult.

**Growth:** Weaning at 5–10 years old, they are fully grown by their late twenties.

**Body temperature:** 36.5 °C.

**Anatomy:** An elephant's trunk is a muscular proboscis formed from a fusion between the nose and upper lip, connected to a bony opening in the skull. It is their most versatile appendage, allowing them to breathe, smell, touch and produce sound. It is capable of lifting a weight up to 350 kg, acts as a snorkel in water, allows them to reach heights of about 7 metres, as well as the ability to perform very delicate tasks such as cracking a peanut, as well as less subtle ones like uprooting small trees. Like horses, they are hindgut fermenters, their intestines measuring about 35 metres. The male's testes are located internally near the kidneys, making surgical castration a very complicated procedure. Tusks are modifications of the second incisor teeth of the upper jaw, and ivory is the dentine layer that remains when the enamel wears off. Just like our teeth, the majority of the tusk has a nerve supply, and the pulp extends about a third of the way down the trunk. Removing the tusks is therefore as painful as extracting teeth. The poaching of elephants for their ivory has already led to the extinction of the genetic pool of so-called 'large tuskers': at the turn of the twentieth century it was common for tusks to weigh in excess of 90 kg, but now most are no more than 45 kg.

**Interesting fact:** Elephants are the only mammals that can't jump.

**Conservation:** The IUCN lists African elephants as 'vulnerable': their 1979 population was estimated to be anything from 1.3 to 3 million; in 2012, this number had reduced to a mere

440,000 individuals – a decrease in the continental population of 66–85 per cent. Sadly, this decline shows no sign of stopping, with an estimated 100 elephants being slaughtered every day in Africa by poachers. At this rate, elephants will be extinct on that continent in just twelve years. Although populations are unsustainably diminishing in East Africa, in South Africa excessive numbers are leading to an increase in human–animal conflicts and habitat destruction for other wildlife. The charity Elephants Alive continues to do vital work in Southern Africa, striving to ensure the survival of elephants and their habitats, and to promote harmonious co-existence between man and elephants. For further information, and for ways to help the conservation of the African elephant, please visit www.elephantsalive.org.

# 7

# CHICKEN

*'The key to everything is patience. You get the chicken by hatching the egg, not by smashing it.'*

Arnold H. Glasow

When we first meet someone, so the theory goes, we only have a seven-second window to make a first impression. Given that we only get one chance at this self-portrayal, it is only natural that we desire to promote ourselves in such a way that those we meet recollect that first encounter with warmth and affection. If, for whatever reason, we fail at this, a lot of time and effort is required to alter a person's initial perception of us. As a vet, to whom people entrust their animals, be they domestic or wild, pet or farmed, it is of the greatest importance to convey a responsible, knowledgeable and friendly professionalism from the very start.

No matter how hard we try, however, there are inevitably days when things conspire against us. The little girl's hamster bites you as you carefully pick it up; the horse bolts past you when you open its stable; the farmer's dog savages your leg as you get out of the car; the sat nav takes you to the wrong farm on the other side of the valley. Usually when this happens, you muddle through the awkward consultation, relieved when it is over, or jump back into the car and speed away at the first available opportunity. On occasion, though, the consultation or visit is more protracted, and then you sometimes have to steel yourself to endure one of the most awkward days of your life . . .

It was often said to me by older, wiser vets that farmers don't suffer fools gladly – but why should they, when you are dealing with their livelihood? The general consensus within the veterinary profession is that you get one chance with them. If you do well, and the farmer likes you, then generosity will often flow abundantly: a joint of beef, a tray of eggs, a box of apples, home-baked scones, lunch or breakfast after the visit, or even an invitation for a day's shooting. If it all goes badly, however, then prepare for an ear-bashing and to be rapidly escorted off the farm with the collies baying at your heels and forever after to read in the large appointments book 'Any vet but Jon' whenever that farmer requests a visit.

'Jonny, I've booked you Mr Howard's TB test for 8.30 a.m. on Monday,' Jackie had said to me before she left work on Friday. 'It's a whole herd test so it'll be about four hundred in total. I don't think you've been there before, but it's quite easy to find. He's a lovely chap if he likes you, but can be quite a character if he doesn't. I'm sure you'll get on just fine.'

It was the usual routine. Jackie would let us know any pre-booked visits for Monday morning in advance so we could either go straight from home or make sure we were in the practice early enough to get organized before the visit. TB was so rife we were inundated with testing, so every vet had at least one large test to do a week, and mine were usually on a Monday. It was very mundane work, but often provided an opportunity to meet and bond with a new client or to find out how things were going with their farm. Having been qualified two years, the TB testing was second nature, so although a boring way to start the week, it wouldn't require any weekend reading and I wasn't on call, so I didn't give the visit a second thought until Sunday night, when I calculated how much time I would need to get there in the morning.

Jackie had reckoned it would take twenty minutes to get to the farm and had given me her usual, precise directions. However, it was the first time I'd visited the farm and so to make sure I wasn't late I decided to leave the practice by 8 a.m. I arrived at a quarter to, collected my equipment and paperwork and, content I had everything I needed, set off.

Jackie's directions were, as usual, spot on. They took me straight to the farm without a problem, so with time in hand, I decided to pull into the layby in front of the farm to organize myself in the ten minutes I had before the appointment. Satisfied that I had all my equipment in order, I pulled out, drove the 200 yards to the large tarmacked entrance of Beech Farm, and proceeded down the driveway between the post-and-rail fencing. Jersey cattle grazed in the fields on either side of the driveway, which was about 100 yards long, and flanked by a dozen 20-foot-high leylandii cypress trees, growing in two groups of six, along both sides. They had presumably been planted to afford privacy to the modern red brick farmhouse at the end of the drive.

As I approached the row of evergreens, about 20 yards from the farmhouse, an eclectic flock of about twenty chickens, of all breeds and sizes, were sauntering across the driveway from my right to left, oblivious to my arrival. They were eagerly hunting out worms and grubs, pecking and scratching on the grass border in front of the fence line. Naturally I stopped to allow them time to pass. It seemed to take them an interminable amount of time to amble the short distance, despite my dog Max's best efforts to hurry them along, barking at them from the passenger seat of my Isuzu Trooper. From my vantage point behind the wheel, my vision was slightly obscured, but at last I could see them all attentively scratching away in the dirt off to my left and so I continued on past the trees and pulled up in front of the house.

Turning off my engine, I stepped out of my car to put on my wellington boots and waterproofs. Walking round to the boot, something caught my eye back down beyond the row of leylandii: a commotion of feathers flapping and jerking all over the place. To my horror, I instantly knew what it was, as my mind flashed back to an incident from my childhood, when I had raised and cared for my own flock of thirty chickens. Occasionally, with an ill chicken or an unwanted cockerel that was fit to eat, I had humanely dispatched them as my father had taught me to do from a young age. On one occasion, though, after I had killed a cockerel, and immediately placed it in the utility-room sink to pluck and gut it for the freezer, the decapitated bird had suddenly jumped out of the sink, over my head, and proceeded to shower the utility room's cupboards, walls and freshly laundered clothes in blood. The neural networks in the bird's spinal cord stimulated exaggerated muscle movements that were no longer being regulated by messages from the brain. My mother had been out at the time, so I had desperately attempted to clean up the devastation before her return.

So now, with a sickening feeling in the pit of my stomach, I knew the flapping and convulsing was not the dance of some sexually charged male in pursuit of an unsuspecting member of his harem, but rather the death throes of their large, ornate, handsome cockerel. I walked as swiftly and casually as I could back to where the deceased cockerel was calming down, praying that by some miracle it was stunned rather than dead, and desperately hoping not to attract the attention of anyone in the farmhouse. However, with its large windows facing down the drive, I was certain I could sense Mr and Mrs Howard observing me intently from the warmth of their kitchen.

Reaching the cockerel, my worst fears were realized. The motionless bird was unmistakably dead, and with tyre marks clearly discernible across his newly elongated neck, it would not require a forensic pathologist to identify the cause of his demise. I stood there frozen to the spot, numb with disbelief, replaying the last few minutes, cursing myself for not getting out of the car to chivvy the flock along to avert this very scenario. Looking down at the cockerel, I saw he was a young, stunning-looking Light Sussex–Maran cross. Or at least he had been. I cursed him for selecting me and my vehicle as his chosen method of extinction. It was a completely unintentional accident, but I felt wretched, and this was the worst possible start to a five-hour-plus farm visit for a client I had never met before. Jackie's words rang in my ears: *'He's a lovely chap if he likes you, but can be quite a character if he doesn't. I'm sure you'll get on just fine.'*

Somehow I wasn't so sure, now. Even if I was escorted off the farm there and then, the best I could hope for would be the relentless gibes I would receive on every farm visit for the next month, since the story would certainly be retold at the Wednesday night skittle league, in which many of our clients participated. It would doubtless spread across the county and farming community like wildfire . . . I looked around surreptitiously. No one had come out of the farmhouse to greet me or to see what was going on. Maybe they weren't in the kitchen, maybe they weren't even in the house – maybe this whole event had passed them by completely, and they didn't even know I had arrived? On the other hand maybe they were even now peering out of one of the windows, watching and waiting to see how I would react.

I was on the horns of a dilemma. Should I pick up the deceased cockerel or leave it where it was? Maybe I could throw it in among the trees, out of sight, where a fox would inevitably remove it in the night. Or should I present it to Mr and Mrs Howard and fess up to my accidental killing of their undoubtedly highly prized cockerel? I knew what I *should* do, but every fibre of my being wanted to absolve myself of the crime and when the cockerel's absence was finally noted in a day or two, the blame would squarely be put at the feet of Mr Fox. Furthermore, the prospect of ringing their front door bell and greeting Mr or Mrs Howard for the first time, introducing myself as the new vet and then highlighting my skills at ending rather than saving life by handing over one of their stock that I had so efficiently assassinated, did not exactly fill me with joy.

Still undecided, I found myself bending down and picking the cockerel up. At the same moment, my quandary was independently resolved when a voice suddenly called out from behind me.

'Good morning, young man. You must be the vet that's come to do our TB test.'

I jumped up, startled, and turned around in the direction of the declaration, the deceased cockerel limply hanging in my left hand. Like a naughty little boy caught red-handed with something nefarious, I tried hiding the cockerel behind my back.

'Yes,' I replied somewhat sheepishly, struggling to find the words to explain why I was holding his dead cockerel.

'What you got there?' was the question that naturally followed as he walked across the gravel drive towards me.

'Um . . . I'm afraid, that I, er . . . appear to have had a bit of an accident . . . with, um, your cockerel. It seems I accidentally ran him over as I was coming down the driveway. I'm – so – *incredibly* – sorry,' I mumbled, preparing myself for the berating I knew I was about to receive.

'Oh? Ha, well that was very skilled of you! Which one is it, let's have a look at him.' Shocked and unsure of this response, I dutifully obeyed. Reaching Mr Howard, I handed over my accidental quarry. Mr Howard studied the bird for a moment.

'Oh, this fella! Don't you trouble yourself at all about that. We've got too many of them. The missus keeps pestering me to knock a few on the head – this one in particular she'll be delighted to see the back of, the savage little brute. He was probably attacking your wheels, which is why you ran him over. No, I reckon you've done us a favour there – but don't you go charging us, mind!'

Reeling from this unexpected reaction, I didn't quite get Mr Howard's joke.

'Charge you for what?' I enquired, confused.

'You know, for the humane dispatch of my killer cockerel,' he said, laughing.

'Absolutely, of course not,' I said quickly, mustering a smile, hugely relieved that this whole unfortunate incident was not, after all, going to destroy my morning or my reputation across the county.

'So you must be Jonathan. I'm Giles Howard, pleasure to meet you,' he said, changing the subject as he switched the carcass into his left hand so he could hold out his right for me to shake.

'Nice to meet you, Mr Howard. Sorry again about the cockerel. It's not exactly how I like to meet a client for the first time!' I responded, trying to match his good humour.

'Honestly, don't worry about it, it was going to happen sooner or later and, as I say, he was a vicious little thing. The wife will be thrilled, and I see you ran over his head and neck, so the rest of the carcass is fine.' He walked over to the side door of the house, which opened into a large washroom. 'Mabel,' he shouted. 'The vet's here, and he's done us a good turn.'

Moments later Mrs Howard appeared. 'Morning,' she said, greeting me and then turning to Giles. 'What did you say?'

'I said Jonathan's done us a favour. He's run over Sid Vicious for you.' He held up the trophy. 'Reckon he's done a pretty professional job, too. We could have it for dinner.'

'Glad someone can do your dirty work for you!' Mabel said with a laugh, then turned to me. 'I'm sure you didn't mean to do it, but thank you all the same. I've been trying to get Giles to sort him out for ages. He seemed to know when I hadn't got my wellies on, and then came out of nowhere, attacking my ankles. I've taken to go outside with a broom to shoo him away!'

Tying some bailer twine around its neck, Giles hung the cockerel among the coats and jackets on the rack by the door out of the reach of the three dogs that had rushed to greet their master ahead of Mabel.

'Fancy a coffee before we start, Jonathan?' he asked.

'That would be lovely, thank you,' I replied, still trying to process the emotional rollercoaster of the previous ten minutes.

As I followed them into the kitchen, Mabel chipped in: 'Giles, how about some bacon and eggs for this young man? He seems like he needs fattening up. I bet he barely has time to feed himself, being so busy.'

'Sounds like a great idea, and I'll join him. We need to get our strength up for the job ahead.'

And there it was, I had somehow found myself in favour with this delightful couple, and their kind generosity was abounding. I certainly hadn't earned it, and I would definitely have preferred not to have started the visit by running over their cockerel, regardless of how vicious it was, but what I had perceived as a terrible first impression was in fact the perfect icebreaker. Tucking into my bacon and eggs and supping on my coffee, complete with fresh Jersey milk, I gushed with gratitude at their kindness, confident the TB test would proceed routinely and without complication.

It did and when I returned on Thursday morning, three days later, to read the test, I was invited to stay for lunch afterwards. With a twinkle in his eye, Mr Howard informed me we would be having roast chicken. It was delicious, but as I devoured it gratefully, I decided not to enquire whether it was Sid Vicious.

# Chickens: fast facts

*Gallus gallus domesticus*: The domesticated chicken

**Distribution:** Chickens are a sub-species of the red jungle-fowl, originally found in South-East Asia, from Nepal down to Indonesia, but now globally dispersed.

**Names:** A male aged less than a year is called a 'cockerel', over a year 'cock' or 'rooster'. A young female is a 'pullet', then a 'hen'. The young are 'chicks'. Adult chickens produced for meat are called 'broilers', those produced for eggs 'layers'. A group of hens is called a 'brood'.

**Life span:** About 5–10 years.

**Habitat:** Originally the jungle, but now wherever humans inhabit.

**Diet:** Chickens are omnivores in the wild, or free ranging, scratching about in the soil for seeds or insects, or eating lizards, snakes and mice. In the broiler industry, their food is the most scientifically researched of any nutrition in the world.

**Incubation:** 21 days: a hen will lay a clutch of about 12 eggs, which won't start developing until she starts incubating them, all 12 thus hatching together.

**Weight:** 30–50 grams at birth, growing up to 0.5–4.5 kg as adults.

**Growth:** Males and females are considered fully grown at 1 year.

**Body temperature:** 40.6–41.7 °C.

**Chickens for food:** More than 50 billion chickens are reared annually for meat and eggs (that's 6.5 chickens per person). Of these, 74 per cent of broilers and 68 per cent of layers are produced intensively. In the commercial UK broiler industry it now takes just 30 days for a bird to reach its slaughter weight of 1.5 kg (in 1925 it took 120 days), and free-range or organic broilers will be slaughtered at 100 days. Commercial laying hens will produce up to 300 eggs in their first year, but after this the rate drops to below commercial viability, when they are slaughtered and used in processed foods. In some other countries, sadly, when laying drops off, flocks are sent into a forced moult by a complete withdrawal of food and often water for up to 14 days, which reinvigorates egg-laying: a major welfare concern.

**Conservation:** With a present conservative estimate of 19 billion chickens worldwide, they are certainly not a threatened species in terms of extinction – but in terms of their welfare the situation remains urgent. As the single largest source of human protein globally, a commercialized poultry industry is inevitable; but we have a duty to uphold the highest welfare standards in this, as in all meat industries. So if you have the time and the inclination, why not give an ex-commercial hen a happy retirement by visiting **www.bhwt.org.uk/rehome-some-hens?**.

# 8
# MANED WOLF

*'A gentleman is simply a patient wolf.'*
Lana Turner

The practice's dart gun had recently been decommissioned after a rather unfortunate incident one Saturday afternoon at a local wildlife park. A heavily pregnant female wolf had just started showing signs of whelping, but despite several hours of restless pacing, panting, discernible contractions and straining, no cubs had yet been produced. The keepers were understandably concerned and so had rung the practice for veterinary assistance, suspecting she needed a caesarean section. Rob was on call so had grabbed the dart gun, some darts and all the other equipment he might require for the procedure and headed over to the park. The wolf had taken to her den, a manmade cave with a vantage point above it, so Rob could get close enough to safely dart her from about 10 metres away. She was in a confined space, and all the wolves were fairly used to interacting with humans, so not easily spooked by the presence of strangers. The conditions seemed perfect for making it as straightforward a job as possible.

Unfortunately, the one element Rob hadn't factored into the equation was the state of the dart gun, which had been converted from an old .22 calibre rifle several years before and was now rarely used. Most of the animals we dealt with at the two wildlife parks were trained either to stand for injections or else to walk into the built-in cages in their enclosures. Rob's first two attempts misfired, resulting in the dart rather pathetically falling out of the end of the dart gun, and his third attempt flew over the wolf's back, embedding in the den wall. His fourth attempt landed 2 feet short of her, but finally with the fifth dart, much to his relief, having waited a further twenty minutes for the now agitated female to settle again, he landed a perfect rump shot. The rest of the procedure went smoothly: she went to sleep nicely, and it was found that a caesarean was indeed required because the first cub was dead and stuck, but the remaining five were delivered fine and healthy. Mum recovered without complication, and the keepers had quickly forgotten the initial problems encountered with the dart gun.

Rob, however, had not, and when Monday morning came, a rather irritated email was circulated advising, justifiably, that the dart gun was not considered safe for use and was going to be sent away for a service and assessment, so would be out of action till further notice. The cost of repair turned out to be prohibitively expensive, however, so a discussion followed as to whether the practice needed to replace it, given how infrequently it was required. The alternatives were to ask the two wildlife parks that we worked for if they wanted to purchase a weapon of their own, or else for us to call in a specialist if and when the situation arose.

Unfortunately, no solution had yet been found when, a few weeks later, we received a panicked phone call from the other wildlife park. One of their male maned wolves was struggling to urinate and seemed to be in a lot of discomfort. The scenario sounded urgent: a suspected blocked bladder or urethra. If he were showing obvious signs of discomfort, then his bladder would already be full, so if the blockage was not resolved soon he could end up with either kidney failure or a burst bladder, neither of which has a good prognosis.

Dave called me from the other surgery and outlined the problem, asking if I was free to assist him.

'Sure, I'll get Jackie to rearrange my morning visits so I can go straight away,' I replied. 'But what on earth is a maned wolf?'

'Imagine a fox on steroids. They're the same colour, look similar, but standing on their back feet they're 8 feet tall.'

'Wow! Interesting . . . Yeah, I'm on my way – but what's the deal with the dart gun?'

'Good question. I haven't really figured that out yet. We might be able to get him into his night-quarters and inject him somehow, or maybe drug his food. There's someone in Somerset with a dart gun, but they'll be three hours away, even if they can come out, or there's Paignton Zoo, but the same problem. So in all honesty I'm not sure . . . I figured we just need to get there, assess the situation and then decide. Any ideas?'

'Remote injection pole? Do we have one?'

'Not that I know of.'

'Maybe we could make one?'

'Not sure how, but if you can figure something out, then great. I've got a case I'm in the middle of dealing with now so I probably won't be able to leave for an hour, but can you get everything together to operate on her, and head over there to assess the situation as soon as you can? I'll join you when I'm finished here.'

I headed to Jackie's office and reported the situation. She kindly obliged in rearranging the three non-emergency large animal visits that were booked in for the morning, thus freeing me up to head out to the wolf. As I started collecting the equipment we might need in the prep room, I was racking my brain for a solution to our predicament. Calling in someone from outside to dart the wolf presented all sorts of problems. Firstly, it would be a minimum of three hours from now, even if they were able to come immediately. I should probably ring them, though, to ask after their availability, and have them on standby if they could come. Secondly, though, that delay would really foul up our day, since all the scheduled visits and appointments would need to be further rearranged, or else someone would be required to cover for us. Neither was ideal, but if necessary, both could be done.

Surely there had to be an alternative solution, though? I remembered a discussion at vet school on the use of remote injection pole sticks as a safe way to inject an animal through a cage or at a distance to avoid being kicked. We didn't have one, but surely I could improvise something? My mind ticked over. How to inject something at a distance? Simply speaking, all that would be needed was a needle connected to one end of a long pipe, with a syringe at the other end. Problem one: how to reinforce the pipe and needle so that I could control where I injected it? Problem two: I needed a pipe to which I could securely connect a needle and a syringe to either end. Problem three: how to control the amount of drug I injected at a distance?

The solution to all three problems came in a flash of inspiration. The practice had an attic space, and it suddenly struck me that the long metal stick used to open the hatch would make a perfect pole. A drip-line extension tube had the right connections for a needle at one end and a syringe at the other, so if I taped the tubing to the pole, with the needle just protruding from the end, it should give me good enough control to safely inject the wolf. I would also be able to draw up the drug through the needle into the pipe and then into the syringe that way. If I calculated how much fluid the tubing could contain, I would be able to compare this to the required drug dose and top any excess space in the tubing with saline. Confident it would work, and feeling rather proud of myself, I rapidly set about constructing my crude injection pole.

Trialling it with some saline, it worked exactly as I had hoped: we now had a method of remotely injecting the wolf. Of course, we would still need to be able to get within a metre of him, but armed with this tool, we would stand a better chance of injecting him through the cage. Even so, I still needed to contact the person in Somerset to see if they could help in case we required it, but with a renewed confidence I set about loading my car with the equipment: the portable anaesthetic machine, surgical kits, fluid bags, drapes, suture material, drugs, and my patient injection pole. I found the telephone number for the capture specialist Eric Jefferies and set off, deciding to call him on the way.

'Mr Jefferies? My name is Jonathan Cranston, I'm a veterinary surgeon from North Devon. We have a situation with a wolf that we may need assistance darting. It's not confirmed yet, but I just wanted to check on your availability to help us with it today.'

'Hmm, sounds an interesting one. I could certainly do it. North Devon, you say?' He paused for a moment, presumably looking at his watch. 'It's ten now, I'm going to be tied up till twelve, so it would have to be between half past one and two before I could get to you, I'm afraid.'

Just as I feared, if we couldn't anaesthetize the wolf any other way, then we would have no choice, but if we had to wait four hours before we even started, it would turn into an all-day job. And besides, could the wolf wait that long?

'OK, thanks so much, that's really good to know. Could you provisionally pencil that in? I'm just on my way to the zoo now, so once I've assessed the situation, I'll have a better idea and will update you then. Is that OK?'

'Sure, no problem either way. I'm here if you need me, Jonathan. And please call me Eric.'

'Really appreciate it, Eric. I'll be in touch soon. Many thanks.'

Twenty minutes later I arrived at the zoo. A very concerned senior keeper greeted me. I had met James a few times before, but he was far from his usual relaxed and jovial self.

'Thanks for coming at such short notice, Jon. He had a similar problem a while ago – Simon saw him – but he was still able to urinate then, his bladder wasn't completely blocked. This seems much worse. Chris doesn't think he's passed anything for twenty-four hours and he's clearly uncomfortable.'

Chris was the keeper responsible for the wolves.

'If that's the case we may need to operate,' I said. 'Dave should be here in about half an hour, but we wanted to get out as soon as we could to assess the situation and come up with a plan of action. You know we don't have our dart gun anymore?'

'Yeah, Simon had mentioned it, and suggested we got our own. We're looking into it, but haven't got one yet. And I'm afraid Marty is the most aggressive of our three maned wolves. What are you thinking?'

'The timing couldn't be any worse,' I said, 'but it is what it is. Anyway, I've teed up a chap in Somerset who has a dart gun

– he's the closest, but he wouldn't be able to get here till two, so if there's another way of anaesthetizing him, it'd be preferable. Look, I've made a crude injection pole so if we could get him close enough to the fence line then we could maybe inject him through it – or would we have access to him through the enclosure? Worst-case scenario, we could put something in his food, but that's a bit hit-and-miss and takes longer.'

'Yeah . . . frustrating about the dart gun. Have a look at Marty for yourself, but I'd personally be worried waiting four hours. I reckon you should be able to inject him from inside the house. Let's go and have a look. It'll give you a better idea of the set-up.'

I followed James through the staff entrance into the zoo, down a gravel path, past the back of the black panther enclosure, before arriving at the door of a red brick building. This was the wolves' indoor housing, a set of three 8-foot by 8-foot enclosures with a narrow alleyway running behind them. We skirted round the house to get to their large outdoor pen, and it was there I got my first sight of a maned wolf. Dave's description closely matched the three animals before me. Their head and ears were those of a fox, and their coat shared that same rustic red colour. But their frame was much, much bigger. As I remarked to James, it almost looked as if a fox were standing on a set of black stilts, so disproportionate were their legs and body to the size of their head, though they were still possessed of an extraordinary elegance and grace.

'Yeah, they're beautiful, all right, and very popular with the public,' he replied. 'Probably because not many people have heard of them. Marty is that one over there.'

He need scarcely have pointed him out, since it was obvious that the animal we were watching was clearly in distress, restlessly pacing up and down the far fence line, stopping occasionally in a vain attempt to void his bladder.

'Yeah, he's definitely struggling. Even if we don't need to operate, we certainly need to have a good look at him and see if we can catheterize him,' I confirmed.

'OK. I think the best option is to get him into his house. If you dart him outside and he goes down, we'd need to separate him from the others, so best to get them all inside first.'

'Agreed. Is that easy to do?'

'Yeah, they're trained to go into their housing quarters. We'll open up all three doors and see which ones they go into. If Marty goes in first, then great, we can close the door directly behind him. Otherwise we'll shut them all in and separate them off once they're shut inside. All three cages are connected.'

He pulled out the two-way radio clipped to his belt.

'Chris? The vet's here. Can you get over to Marty's enclosure?'

'Be right with you,' a voice crackled back.

Moments later Chris arrived, an athletic man in his late forties, about 6 feet tall, with short greying hair.

'What do you think, Jon?' he said, getting straight to the point. 'He's not happy at all, is he?'

'No,' I agreed. 'We certainly need to have a closer look at him.'

'Can we get him in, Chris?' James asked.

'No problem, give me a moment.'

He disappeared round to the side of the brick building, and a few minutes later the far-right pen door opened and we could hear Chris calling to Marty. The wolf responded surprisingly quickly, trotting gingerly over to the open door, with the other two wolves following behind. It suddenly dawned on me that Marty was the alpha male, which would make it easier to separate him. As Marty got to the entrance of his enclosure, he hesitated for a moment, obviously confused by this change to his normal routine, but after a brief interlude sniffing around, he slowly padded inside. Chris was obviously watching and waiting behind the door, because as soon as Marty had disappeared from view, it shut behind him.

'That was pretty straightforward,' I said to James. 'So Marty is the alpha, is he?'

'He sure is, and quite the dominant one.'

We headed back around the building, following Chris's direction through a dark 3-foot-wide corridor. The three wolves' cages ran down the right-hand side, the left wall was exposed red brick, and the floor was polished concrete, with a gutter on the left running along the length of the building. To the left of the door that led into Marty's cage was the pulley system, which controlled the outside door to the cage. Chris had just finished securing it as we walked in. We could now hear Marty snarling and growling.

'He's not happy with us,' Chris observed.

'Yeah, but you can't really blame him,' said James. 'He must be in one hell of a lot of pain and doesn't realize we're trying to help.'

'That's for sure,' I said.

'OK, so what's the plan?' Chris asked. 'Do you have a dart gun or is it still out of action?'

'I was telling James, ours has been decommissioned. I've got a guy in Somerset on standby if we need him, but he can't get here till two. I've made an injection pole that would allow me to inject from about a metre away, but –' I looked at Marty prowling around the cage complaining vociferously – 'there's still too much space in here for me to be able to do him like that. I don't suppose there's any way of confining him in a smaller space, is there?'

'Not really . . .' Chris replied, looking at his watch. It was now nearly eleven. 'But two o'clock is a long time to wait.'

We all stood there for a moment in silence, pondering a solution we were sure existed somewhere. Chris was the first to break the silence.

'Do you remember that mattress that we used for the impala to stop them hurting themselves when we blood-sampled them?'

'Yeah, what about it?' James replied.

'Couldn't we use it to pin Marty into a corner so that Jon could quickly inject him?'

Chris's suggestion hung in the air for a moment as James and I processed the full implications of what he was proposing. The anguished growling emanating from the cage next to us served as a reminder of what this notion entailed.

'Oh, I see.' James breathed out through his teeth. 'I guess that could work. What do you think, Jon?'

'Um, to be honest, it doesn't sound the safest plan I've ever heard. It'd be great if it worked, but just now I can only see the dangers and pitfalls.'

'Yeah, but don't you think Marty will just cower under the bench, rather than come out fighting? He's really not well enough, and this growling is just a kind of protest, isn't it?' Chris was clearly set on the plan, and I could see James coming round to the same idea.

'I think you're probably right,' he said. 'We can at least give it a go. I mean, what have we got to lose – other than an arm, I mean, and the risk of a major wound? Where's the mattress?'

'I think Jenna knows where it is.'

Chris reached for his radio to ask.

'I think it's in the storeroom,' came the crackling reply. 'Do you need a hand with it?'

'Thanks, Jenna, that would be great. I'll meet you there in a minute – if you're free now?'

'Sure.' With that Chris disappeared.

'Are you really sure about this?' I asked James hesitantly, after he'd gone.

'Yeah, I'm sure it'll be fine . . . Maybe if you just stood ready by the outside door, then if there are any problems you can just open the hatch? If he does decide to attack, it'll be a fear aggression, so with the door open, I'm sure he'll just want to run away.' James sounded confident enough, but I wasn't sure whether he was trying to convince me or himself.

I didn't quite know what to do. Surely the sensible thing would be to veto this plan now, or at least urge them to await the arrival of my colleague Dave, who would certainly see sense. On the other hand, a part of me was beginning to be persuaded by it. I mean, could a maned wolf *really* be much worse than a particularly aggressive large dog? And with the injection pole, we didn't need to restrain him much: the mattress should be enough of a shield, shouldn't it? I am ever the optimist, but that can be a dangerous attitude in a situation like this. If it went wrong, it could go spectacularly wrong – a severe mauling, injuries, maybe even death. Were those genuine risks or was I exaggerating them? I just didn't know. *Well, if you don't know, then err on the side of caution*, I told myself. But if we don't do it this way, then we've got a three-hour wait and that could simply be too long for Marty in his current state. Besides, I'm sure James was right, and if things started to go wrong, I could always open the hatch, and Marty would be sure to run off. All these thoughts were whirling around my mind when Chris and Jenna returned with the mattress. I could see that they were all still committed to the plan.

'What do you need it for?' Jenna asked as she and Chris placed it in the corridor.

'You don't want to know,' James replied, 'but if anything happens, just tell our wives we love them.' He and Chris laughed.

'What?' Jenna said with shock and concern.

'Don't worry, I'm joking, it'll be fine. We just need to inject Marty.'

'I'll just pop to the car and get the injection pole and my kit,' I said, decisively committed now to Chris and James's plan.

'I might go and get us some gauntlets to protect our hands,' suggested Chris.

'Yeah, good idea, and maybe grab my Barbour jacket as well.'

'Oh yeah, I'll bring mine as well. Zipped up with the collar up, it'll cover our necks.'

'You guys are nuts!' Jenna exclaimed.

*Were we really going to do this?* I pondered, having second thoughts as we headed back to my car.

A few minutes later all the equipment was lined up along the corridor, Chris had returned with the Barbours and gauntlets, and Jenna had disappeared, too anxious to watch.

'How much do they weigh?' I asked as I selected my drug concoction.

'About 25 kg,' Chris replied.

'Wow, is that all? Given their size, I thought it'd be more than that.'

'Yeah they are tall, but have a very slender frame.'

'OK, thanks.' I calculated my dose and then drew up the combination into a syringe. I discarded the needle, attached the syringe to the extension pipe and filled the pipe with the drug. Refilling the syringe with saline, I reconnected it to the pipe and depressed the plunger until the drug was down to the far end of the pipe where the needle was. With the pole syringe primed, if I pushed the needle into the wolf and depressed the syringe, the drug would be injected into him.

As I was occupying myself with this, James and Chris were readying themselves; wearing their Barbours, gauntlets and Australian bush hats, only their faces were exposed.

'Are you ready, Jon?' James enquired.

'Yeah, are you sure you want to do this?' I said in a final moment's hesitation, but with the wheels already set in motion, and adrenaline and testosterone pumping, there was no way they were changing their minds now.

'Yeah, it's fine. Don't worry, we won't blame you if something goes wrong!' Chris said laughing.

'No but your wives might,' I shot back.

'OK, here goes. We'll tell you when it's safe to come in, so just close the door behind us initially,' Chris said as he picked up the mattress, slowly opened the cage door and stepped in with James hot on his tail.

As they disappeared into the enclosure, Marty's snarling and growling intensified. I pulled the door to behind them, conscious that it only opened inwards so if one of them got stuck behind it, it would be impossible for me to safely get them out without going into the cage myself. I tucked myself round the corner, suddenly too fearful to watch as the noise intensified. My mind suddenly flooded with the range of horrific scenarios that could unfold, but it was too late to do anything about it now, I just had to stand there and pray that it all went to plan.

It was probably only a matter of a minute or two, but it felt like a lifetime. The level of ferocity escalated and then died away to a low growl and then I suddenly heard James's voice.

'We're ready for you, Jon.'

Had I heard correctly? Had it worked? I dared not believe it, but then James repeated, more urgently now, 'Jon we've got him, you can come in.'

I unlatched the door and walked in, injection pole at the ready. Chris and James were in the near corner, pushing against the mattress, which was partly wedged under the wooden shelf that ran the full length of the back wall as James had said earlier. Marty's rear end and tail were just visible against the wall. I didn't hesitate, quickly jabbing the pole needle into Marty's rump and injecting.

'OK, all done,' I said, stepping back and retreating out the door.

'Is that it? We're done?' Chris said, surprised.

'Yup.'

'Wow, you didn't hang about,' James added. 'OK, Chris, one, two, three, and then we retreat, OK?'

'OK.'

'One – two – three . . . go!' They said in unison. Once outside we shut and bolted the door.

'Wow, well that went better than I thought,' said James.

'Yeah, it certainly did,' Chris agreed.

'Now we just need the injection to work and for him to go to sleep,' I added.

'Oh it'd better. I don't think my heart could cope with having to do that again. I won't lie, I was fairly terrified,' James now revealed.

*That really was not a sensible plan*, I reflected, feeling that we'd had a lucky escape. Just as well Dave hadn't arrived halfway through it.

It was difficult to assess Marty through the narrow window bars of the cage door, but his growling and snarling slowly abated till, after about five minutes, it had ceased all together. We gently opened the door wide enough for me to lean in and probe him with the pole. He didn't respond.

'He's out,' I said, with a huge sigh of relief. It was done. Marty was asleep and no one was hurt.

'Great.'

'Good job, good job.'

The release of tension was visible on all our faces, but we knew it was only the first hurdle. We still had to figure out what was wrong with Marty. Chris, still tentative, set about cautiously removing the mattress, ensuring that Marty didn't stir and that he was in fact asleep, which he thankfully was. No longer fearful, we lifted him onto the shelf to use as a worktop. I then wheeled the portable anaesthetic machine into the cage. I needed to intubate him before I could properly connect him up, but in the meantime I used a mask over his mouth and nose.

Into the midst of this busy scene Dave now arrived. The shock, disbelief and confusion on his face when he realized that we had already anaesthetized Marty was a picture.

'How did you do it?' he enquired.

'I made an injection pole and used that,' I said casually, not wanting to go into too much detail, aware of the disapproval that it would be greeted with. Fortunately, Dave was quickly distracted by the job in hand, assisting me to intubate and catheterize Marty.

'Dave,' I said. 'Are you happy for a moment? I just need to ring the capture specialist in Somerset and tell him we don't need him. I had him on standby just in case.'

'Oh, that was good thinking. Yeah sure, go call him, I'll take over here.'

'Thanks.'

And with that I headed out of the building to call Eric.

I walked back down the corridor to the cage doorway. Dave looked up at me, giving me a knowing, disbelieving look. Clearly James or Chris hadn't felt the same reluctance about sharing our unconventional, high-risk injection strategy as I had. Obviously he'd be having words with me later, but for now we were focused on the patient before us. I handed Dave the urinary catheter. It took several attempts and a few patient minutes, but suddenly it advanced and with it a stream of dark, foul-smelling urine flowed forth.

'Good job,' I said to Dave.

'Yeah, he was definitely blocked and I wouldn't be surprised if he had a bladder full of stones, but there's no way of telling without X-raying him, so I reckon now that we have him anaesthetized and stable, we open him up and flush out his bladder. What do you think, James?'

'Whatever you think is best.'

'Jon?' Dave said turning to me.

'Yeah, I agree. He seems stable and we'd be kicking ourselves if he reblocks in a day or two.'

'OK, are you happy to do the anaesthetic if I do the surgery?' Dave asked me.

'Yeah, no problem.'

'Perfect.' Dave picked up the clippers and started clipping the hair away from Marty's belly where he would make the incision.

'Anything we can do?' James asked.

'Could you grab a jug of warm water?' I suggested.

'Sure,' James replied and disappeared.

I turned my attention to checking Marty. He was breathing steadily, heart rate was 80 and he had no blink reflect; he was nicely asleep and stable.

James returned a few minutes later with the jug, Dave had finished clipping, so having added some iodine solution to the water, I started scrubbing the now exposed skin to clean it and prep it for surgery. Once finished I sprayed it with spirit while Dave used an antiseptic gel to sterilize his hands. I then opened the surgical kits so he could gown and glove up. With

Marty draped, and Dave's instruments laid out next to him, I provided him with a scalpel blade and suture material and he was ready to go. I did a final check to make sure Marty was fully under and then Dave proceeded.

It turned out that Marty had a bladder full of a gelatinous material, rather than the classic stones we were expecting, but nevertheless the find confirmed the need for the surgery. Having removed them and flushed through his bladder, Dave closed his bladder and then his abdomen and finally his skin, using buried stitches so they wouldn't need removing.

'Well that went pretty well,' Dave confirmed as he removed his gloves and packed away his surgical instruments.

'Thanks, guys, it was definitely the right call,' Chris said.

We cleared all the equipment out of the cage. Once the room was empty, I turned off the anaesthetic machine, disconnected it and wheeled it out. Dave drew up the reversal agent and after I had removed Marty's endotracheal tube, injected him. We both retreated, closing the cage door behind us to wait for him to wake up.

Ten minutes later he stirred, and within minutes was then up and about, prowling around the cage.

'You should keep him in for a few days, so maybe allow him access to the neighbouring cage as well.'

'Sure,' Chris agreed. 'Does he need any follow-up meds?'

'Yeah. I'll get them put up at the practice for someone to pick up later.'

'Perfect, thanks.'

We carried all the equipment back to the car, loaded up, said our farewells and headed off.

The next day, Simon called me into his office.

'Jon, Dave told me about yesterday . . .'

He left the sentence unfinished. We both knew what he was alluding to.

'Yeah, probably not my finest hour, sorry.'

'You realize how serious that could have been? And as the vet in attendance it was your responsibility.'

'Yeah, I know. Lesson well and truly learned. Sorry.'

'Good, that's all I needed to know. A mattress and a home-made injection pole were pretty ingenious, but I think a dart gun is preferable in future.'

'Agreed,' I replied. 'But only if it shoots straight.'

# Maned wolves: fast facts

*Chrysocyon brachyurus*: The maned wolf

**Distribution:** South America, south and central Brazil, Paraguay, northern Argentina, Bolivia and south-eastern Peru.

**Names:** A male over a year is called a 'dog', the female a 'dam', and their young are called 'pups'. A group of maned wolves is called a 'pack'.

**Life span:** About 12–15 years.

**Habitat:** Semi-open areas of grassland, savannahs and forests.

**Diet:** Maned wolves are omnivores, solitary hunters of small to medium-sized animals such as rodents, rabbits, birds and fish, though more than 50 per cent of their diet is from vegetables and fruit (including lobeira, the so-called 'wolf-apple').

**Gestation:** 65 days with a litter of between 2 and 6 black-furred pups.

**Weight:** About 450 g when born, reaching about 23 kg as adults.

**Growth:** Pups nurse for 4 weeks, develop their distinctive fox-red coat at 10 weeks, wean at 4 months, are fully grown at 1 year when they leave their parents, and reproduce from 2 years of age.

**Body temperature:** 38–39 °C.

**Facts:** The maned wolf is the largest canid in South America. Although it resembles a fox with long legs and is commonly known as a wolf, it is actually neither, but a distinct species: the only member of the genus chrysocyon. They are mainly nocturnal with crepuscular (twilight) peaks in activity and live as monogamous pairs sharing about a 10-square-mile territory, but hunt, travel and rest in solitude, and out of the breeding season will seldom meet. They mark their territory and communication with powerful-smelling urine that is said to resemble a skunk's spray. The female enters oestrus once a year for about 5 days between April and November. Females rear the pups, but males provide the food, which is regurgitated, to the young.

**Conservation:** The IUCN considers the maned wolf as 'near threatened', although it is considered endangered in Brazil, and it is estimated that only about 25,000 remain in the wild. Habitat destruction for agriculture and highways, disease from domestic dogs, poaching for body parts and traffic fatalities have all led to a decline in their number. The World Association of Zoos and Aquariums has instigated a Maned Wolf Conservation programme to promote the survival of maned wolves in Argentina by involving local people: **www. waza.org/en/site/conservation/waza-conservation-projects/ overview/maned-wolf-conservation**.

# 9

# HOLSTEIN COW

'Moo *may represent an idea, but only the cow knows.*'

Mason Cooley

'You can't go wrong, it's really easy to find,' Amber had said. Her words were ringing in my ears as I set off bleary-eyed from the backpackers' hostel where I was staying in Greymouth, in New Zealand's South Island. It was 3 a.m.; my job was to vaccinate 700 cows on a farm just over an hour away. 'Head north out of Greymouth on the seven, drive for about forty-five minutes until you get to Mawheraiti, take the only left in the town and then the second left and drive all the way down that track. It ends in a farmyard.'

'Sounds pretty straightforward,' I'd said. 'Seven north, Mawheraiti, left, then second left and drive to the end of the track. Yup, shouldn't be a problem and I need to be there for 4 a.m. when they start milking, is that right?'

'Yeah, they have a big rotary parlour, so they'll set you up on a platform and leave you to it. They start milking at four, so they want you there then to inject the cows as they're milked. All the vaccines are in the cool box, along with the injection guns. There's a strap to go over your shoulder. I tend to have two on the go, one in each hand, but do whatever works for you.'

'No problem. I should be able to manage that.'

'It's as dull as anything and will probably take four or five hours, non-stop without a break so take your iPod and make sure you've got something good to listen to!'

'OK, thanks.'

And with that I had headed back to my hostel for an early night.

It was going to be nice to do some vet work again. It had been about five months since I last had anything to do with an animal in a professional capacity. Sure, it was going to be boring, mundane work, but it would ease me back into it, physically tiring, but not mentally. There were no drug doses to remember or complicated surgery to perform, just the simple routine of vaccinating cow after cow for five hours, and then I could come home and chill out for the rest of the day. Besides I needed the money. Five months of travelling through Southern Africa and Australia had drained the bank. I had intended to do more travelling in New Zealand, California, Canada, and then head home, with no plan to work in any of these countries, but my budgeting had gone pear-shaped. Landing in New Zealand, it was either a case of three weeks sightseeing and then back to England, or else try to find some work.

The privilege of the MRCVS qualification is that it is recognized in many countries across the world, including New Zealand. I was under thirty so I could get a working holiday visa without too much trouble, and so with a letter of good standing from the Royal College of Veterinary Surgeons, I could register with the New Zealand Veterinary Association and be good to go.

I just needed to find work. There were plenty of locum agencies looking for keen vets, and with over three years' mixed animal practice experience, I would be reasonably employable, but my first phone call was to a great university friend who had gone out to New Zealand for nine months, three years ago, and never come back. She was now running a small mixed animal practice in Greymouth.

'Hey, Amber, it's Little Jon. I've just got to Christchurch, planning on coming to visit you, but I don't suppose you need an extra vet anytime soon, do you?'

'You finally made it! Amazing! It'll be so good to catch up. Regarding work, we are actually just getting to lepto vac time. We've got twenty thousand to do in the next six weeks, so an extra pair of hands would come in very useful.'

'Lepto vacs? What's that all about?'

'Government policy. All milking cattle have to be vaccinated against leptosporosis to try to minimize animal-to-human transmission and vets have to sign off to say that it's been done, which means we have to do the vaccinations.'

'Seriously? Sounds like a good policy, but a lot of work for you.'

'Well, with 40 per cent of New Zealand's GDP coming from farming, and most of that being milk export, we can't afford any disease scares. Besides, the government pays us to do it so it's a good income stream for each practice. Bit like TB testing in the UK.'

'Sure, I can see that, but don't you have to TB test as well?'

'We do, but that's mainly done by specialist TB testers. We don't do too much as a practice.'

'Great, well I'll take it. Thanks, Amber, I really appreciate it. I can't wait to catch up.'

'Hey, what are friends for!'

Two weeks later I arrived in Greymouth raring to go, complete with a white, automatic Subaru Legacy with a broken gearbox that meant its top gear was third. At 30 mph and 4,000 revs, it wasn't the most economical vehicle I had ever owned. Of course, I'd test driven it, but only around the block, so the gearbox issue only became apparent on the journey back to my friend's house, by which time I had parted with the cash and the bloke had done a runner. It had not been my finest purchase. Still, I had wheels, and they had got me over Arthur's Pass. More importantly, I had my veterinary registration certificate, so I was official. Furthermore, I had been to a local charity shop and picked up the statutory vet's uniform of khaki chinos, checked shirt and gilet, so I looked every inch the professional.

The alarm had gone off at 2.30 a.m. I'd had five hours' sleep, and after months of not being on any real schedule, it was a complete shock to the system. With that nervous panic that comes from a first day on a new job, however, I found myself wide awake, and jumped out of bed, dressed and headed for the kitchen to make myself a coffee for the journey. A shower could wait. By 2.45 a.m. I was in the car and heading out of the hostel. Amber had reckoned it was no more than an hour to the farm, and the directions certainly seemed straightforward enough, but from previous nightmares as a new graduate, I had a healthy phobia of getting lost and so always tried to allow a bit of extra time for a new visit, and particularly as this was my first job for Amber.

The roads were empty save for the odd lorry, and Amber, having taken pity on me for the disaster of a car I had purchased, had lent me hers, so I made good time and reached Mawheraiti in forty minutes. It was still pitch dark outside so as I saw the sign welcoming me to the town, I slowed to a crawl to ensure I didn't miss the turning. I needn't have bothered because the town's one solitary street lamp shone over the turning. At this point tarmacked road became gravel road and so, as I headed along it, headlights reflecting the plumes of dust that the car generated, I continued at a snail's pace, so as not to miss the turning – second left, I recalled from Amber's instructions. The first left came immediately after I turned off the main road, but it was another mile or so to the second turning. I was starting to second-guess myself. Had I missed it? Or had I got the directions wrong? But then, there it was, and I sighed in relief as I turned down it. *Just drive to the end of this road and you're there,* I thought. It was 3.40 a.m. I was in good time. It couldn't be too far down this road so I should be there promptly for a 4 a.m. start. I always like to give myself every advantage for making a good first impression. Arriving late the first time you meet a client can be a disaster. Not only is it unprofessional, it also means you have to work twice as hard to leave the client feeling satisfied and confident in your abilities.

The road wound its way through invisible countryside as I drove further and further into the blackness. It was eerie. There wasn't a soul in sight, or any indication of life anywhere. The headlights of my car just picked out the dusty gravel track and the hedgerow either side of me. As I once again started doubting myself, I suddenly saw a light in the distance: that had be the parlour. The road brought me closer to that light, and eventually I came to a set of galvanized metal gates to the right of the track. The gates were open and led into a sizeable farmyard illuminated by the floodlight I had seen on top of the large shed, which I assumed was the milking parlour.

As I drove in, my arrival caught the attention of one of the workers who came over to greet me.

'I've come to vaccinate the cattle,' I said, winding down my window. 'Where should I park?'

'The manager didn't say anything to us about it.' He scratched his head for a moment in confusion, looking at the ground. 'I mean, the cattle need doing, but I don't think he told us, but then I guess he sometimes forgets. Anyway, who are you? I don't think we've met before.'

'I'm Jon, a vet from England, I'm doing some locum work over here for a bit.'

'Nice to meet you, bro, I'm Nathan. You best grab your stuff and we'll get you set up. Mike and Darren are just bringing the cows in so you're in good time, we haven't started yet.'

I grabbed the cool box and Nathan helped me with the rest of my equipment and headed into the parlour, a large, square space with the fifty-cow rotary parlour in the centre, leaving only a 2-metre gap all the way around.

A rotary parlour is a clever, but simple design. The raised central platform constantly rotates at a slow, steady pace, the cows walk onto it, facing inwards. The milker, standing outside the platform in the pit below then cleans the teats and places the clusters on the cow as she passes by. Regardless of how long the cow takes to be milked, she stays on the platform until it has completed a full revolution and then she backs off the platform and back into the yard and then out into the field.

'Best put you about here, I reckon,' said Nathan. 'You'll be out of Darren's way, but the cows will only be halfway round so if there are any problems or you miss one as you're reloading, you should have plenty of time to catch up.'

'Sounds ideal, thanks.'

From one corner, Nathan found a large metal trolley on wheels and brought it over to me, putting the brake on and making sure it was pretty sturdy.

'Will that do you, bro? Give you enough space? It should be the right height, it's what we use if we need to do anything to the cows when they're on the platform.'

'Perfect, thanks,' I said, loading my stuff onto it.

'So how you finding New Zealand then? Explored much?'

'Only arrived two weeks ago and just been sorting out my vet licence, but I was here in 2005 for the Lions Tour.'

'Ha! Didn't go too well for you guys, did it! Still, you boys were a great crack and we loved having ya. The country was heaving with you Lions fans, but it was awesome.'

'Yeah, I travelled around most of the South Island then and knew I had to come back.'

'Well enjoy it, bro. They call it God's country for a reason!'

And with that he headed off in the direction of the high-pitched piping of the quad-bike horn and the mooing that heralded the arrival of the cattle.

I busied myself setting up my equipment, attaching the vaccine bottles to the pipe that fed into the injection guns. The guns could be adjusted to repeatedly inject the same volume: squeezing the handle injected the vaccine, releasing the handle drew more into the gun from the bottle. Each cow required 2 ml injected into the muscle, so I adjusted to this level, testing both syringes by discharging onto the floor. They were both working fine, I slung one over each shoulder like a veterinary Rambo and climbed onto the trolley to see if I could see how things were progressing with the cows. The first ones were just walking up the ramp onto the platform. I double-checked I had everything I might need for the next four hours and then dug out my iPod, found my favourite playlist and I was ready to go.

It took me a bit of time to get into a routine, but then I was away. Jab, jab, jab, jab, jab – it was indeed easy and tedious work, but it was nice to be back out with animals and doing some form of veterinary work, even if this particular job didn't require five years of training. Time passed painfully slowly. There were the odd couple of minutes of frantically changing onto the next vaccine bottle and then having to move the trolley and catch up on the cows I had missed in that short delay, but otherwise it was pretty mindless work.

I kept myself amused by playing games with myself, scoring the cows on their beauty: which ones would I want in my imaginary herd? They were all Holsteins, a tall, skinny black-and-white cow, often crossed with the Friesian, which is a smaller, stockier cow of the same colouring. I generally preferred the Friesian's characteristics to the Holstein's, which often look very bony, but the Holsteins were absolute milking machines, often expending all their energy on milk production rather than themselves. Their diet had to be managed well to stop them having a metabolic crisis during their lactation. Some of these Holsteins, though, were stunning breed examples: good leg formation, a nice, even udder, not too bony … 'She'd be a good addition,' I said to myself as I studied a few more carefully. 'She's pigeon-toed; no good. Horrible bony hips; nope. Clearly had mastitis in that left hind quarter; nope …' I pulled myself up: if someone could hear me talking to myself in this way they'd think I was seriously weird. With that thought, I had an urge to check behind me, making sure that Nathan or Mike hadn't snuck up on me, laughing at my professional admiration for bovine breed traits.

On and on it went. At about 6.30 a.m., the sun started to rise and for the first time I got to see my surroundings. It was breathtaking. There was no side to the parlour where the cows walked on and off the platform. As the mist hung over the dew-wet grass, the West Coast Mountain range slowly revealed itself. It was a truly magical sight, and the tedium of the job at hand suddenly evaporated like the morning dew. I savoured the view, watching as, bit by bit, the scene evolved as the curtain of mist retreated and the natural splendour fully emerged.

The sunrise gave me an injection of my own, a burst of energy at knowing that I had broken the back of the herd and was on the home straight. There couldn't have much more than an hour to go. Then, before I knew it, I saw the last cow stepping onto the platform and then no more. Slowly the platform rotated, and she crept nearer and nearer, and then – jab – and it was all done: 700 cattle vaccinated. Looking at my watch it had just gone 8 a.m. Good job, boy! Find a nice café on the way home for a well-earned breakfast, and then see if Amber has anything else. Hopefully, though, I'd have the rest of the day to myself.

I packed away my kit and took it back to the car in two loads. Nathan and Darren had already started hosing down the parlour, and I heard the engine of the quad bike start up. I guess Mike was getting ready to shepherd the stragglers back to their field and shut the gate. I washed myself off, made my farewells to Darren and Nathan and headed for the car.

I set off out of the farm, down the track, planning to grab a coffee and check in with Amber once I got into Mawheraiti. With that job behind me, I felt pleased with myself. The sun shone through the mist, and the scenery, which had been hidden in the dark, was now visible in its full glory. I wound down the window, turned on the radio and trundled back down the lane. What a great morning!

There didn't seem to be anywhere to get a coffee in Mawheraiti at that time so I pulled into a layby and found my phone. Odd: I had five missed calls from Amber. I looked through them; first one was at 5 a.m., then 5.10 a.m., 5.30 a.m., 7 a.m. and 7.30 a.m. She must have just been checking I got there OK. I pressed RE-CALL. Amber answered.

'So how are you? And where have you been?' she enquired. Odd question, I thought.

'Fine, fine, job done, all seven hundred cows vaccinated, just in MawHerAteEE, or however you pronounce it.'

'Mawheraiti! What . . . you've been on the farm and vaccin-ated all the cows?' she said, bemused.

'Yup, all done. Went pretty smoothly. They weren't expecting me, but it was all fine in the end,' I said feeling a surge of pride.

'Interesting,' Amber replied, then after a pause, 'How odd. Martin, the farm manager, rang me at 5 a.m. asking where you were.'

'Odd indeed. Well, I didn't see a Martin, but I was there, all right, I've got seven empty vaccine bottles to prove it!'

'You found it OK then?'

'Yup, not a problem. Left in Mawheraiti, second left and then drive to the end of the track.'

'Yeah, that's right. How strange. Martin was adamant you weren't there. Maybe you just missed each other, but I'm not sure how. Let me just call him. I'll call you right back.'

'OK,' I said, and hung up. What was Martin playing at?

Five minutes later my phone rang. It was Amber. She was laughing.

'Jonny, I've just spoken to Martin. I don't know where you've been, but you were definitely not on his farm!'

'What?' I said in disbelief. This had to be a wind-up.

'You've just vaccinated 700 of the wrong cattle.'

'How have I managed that?' I asked, reeling from this revelation.

'If you followed my directions, Martin said it must have been his neighbour's farm.'

'But how? I followed the track to the end of the road.'

'Did you turn right into the farmyard through some new galvanized metal gates?'

'Yeah . . .' I said, starting to realize that this might not be a wind-up.

'Yeah, that's Martin's neighbour. His parlour is on a 90-degree bend. The track continues for another 2 km and ends in Martin's yard.'

'You're kidding me! But I didn't see any other lights from another parlour when I was heading down that track at 4 a.m.

It was pitch black, no light pollution, so surely I would have seen the lights from Martin's farm?' I gabbled.

'Martin's farm is in a valley over the hill, so you wouldn't have seen the lights.' She was trying to sound sympathetic, but was still in hysterics. 'Jonny, you're hilarious. I told my boss in Invercargill that my very good and experienced friend from England was coming to work for us for a bit and he was delighted. Day one, and you've vaccinated 700 – not just one or two, but SEVEN HUNDRED of the wrong cattle . . . You've got to see the funny side to that!'

'Yeah, I suppose so!' I said, beginning to smile.

'Didn't you think it was odd that they weren't expecting you?'

'Well, not really, because one of the guys said that the manager often forgets to tell them stuff like that.'

'On the bright side, you've just earned the practice an extra couple of thousand dollars! Although Simon won't be too happy when I tell him we've just pinched some of his government work! I'll blame it on my English locum . . . I don't think I'll tell him we were at college together!'

'So you know whose client that farm was?'

'Yeah, they're clients of Dixon Park Vets, Simon Harwood's practice. He's always accusing us of trying to steal his clients!'

'. . . Sorry,' I mumbled.

'Don't worry about it, I'm going to get so much mileage out of telling this story it's well worth an awkward five-minute conversation. Oh, and you know what you're doing tomorrow morning, now don't you?'

That realization suddenly hit me, I would have to trek all the way back out here at 4 a.m. tomorrow to vaccinate the right 700 cattle.

'Yes,' I said with a groan. 'I'm rather afraid I do.'

# Holstein cows: fast facts

*Bos taurus*: Cattle

**Distribution:** There are two living sub-species of the modern domestic cow – *Bos taurus indicus*, the zebu, which originated in Pakistan, and *Bos taurus taurus*, the European cow, which originated in south-east Turkey – but between the two *Bos taurus* now exists in virtually every corner of the world.

**Names:** An adult male is called a 'bull', a young bull a 'bullock', and a castrated male a 'steer'. A female that has had more than one calf is called a 'cow', a female under three that hasn't calved is called a 'heifer' and the young are called 'calves'. Cattle that are used for draughting are called 'oxen'. A group of cows is called a 'herd'.

**Life span:** About 18–22 years.

**Habitat:** Open grasslands, but in the wild they will also live in forested areas.

**Diet:** Their natural diet is grass, but to enhance milk or meat production or when grass is not available, their diet is supplemented with silage (a fermented high-moisture grass crop) or grains (a mixture of corn, oats and barley).

**Gestation:** 283 days, giving birth to 1 or 2 calves.

**Weight:** Varies between dairy and beef animals, between males and females and between breeds. A calf can weigh anything from 25 to 75 kg at birth, reaching an adult weight of 270–1,200 kg.

**Growth:** Calves feed on milk for the first 5–6 weeks, then as their rumen develops, can start grazing and will naturally completely wean by 7–8 months. Both males and females become fertile at about 7 months, but are not fully grown till 2 years. In the dairy industry the aim is for a heifer to have her first calf at 2 years old, which means mating her at 15 months. In the beef industry animals tend to be slaughtered between 18 and 24 months.

**Body temperature:** 38–39.3 °C.

**Facts:** Cattle can be divided into two groups, dairy cattle and beef cattle, though the two industries overlap. In the dairy industry, every cow has to produce a calf a year to maintain its milk yield, but not all the calves produced will join the milking herd. Half the calves will be male, and these will then be sold on to rear as beef or as veal calves. Of the remaining female calves, only around half will be required as replacements. With beef cattle, a good beef rearing mother is a cow that calves easily and produces a lot of milk, but at the same time will pass on the genetics of a good meat producer, and will often be a cross between a dairy and a beef animal, a Friesian–Hereford being the commonest breed in the UK.

**Conservation:** With an estimated 1.47 billion cattle worldwide they are not endangered, but with these numbers come concerns about their welfare, human welfare and the environmental impact. Cattle are thought to be responsible for 18 per cent of global greenhouse gas emissions through methane production when they eruct during rumination. In the developing world cattle are often a sign of wealth, and are closely guarded which means that humans and cattle often co-exist in close proximity, leading to a two-way transmission of zoonotic diseases, most notably tuberculosis. TB kills over 4,000 people globally every day and awareness is growing of the contribution of bovine or zoonotic TB in this epidemic. The World Health Organization has set a target to reduce TB deaths by 95 per cent and to cut new cases by 90 per cent by 2035. See: **www.who.int/tb/areas-of-work/zoonotic-tb/en/**.

# 10

# RHINOCEROS

*'I wish that people would realize that animals are totally dependent on us, helpless, like children, a trust that is put upon all of us.'*

James Herriot

shuddered as I gazed at the item in my hand: a coarse, disagreeable material, with an unpleasant odour. The myriad of emotions was overwhelming: helplessness, disgust, bewilderment, confusion, and an anger that only a deep injustice can bring.

I turned the item over and over in my hand, studying its every facet; I felt the barbarity, suffering, cruelty and death of what had gone before. But at the same time the item created a glimmer of hope in the darkness, a sign that despite the depravity of human nature, there would always be a fight against it.

The item was maybe 6 inches long by 6 inches at its base, a dark grey almost black in colour, rough on all but one side and conical in shape. It might have resembled a large chunk of laval rock, but for the unique and distinctive smell. The smell was undeniably animal in origin, a noxious, stale, earthy dung recently infiltrated with the pernicious stench of burnt hair.

Moments before, Geoff had casually thrown the item to me as nonchalantly as if it were indeed worthless rock. But this was far from worthless, and it was not a rock of any kind. It was in fact one of most expensive commodities on the black market, more expensive than heroin or cocaine, and its illicit and illegal brutal trade was bringing a species to the brink of extinction.

I was holding about a kilogram of rhino horn, which at current valuations was worth about £65,000. Just minutes earlier, it had been the property of the large female white rhino that was lying metres from where I stood.

She was lying on her chest, her front and back feet tucked under her, her head swaying gently, inches from the ground, as she snorted in an anaesthetic stupor. A blindfold covered her eyes, and an old pair of tights stuffed with padding made convenient earplugs. A dozen people busied themselves around her, some monitoring her heart rate and breathing, others adjusting the intravenous catheter in her right ear which was connected to a 5-litre bag of saline being held above her head. The dart that delivered the Etorphine and Azaperone drug combination to induce anaesthesia had been removed, and the resulting wound had been injected with penicillin to prevent infection. Several of the farm workers were pouring large drums of water over her to prevent overheating in the sweltering African sun. Every procedure required serious manpower. Another group held taut a thick rope that looped around one of the rhino's back legs – the full extent of African health and safety! We were in exposed bush, with no trees to climb or obstacles to hide behind. If the rhino suddenly awoke, the rope would give us the crucial momentary advantage we would need to retreat. Weighing close to 2 tonnes and reaching speeds of up to 40 mph, a rhino is not to be trifled with. We all knew that this ostensibly very organized, controlled, routine procedure could, in an instant, turn into a very dangerous life-threatening scenario. I had learned never to be complacent around animals, and never more so than when it was a wild animal of such immense strength and speed.

Geoff, the farm manager, had just finished removing the secondary horn with his Black & Decker cordless reciprocating saw. He threw the horn to one of his colleagues as he stood up, groaned, and stretched, rubbing his lower back. Dressed in his obscenely diminutive blue light cotton shorts, with the typical safari thick khaki cotton short-sleeve shirt and khaki ankle boots, he was in his mid-sixties. A true Afrikaaner farmer, he was rough and tough, but with a huge heart and a gentle soul. From a lifetime of working with wildlife he had become hardened to most things, but the horrific reality of being on the front line of rhino poaching was taking its toll. Every morning when he went out on his daily check of the 200-hectare game farm, he feared what he might find. I had only ever seen pictures before and that was shocking enough. To actually find the mutilated body of an animal that you had known from a calf, had watched grow, then produce a calf of its own which it nurtured and raised, I could not begin to imagine. On top of that, to know how much it must have suffered before it died would make you physically sick. Geoff said it often did.

The reason for our presence there that day, and for our involvement in the risky anaesthesia of a healthy animal, was as part of a dehorning programme, designed to prevent the rhinos on the farm being poached. The hope was that if the horn were removed back to its germinal base, the remaining horn tissue would be of insufficient size to be worth poaching. The dehorning of rhinos was stringently controlled. A rhino owner needed to apply for a specific licence from the Parks Board to allow them to dehorn an animal. Once granted, the procedure required the attendance of a State Vet to supervise and document the operation. Delaray was the State Vet today, a tall, slender, youthful chap. It was his first job out of vet school, and as such it could have been a very tough first gig, having to lay down the law with some of these toughened farmers. But he was a warm, friendly, likeable chap and it was immediately apparent on first meeting the group that day that Geoff and the senior farmhands had an immense respect and affection for him.

As Geoff finished the dehorning procedure, Delaray and a couple of vet students busied themselves around the rhino's head, variously taking blood from an ear vein, collecting hair and toenail samples, gathering up any remnant fragments of horn, and tagging and photographing the rhino. It was all part of the DNA identification record that allowed each and every horn to be traced to the farm, with details of the animal, and the date and time that it had been removed. With the horn being so incredibly valuable, the paper trail had to be impeccable to prevent even a sniff of corruption or any horns inexplicably 'disappearing'. Even so, and despite every effort to the contrary, corruption was still heartbreakingly rife. With its value of £65,000, each kilogram of horn was worth more than most Africans would earn in a lifetime. This was often just too tempting to resist. I remembered a conversation I had had two years previously with a ranger at Chobe National Park in Botswana, when we were out on a morning game drive. It was my first trip to Africa and I was intent on learning more about the poaching problem. He told me that just a few months previously the park had lost its last black rhino to poaching, an utter devastation for all who had fought, quite literally, to prevent such a scenario. But to add insult to injury, when they located the horn using the tracker that it had been implanted with, it was under the bed of one of the park security guards. 'You can't trust *anyone* in this game,' he had said.

Geoff stepped back from the rhino, his task now done for this one, but we were only just getting started. With nine more to go, it was going to be a long day. He glanced over at me; I was still holding the horn he had thrown to me. As he caught my eye, he read my thoughts.

'You are wondering how anyone could mutilate such a beautiful animal for something similar to our fingernails? Or something like that?'

'Something like that,' I acknowledged. 'This must taste disgusting, and you've got to be pretty stupid to think it has any medicinal properties. I just don't get it.'

'It is desperation and three thousand years of tradition tied up in one. It's impossible to counter, and they don't have a clue about the brutality involved in obtaining it. Then at this end, the guys doing the dirty work are on the breadline, struggling to feed themselves and their families. Someone comes along and offers them more money than they will ever otherwise see, for some information or one night of work. It's no wonder they jump at it. We can condemn them, gasping in disgust and shuddering in disbelief that a fellow human could be so callous and brutal, while we lie in our comfortable beds, watch TV in our cosy homes, and shop in food halls stacked with every food choice known to man. We don't know the desperation of wondering where the next meal will come from. For them the choice is simple, it's "the animal or me". For every poacher killed, there are a hundred more lining up to take his place.'

It was a perspective I hadn't considered before. It was humbling, in a way, given what he had seen and experienced. Suddenly the problem was opening up to me in a way I hadn't understood before. I felt ashamed as a foreigner to be coming in with all my preconceptions and prejudices, ignorant of the nuances of the problem. It was an abhorrent illegal trade that was bringing a species to the brink of extinction, there was no question about it, but there was also never going to be a simple solution. There were so many layers to the problem and I was only just starting to understand them.

'It's the depraved, malicious, pitiless, bloodthirsty, inhuman gang leaders that run the cartels that I want to get. String 'em up by their balls and let's see how they like being slashed around and shot at before having a chunk hacked out of their face.' The emotion was raw and the words just splurged out. It wasn't pleasant to hear, but I felt the same visceral emotion – and I hadn't even confronted the reality in the flesh.

Three years later I was back in South Africa. The morning had begun rather sedately with a relaxing breakfast; there was no tight schedule, nothing much on the agenda for the morning. We were a mixed group of seven vets from America, the UK and South Africa. It was to be a morning of sharing research, experiences and knowledge. Half an hour in, though, it all changed. Derik received the phone call he always knew might come, but had hoped never would.

Sabi, the three-year-old white rhino that he and Cobus had rescued and nursed back to health after it had been shot while his mother was poached, had himself been poached in the night.

Sabi had been just weeks old when rangers had found him trying to nuzzle the mutilated body of his mother. He was in a bad way, having been shot three times. But despite the poachers' efforts to kill or scare him off, he had remained by his mother's side as she had been peppered with machine-gun bullets and slashed across her back and legs with machetes. She then had her horn hacked off before being left to die in utter agony.

At just weeks old he was completely helpless, so when Cobus arrived on the scene he knew Sabi's only chance of survival was 24/7 care. They took him back to the vets' base and nurtured him back to health, feeding him every few hours and often sleeping with him to keep him company. Incredibly, and against the odds, he made a full recovery and grew well.

At six months of age he was sufficiently independent that they felt it best to relocate him to a secure facility where he could be socialized with other rhinos. It was here, two and a half years later, that Sabi once again had to experience the callous, depraved brutality of human greed, and this time it cost him his life.

As Derik hung up the phone, his shock and disbelief were evident; he struggled to find the words as he fought back the tears. He had experienced the realities of rhino poaching countless times, but this had a personal element to it. He reached into his top pocket, pulled out a cigarette, and turned to walk out of the room as he fumbled in his pocket for his lighter. The atmosphere in the room, which only moments before had been light-hearted, full of jokes and laughter, was now an eerie silence. We exchanged glances, but none of us could speak for shock, and anyway, there didn't seem to be anything to say. We heard Derik's phone ring again from the veranda outside the meeting room and then the distinctive guttural sounds of Afrikaans. The smell of cigarette smoke now permeated the room. We remained in silence, each immersed in our own thoughts. When the phone call had ended and the cigarette extinguished, Derik rejoined us.

'They want us to go and help with the post-mortem,' he announced. 'The police and forensics need to examine the scene and gather evidence initially, and then it will be over to us. I warn you, it won't be pleasant, but this is reality. We'll leave in half an hour.'

The journey was a bizarre experience. Large portions of it were conducted in silence, each of us lost in our own thoughts as we gazed out the window at the passing African landscape. Conversation, when it did come, ranged from trivial small talk to an emotive discussion about how to deter poachers, protect rhinos and whether legalizing the trade in rhino horn was the solution or whether we were just being naive and the battle was already lost.

Three years before, I had been convinced that legalizing the trade of rhino horns was the answer. Allowing people to farm them like any other animal product would flood the market, reduce the price, and thus reduce the incentive to poach them. It seemed a painfully simple solution to a dire problem. If asked, I would have invoked the regulations implemented by CITES (the Convention on International Trade in Endangered Species of Wild Fauna and Flora) in the 1970s that promoted crocodile farming – a system of captive breeding that sought to prevent crocodile ranching and the theft of eggs from the wild, and how this brought the Nile crocodile back from the brink of extinction. If it worked for crocodiles, wouldn't it work for rhinos, too? As is often the way, though, the more ignorant you are, the simpler the solution can appear to be.

Unfortunately, the solution to these problems is invariably multifactorial. They involve predicting an outcome that will only be able to be proven after it has been committed to and is impossible to undo. Get it wrong, and you are faced with a new problem, which may be worse, perhaps catastrophically so, than the first.

So is legalizing the trade of rhino horn the answer? Three years on, I was more sceptical. In 2001, three rhinos were poached in the whole of South Africa, in 2016 nearly three rhinos were being poached *every day*, an unsustainable increase that will see the species extinct in twenty-five years if something dramatic isn't done to stop it. So what has led to this exponential increase? For hundreds of years the horn of this exotic creature from lands far away has been believed to possess medicinal properties, ranging from curing rheumatism, gout and typhoid, to snakebites, food poisoning and even cancer. With the increase of wealth in Asia, more and more people purchase rhino horn as a status symbol, simply to show that they can, and thus the demand has increased dramatically. The current annual global demand for rhino horn is estimated at around 16 million tonnes, and it is thought that there are around 40 million tonnes stockpiled in vaults from animals that have been legally dehorned for their protection. If the trade were legalized, this stockpile could be used to supply the market and thus reduce the poaching demand. But there are two possible fallouts from this. Poaching would indeed be reduced as this stockpile replaced it, but it would be used up more quickly than it could be replenished. The current stockpile has taken fifteen years to accumulate, and once used, at present levels of demand, poaching would return to the same level as before. Alternatively, poaching levels might remain high as legal horn hit the market, the sale price of it would then fall, making it affordable to a wider population, thus increasing the demand from 16 million tonnes a year to maybe 20 million or even more. It takes about eighteen months for 1 kilogram of horn to grow on an adult rhino, and it is estimated that there are 29,000 rhinos left in the wild, so the current demand is impossible to match sustainably with these numbers. Two things need to be achieved: the current demand needs to decrease, and the birth rate of rhino calves needs to exceed the rate at which they are being killed.

Legalizing the trade of rhino horn may be one component of the answer, but education and awareness have to penetrate the heart of these communities too.

When we arrived at the farm, we parked some distance from the bomas (enclosures) where the rhinos were kept at night. Lisa, who ran the sanctuary, greeted us. She had obviously been crying, and composed herself as she politely met us, but as soon as she made eye contact with Derik the tears started flowing again. There was a deep, raw, emotional grief shared between the two of them, almost like that of bereaved parents. As they hugged, the grief turned to anger as Lisa exploded in a burst of Afrikaans that we didn't need translating to comprehend. Lisa had been heading up this secure, highly confidential sanctuary for nearly ten years. The sanctuary served two purposes: as a safe house that rhinos could be moved to when a reserve was hit by poaching, and as a place that rehabilitated and cared for rhinos that had suffered injury from poaching. The work Lisa and her team did was invaluable in the fight against the seemingly unstoppable force of the poaching cartels. But all of this was now severely threatened. The tragedy of Sabi was utterly devastating for all those involved, but the wider implications for the sanctuary were completely shattering; every remaining rhino was at extreme risk of a similar fate, and it was now a race against time to come up with a strategy to protect them.

The police and forensic teams were already at work combing the area for clues. We could see them in the distance: it was going to take some time to complete their task and until then we had to keep well clear for fear of contaminating the crime scene. Our attention was quickly drawn to an enclosure close to the house, containing two rhino calves that couldn't have been more than a few months old. Like magnets, we were irresistably drawn to them. Having regained her composure and assuming the role of hostess, Lisa followed us.

'These are Sethemba and Isibindi. Their names mean "hope" and "courage" in Zulu. Both of their mothers were killed by poachers. Sethemba had her ears hacked off in the process and Isibindi had several deep wounds to her head and side caused by machetes. It's a common occurrence. The poachers view these young calves as a nuisance, so they try to scare them off and attack them wildly. Sometimes they kill them, but more often they are just severely maimed.' She paused for a moment, collecting her thoughts. 'So strong is the mother–calf bond that despite the extreme trauma they suffer, they are always found together in the morning. Often it is apparent that the mother has used every last ounce of her strength to protect her offspring, dragging her mutilated body through the bush to where her calf has retreated to shelter. The mothers rarely survive the night due to the extent of their injuries, so in the morning the calves are usually found nuzzling their mother's head, crying for her to get up and confused about why she hasn't. I don't think there can be a more distressing sight in all of nature than a baby mourning its mother. Their high-pitched squeak or whine cuts right through you. You'd have to be inhuman not to weep.'

As we surveyed the two little rhinos, seemingly happy and content charging around, playing with each other, oblivious to our watching eyes, it was hard to comprehend the suffering that they had already endured in their short lives. What more did they have to face? How would the situation play out for their species? Their generation exists at a critical time: will they see their extinction averted or will they both just become two more gruesome poaching statistics as the species is eradicated by human greed?

A further two hours passed before the forensic team had finished their work. The senior police officer strode over to Lisa's house where we had been waiting. He engaged Lisa and Derik in a long conversation in Afrikaans, obviously explaining the team's findings. Although we were unable to understand the details, their expressions gave us a stark insight into what they were hearing. It was as if they were hearing the last movements of a gallant son killed in action. Grief, anger, despair and guilt were all there on their faces.

We later learned the full story of what had happened. There had been a full moon. Poaching goes up threefold on a full moon because of the increased visibility. There had been two perpetrators, and all the evidence indicated that they were very familiar with the set-up at the enclosures and with Sabi himself. The tracks led directly to Sabi's enclosure. They had known exactly which animal they were going for and where he would be. It had been an inside job. Geoff's words echoed in my head from three years before: 'You can't trust anyone in this game.' Standing at the inside feeding hatch, they had lured Sabi into his shelter with food, and then shot him twice in the head at point-blank range. However, these first shots didn't kill him, and instead he turned in fright to flee. The poachers then shot him three more times: the first in the top of his neck, the second across his mid-spine, and the third into the side of his head. He had managed to stumble 10 feet out of his shelter before he had finally collapsed and died.

It was in a sombre and apprehensive mood that we made our way to the enclosure, trying to picture in our minds the scene that would greet us, so that we could mentally prepare ourselves. Nothing could prepare us for it, though.

We walked into the boma from the end furthest from the shelter. Several members of the police and forensic teams were still gathered around Sabi, obscuring most of his body, so all we could initially see were his hindquarters. From that angle he could have just been another anaesthetized rhino. Moving round the enclosure, we could see glimpses of bright red contrasted against his dark grey skin. But it was when the party gathered around Sabi noticed our arrival and turned to greet us that we saw the full extent of the horror. The front of his head had been hacked off, from below his eyes to above his nose. Where his nose and two horns should have been was now just a mess of bone, blood and tissue. Congealed blood covered the sides of what remained of his face. There was one solitary marker protruding from a bullet wound on the side of his head, from which a trickle of blood had run. The marker indicated the fatal shot. An additional and unexpected cause of revulsion was the exposed mess of bony flesh where the right foot should have been. We found out later that because of an increasing trade in fake rhino horn, it was now commonplace for the poachers to hack off a leg as well, as evidence that the horn had indeed come from a rhino.

As the scene before us began to sink in, there were no words. It was a bizarre juxtaposition: Sabi seemed so peaceful lying there, and yet the starkness of his mutilations told of the suffering he had endured and the depravity and greed of mankind. The farm workers, Derik, and the rest of the team, started on the post-mortem under the supervision of the police. To our great relief we were not required. We sat down on the dry, dusty dirt of the enclosure, a few metres from where Sabi's body was slowly losing its majestic identity in a procedure familiar to all of us. No words were exchanged. Once again, we were each of us lost in our thoughts, processing and trying to come to terms with it all. As a group of six vets, we had all seen hundreds of dead animals, witnessed hideous injuries and experienced desperate sadness in our careers to date, but this was different: a deliberate, targeted, malign and murderous cruelty, driven by grotesque human avarice, and meted out on an innocent and beautiful animal.

We were just about holding it together, each of us masking our anguish with a feeling of outrage. Or at least we were – until we started hearing a high-pitched, mewing cry. At first we were clueless as to its origin or significance. It was a rather irritating, uncomfortable sound, but as it persisted, it dawned on us that this was the distressed rhino cry to which Lisa had earlier alluded. Peering between the wooden posts separating the two enclosures, we could just make out the rhino next door. He was repeatedly, obsessively, pacing up and down against the fence, crying out unremittingly in an impassioned whimper. We will never know exactly what those cries signified, those visceral, emotive, childlike cries. And though it is always dangerous to anthropomorphize, it was impossible not to hear these cries as heartfelt and agonizing – cries of confusion, cries of grief, cries of concern. Why was his friend not responding? Why was there so much human activity around him? Why was there that distinctive smell of blood that he could only recognize intrinsically as danger, a sense that all was not right?

For us, though, to hear such a pathetic and feeble noise emanating from such an immensely large and powerful creature was the last straw. It was as though he were begging us, on behalf of all rhinos, to *do* something. Turning away, I was glad of the sunglasses masking my eyes. There was no holding back the tears anymore.

# Rhinos: fast facts

*Ceratotherium simum*: The white rhinoceros

**Distribution:** There are five distinct species of rhinoceros, two native to Africa and three to Southern Asia. 98.5 per cent of white rhinos live in just five countries (South Africa, Namibia, Zimbabwe, Kenya and Uganda).

**Names:** An adult male is called a 'bull', a female a 'cow', and the young a 'calf'. A group of rhinoceroses is called a 'crash'.

**Life span:** About 40–50 years.

**Habitat:** Mainly open, grassy plains, though other species prefer swamps or forested areas.

**Diet:** The white rhino is a grazer, and is distinguished from the black rhino, which is a browser, by its wide flat upper lip, which allows it to pull up even short grasses.

**Gestation:** 16–18 months.

**Weight:** Newborn calves weigh 40–65 kg, reaching an adult weight of between 1,700 kg (females) and 2,300 kg (males).

**Growth:** Females tend to live in crashes of up to 14 animals; males are usually solitary, but will stay with a female for up to 20 days at mating. The female raises a solitary calf, only giving birth every 3 to 5 years. The calf will stay with the mother until about 3 years. Females reach sexual maturity at about 5 years, while males reach sexual maturity at about 7 years.

**Body temperature:** 36.6–37.2 °C.

**Interesting fact:** Contrary to popular belief, the name 'white rhino' doesn't refer to its colour, but comes from a mistranslation of the Dutch word *'wijd'*, meaning 'wide', referring to the width of its mouth which distinguishes it from the narrow pointed mouth of the black rhino.

**Conservation:** Of the five species of rhinoceros the IUCN identifies the black, Javan and Sumatran as 'critically endangered', the Indian as 'vulnerable' and the white as 'near threatened'. The statistics surrounding rhinos are horrifying: only about 275 Sumatran rhinos and a mere 60 Javan rhinos remain in the wild; between the 1960s and 1990s black rhino populations fell from 70,000 to 2,410, and the Indian rhino to about 1,870. In 2007 13 rhinos were poached in the whole of South Africa; in 2014 the number reached 1,215, which equates to more than 3 a day. So although there are estimated to be around 20,000 white rhinos in the wild, and about 4,500 black rhinos, at current poaching rates rhinos will be extinct from Africa within 25 years. What is more, the manner in which these animals are brutally slaughtered leaves them to suffer and die in agony. Saving the Survivors is an incredible charity whose focus is on the treatment and care of all wildlife, but particularly rhinos that have fallen victim to poaching or traumatic incidents. See **www.savingthesurvivors.org**.

# 11

# DONKEY

*'I hope you heard that? She called me a noble steed. She thinks I'm a steed.'*

Donkey in Shrek

It's John from the donkey sanctuary here,' came the familiar Wiltshire accent over the phone.

'Hi, John, how are you?'

'Oh, very well, sir, very well, thank you – and you?' came the usual reply. Born of a lost generation where manners were everything, it was always so humbling when an older gentleman to whom I felt a natural deference, addressed me with such regard. In John's eyes, though, as a veterinary surgeon I deserved respect. In turn I admired and respected John immensely for his lifetime of unassuming, selfless dedication to the care of neglected animals, and in particular, donkeys. It was this mutual respect that was central to our working relationship and served to benefit the goats, pigs, sheep, dogs, cats and 120 donkeys at the sanctuary John had established over thirty years before.

'I'm well, thanks. The usual problem of not having enough hours in the day!'

'Indeed, Jon, indeed, always too much to do when it comes to caring for animals.'

'How can I help?'

'Jon, it's Pollyanne. She's gone lame again on both front feet. It's a worry with *Carmen* coming up in a couple of months, she needs to be sound and ready for that. It's the last run and they'll be devastated if she can't be on stage.'

Pollyanne was, without question, the star and public face of the donkey sanctuary. John had rescued her from Salisbury Livestock Market in 1997, where he had found her distressed, severely neglected and destined for imminent slaughter. Appalled by her condition, he had immediately offered to buy her there and then, and taken her home. It had taken a huge amount of work to gain her trust, and a long programme of farriery to rectify the years of neglect to her feet, but after many months' care she had come round, and she and John had formed an inseparable bond. Thriving on attention, she soon became the natural choice for Nativity plays, Palm Sunday services and any other event where a donkey was required. From the sanctuary's perspective too, she exemplified everything it stood for and was striving to achieve: providing a home for neglected donkeys where they were cared for, nurtured, and encouraged to trust humanity again.

Pollyanne turned out to be such a natural performer, in fact, that after being talent-spotted at an event, she was signed by a specialist agency providing animals for TV, film and theatre. Her first professional role was at the Royal Opera House, Covent Garden, starring alongside Plácido Domingo in *I Pagliacci*. On one notorious occasion she even upstaged him from the wings by braying noisily as he was singing one of his arias leading him to call her 'a great scene-stealer'.

Nevertheless, Pollyanne went down a storm, and so when a donkey was sought for Francesca Zambello's 2006 production of *Carmen* to mark the sixtieth anniversary of the founding of the Royal Opera, Pollyanne was a natural choice.

Fast-forward nine years, and Pollyanne had appeared every year in the celebrated production of Bizet's Spanish master-piece, but 2015 was set to be its last run. Pollyanne had been so popular, among the cast and audience alike, that for her not to be able to perform in *Carmen* was unthinkable.

'I think it's her laminitis flaring up again, but it seems worse than normal,' continued John. 'I've tried to bring her into her stable from the paddock, but she's so sore she doesn't want to move.'

'Poor Pollyanne! I've got a few things on this morning, but I could come out this afternoon about three o'clock. How would that suit?'

'That would do nicely, thank you, sir.'

'Great. Meawhile, give her half a sachet of painkiller and see if that makes her comfortable enough to bring her into her stable in an hour or so.'

As a result of her years of neglect, Pollyanne had periodically suffered from bouts of laminitis, a painful inflammatory con-dition of the tissues that bond the hoof wall to its pedal bone. Over the years John had learnt how to manage these flare-ups in her condition through a combination of painkillers, diet and a bed of deep shavings for a couple of weeks until things settled. However, they had occasionally been so bad that she required more intensive treatment, and it would take much longer for her lameness to fully resolve. If that was the case this time, there really was a genuine question as to whether Pollyanne would be healthy enough to make the two-hour lorry journey to the Royal Opera House in a couple of months' time, so I fully understood John's concern and prayed it wouldn't be that serious.

It was a little before 3 p.m. when I drove down Old Didcot Road and turned into the donkey sanctuary. John was waiting as I pulled up at the gate into the yard, and he came striding over to open it. Then in his mid-seventies, he was still incredibly fit, but that was hardly surprising: he was a true worker, so passionate about his donkeys and other animals that to him his job was as pleasurable as a hobby. I was sure that in the thirty-two years since he had set up the sanctuary, he could count the number of days' holiday he had taken on two hands.

As I got out of the car, he greeted me with his usual broad grin and firm handshake. Dressed in his customary heavy-duty black ankle boots, brown corduroy trousers, checked shirt, grey knitted V-neck sleeveless jumper and his faithful flat cap, he was ever the country gentleman, although his clothes, like his hands, told the same story of years of toil and hardship.

'Good afternoon, sir. Thank you very much for coming.'

'It's a pleasure, John. Now, how is she?'

'Oh, not very good . . . not very good at all.'

'Did you get the painkiller into her, and did you manage to get her in from the paddock?'

'I did, yes, she's had half a sachet of Bute, and Linda and I managed to walk her in an hour ago, but she's still incredibly sore.'

'Let's have a look at her then.'

We strolled over to the old ramshackle wooden barn next to the staff room, which was used as the infirmary. Full of cobwebs, with a pen for a sheep and goat, chickens nesting among four square straw bales, the odd farm cat peering out from behind a bag of corn, and a pile of baler twine and empty feed bags in the corner, it was an image of a forgotten time. For that very reason, it was my favourite place at the sanctuary and, of course, where I ended up spending the majority of my time.

Pollyanne was in the first of the two stalls. Despite the painkillers, and the deep straw bedding to cushion her feet, she was in obvious pain. Standing with her forelegs straight in front of her, resting her weight on her heels, she had the classic laminitic stance. There was none of the friendly, inquisitive nuzzling with which she usually greeted strangers as I stepped over the three-foot stainless-steel sheep fencing into her pen. Instead, her ears were down, and her eyes bulging, emphasizing the discomfort she felt.

'I see what you mean, John. She really is struggling, isn't she?'

'It's the worst I've seen her in eighteen years.'

Never one to exaggerate, John didn't say that lightly. I bent down and felt for her digital pulses. They were pounding, and there was also noticeable heat in her hooves. I was keen to lift up her feet to have a look at her soles, but transferring further weight onto an already painful foot was something she firmly resisted and thus didn't warrant the further distress it would have caused.

'Yeah, it's laminitis all right, and given how painful she is, I think we should X-ray her feet and make sure nothing catastrophic is going on in that hoof.'

'Whatever you suggest,' John replied.

'I could borrow our practice's machine, but I won't be able to get back out with it again until Thursday at the earliest, so I think it's best if I refer her so we can get the ball rolling as soon as possible.'

If her pedal bone was rotating and slipping through the hoof, then Pollyanne's condition was extremely serious and would need intensive remedial work by a farrier to address the problem. The only way of accurately assessing whether there was any rotation, and if so how much, was by X-raying the feet. It was a simple job, but because she was in so much pain, she was unfit to travel and so the X-raying would need to be done at the sanctuary, and this required a portable machine. There was a very good equine specialist hospital not far away and they had a very experienced farrier who would be able to manage her feet and give her the best chance of a speedy recovery.

'I'll give them a call now,' I explained to John, 'and see if someone can come out to X-ray her feet this afternoon. Then we can take it from there. In the meantime I'll give her a sedation and some more pain relief and put some temporary cushioning pads on the bottom of her feet. Hopefully that'll help her a little.'

Returning to my car, I made the call, grabbed some bandage material and soft supportive pads, and drew up a couple of injections, which I then administered. After a few minutes Pollyanne was sleepy enough for us to lift each front foot in turn so I could bandage the cushioning in place. Ten minutes later the job was done.

'I'm much obliged to you,' said John, handing me a coffee. 'You know what Pollyanne means to me. They're all special, of course, but I've never had a donkey like her . . . She really is a special one, all right.'

'Someone will be out between about five and five thirty this afternoon,' I reported, taking a sip.

'Very good, very good. Thank you.'

'They'll let me know what they find, and then we'll take it from there. I can come back out in due course to check on her, but they'll probably manage her from here on.'

'Right you are, Jon.'

So after my coffee and my usual enjoyable chat with John, I bid him farewell and headed off in my car.

That evening I got a phone call from the vet with the results of Pollyanne's X-ray. There was a small amount of pedal bone rotation in both feet, he told me, but fortunately she wasn't in imminent danger of her bone slipping through her sole. She would need some remedial care to correct and settle things, which would take time to resolve, but he was optimistic that she would be sound in plenty of time for the opera. It was encouraging news and, although he'd already told a very relieved John, I rang him to check in.

'Hi, John, I've just spoken with the vet. It sounds like it's really the best possible news.'

'So it is, Jon, I'm mighty relieved and very grateful to you for your help. If all goes to plan, there'll be no holding her back in six weeks.' The anxiety I had heard in his voice that morning had gone. 'And Jon? As this is the last year she's performing, you'd be more than welcome to come up with us to one of her performances and be with us backstage.'

'I would love that, thank you!'

'That's settled then. It's the least I can do. I'll get Wendy to send you a list of possible dates and then you can let me know which one suits you.'

'Perfect, I'll really look forward to that.'

'Good. It's quite an experience – and you'll have to excuse my outfit.' He laughed. 'I look quite the character when I'm all made up.'

'I'll wait to hear from Wendy. Thank you, John. And let me know if I can help any further with Pollyanne, but it sounds like she's in good hands.'

After a couple of weeks' slow progress, Pollyanne suddenly turned a corner, and a month later she was back to trotting around the field as though nothing had happened and, much to everyone's delight, the opera was back on. Wendy sent me a list of dates when Pollyanne would be performing, and I was pleased to see that I'd be in London for one of them, which sounded like a fun way to finish a day of meetings.

And so on a cold, crisp Tuesday evening in November I found myself turning off Bow Street into a virtually deserted Floral Street. Parked up next to the tall black double doors of the backstage entrance, John's elderly maroon converted Ford Transit horsebox looked entirely out of place. The stage doors were so tall you could walk a giraffe in through them with ease. A security guard stood on patrol, eyeing me suspiciously as I headed over towards the trailer, but before he could engage me, John appeared out of a nearby door, wiping his mouth with a handkerchief.

'Perfect timing, Jon,' he said, shaking my hand. 'I've just had a lovely dinner courtesy of the Opera House in their restaurant. Have you eaten? They'll feed you if not? You have? Oh, very well, very well.' He turned to the trailer. 'And what about you, Pollyanne, is it time for your pre-performance snacks?' The trailer shook as she stomped inside, responding to the familiar voice. 'You've been a very patient girl, as always.' He started unbolting the backdoor to the trailer.

'Are you ready to take her in, John?' the security guard suddenly piped up.

'Yes please, Keith,' John shouted back.

'Right you are.' He spoke into a receiver on the wall. 'Lift for John and Pollyanne coming onto stage.'

John had meanwhile lowered the ramp and was climbing onto the trailer. 'Jon, would you mind taking some of the chickens over to the lift?' he said, handing me a crate containing two live chickens.

Somewhat baffled, I did as I was told. Returning to the trailer, I could see that Pollyanne was getting impatient now, stomping and braying.

'All right girl, I'm just coming,' John assured her, handing over a second crate of chickens. 'Jon, can you close up the trailer behind me?'

He handed me the keys before climbing back onto the trailer, untying and leading Pollyanne down the ramp. It was such an incongruous sight that my brain could scarcely process the image I was seeing: a donkey trotting the streets of London. I lifted up the ramp to close and lock up the trailer and joined John in the elevator. This was already becoming an evening of firsts; I was now in a lift in the Royal Opera House, with four chickens and a donkey . . . It felt like the start of a joke. Keith shut the doors behind us and with the press of a button sent us on our way, up to the stage floor.

The stage manager, dressed in black jeans and a T-shirt, complete with clipboard, a radio and earpiece, greeted Pollyanne warmly.

'Here she is!' she said, ignoring John and myself as she opened the elevator door. 'I've missed you, Pollyanne.' There was obvious affection in her voice as she rubbed Pollyanne's mane. Pollyanne responded, with equal affection, nodding her head and nuzzling into the stage manager's arm, but then she started sniffing her pockets for a treat. They clearly had an established routine. 'OK, OK, here it is,' she said, pulling out a carrot, which she grabbed before it was offered. 'You only love me for my treats, don't you, Pollyanne?' she said with an air of pretend resentment. Greetings done, she turned her attention to us. 'Evening, John. You're in the same place as usual, let me know if there's anything you need.'

'Thank you, Emily. On top of things as ever, I see! Can I introduce you to Jon? He's Pollyanne's vet. He couldn't miss her last season performing.'

'Welcome, it's a pleasure to meet you. I'm sure John will show you the ropes, but if there's anything you need just let me know.

Feel free to watch the performance from the wings. You'll see some tape on the floor. Anyone past that line can be seen by the audience, so can I just ask you not to go beyond it at any time.'

John stepped off the elevator platform leading Pollyanne, and I followed with one of the crates. As we came out from behind a black screen, a hive of activity greeted us and I realized we were actually already back stage. To the right of me was the stage itself, but the large forty-foot-high set panels blocked my view of it. The high ceiling was full of scaffolding on which the lighting rigs could be hung and moved. Cables ran along the floor in all directions, taped down at regular points to prevent people tripping on them. Messages, instructions or directions were chalked on the floor at various points. A lady attended to a rack of costumes and table of props. A multitude of people dressed in black like Emily were all busy at work on their various jobs. On this side, the back stage area was probably 15 feet wide. Halfway along it, a 6-foot by 6-foot pen had been erected, complete with straw bedding and a bucket of water. Next to it hung a rack with John's costume. He opened the pen and Pollyanne sauntered in with an eager familiarity. The lady on the props table walked over to join us.

'Evening, John. Your costume is all here, do you want assistance dressing this evening?'

'Thank you, Mary, I'll be fine.'

'No problem,' she said, disappearing back to her table.

'When I first started doing this, I used to be dressed every night like some earl,' he whispered to me. 'It was all very odd, but now I know how to put it all on, I prefer to do it myself.' He busied himself getting Pollyanne settled with her hay net and unpacking her bag of brushes. Meanwhile I returned to the elevator to grab the other crate of chickens. 'There's a little drinker and a bottle of water you can fill up for each of the chicken crates,' John instructed me.

As we settled our charges into their temporary accommodation, the stage workforce were increasingly distracted by our arrival, coming over to greet Pollyanne enthusiastically. It was evident that she was a very popular addition to the performance. One old chap suddenly appeared with two carrier bags, full to bursting, one with sweets and the second with apples, carrots and other such donkey delights. 'Here you go, John, your evening supplies.'

'Thank you kindly, sir,' John responded as he took them, then turned to me and whispered, 'That's Richard, he's the same every time. Brings all these sweets for us. I can never eat them, but he insists we take them home for all the volunteers at the sanctuary, and of course Pollyanne gets her own bag.' Then in a slightly serious tone, he added, 'As you can see, everyone is so eager to spoil her, I actually have to monitor what she gets, to make sure she doesn't get overfed.'

Among the small crowd of well-wishers, a lady now appeared who, from her appearance, did not seem to be part of the stage crew.

'Evening, John, all OK?' she said, before turning to greet Pollyanne.

John looked up and, as he recognized her, a warm smile spread across his face. 'Hi, Kay, I'm fine, just fine, let me introduce you to Jon, he's our vet at the sanctuary, I thought I'd bring him to show him our star at work!' He turned to me. 'Kay is Pollyanne's agent, the one that got us into all this nearly twenty years ago, can you believe it?'

'Pleasure to meet you,' I said, shaking her hand.

'How lovely you could come this evening. You must go and meet Louis, the gentle giant, he's the other star of the show.'

'Yes, Louis is beautiful,' John agreed. 'In fact, Kay, would you mind staying with Pollyanne for a minute so I can show Jon around?'

'Of course, no problem,' Kay said, and immediately turned her attention to fussing over Pollyanne who was now more interested in her hay net.

'Come on, Jon, it's only six thirty, so there's plenty of time to show you around before I need to get ready.'

First he led me towards the front of the immaculately pre-pared stage, where a small team of stagehands were attending to last-minute jobs. The vast crimson red stage curtain was down and there was as yet little noise coming from the other side of it. Any punters who had already arrived were clearly occupying the bars and restaurants rather than their seats. I noticed the yellow tape on the floor that Emily had mentioned. Despite it being set about a metre back from the stage entrance, the vantage point still afforded a view of over half of the stage. Six chairs were lined up in two rows of three, in the corner, behind the line.

'You're more than welcome to watch the performance from here,' John told me. 'These are for special guests of the performers.'

Then he led me back past Pollyanne's pen to the back right of the stage, which opened out into a much larger area. A large, majestic, jet-black shire stallion stood in the middle of his roped-off area as his owner brushed and groomed him.

'Good evening, Samantha, are you well?' John said, greet-ing her and introducing us.

'This is Pollyanne's mate, Louis,' she told me. 'The two of them have been in every performance of *Carmen* since it started, haven't they, John?'

'Indeed, they both love it.'

'What a beautiful animal,' I said, stroking him.

'Thank you, he's such a star, even if I do say so. Never put a foot wrong in nine years.'

'Louis plays a horse belonging to Carmen's lover, the bull-fighter Escamillo,' John explained. 'He has to carry Escamillo around the stage while he sings "Toreador". It's pretty impressive to watch.'

I wondered how many opera singers imagine their career will involve performing on horseback. We left Louis, and John led me further back. It was only now that I began to fully appreciate just how large the stage was, but just when I thought we had reached the back of it, we came to a huge doorway. Walking through it, I realized we were on another enormous stage, and beyond that a third stage piled high with an array of sets: a throne room, a balcony, vast paintings, spectacular painted vistas.

'It's incredible, John,' I said in disbelief. 'I would have never known the back stage area was so vast.'

'Yes, this area is even bigger than the front of stage, apparently, and these stages are on a huge turntable system so parts of the floor or whole stages can be interchanged between scenes or performances. They can store multiple different sets at the same time, which means they can have several different performances running together. It had a huge overhaul in the late nineties, and that's when they added a lot of this. Well, I guess I'd best be getting ready, and Pollyanne will be eager for a brush,' he added, bringing me back to the whole purpose of why we were there. We retraced our steps, and found Kay sitting on a chair outside the pen, busy on her phone, while Pollyanne was still happily tucking into her hay.

'Thanks, Kay,' John said, gathering together his outfit from the rail. 'I'd better go and get changed now.'

'Do you want me to give Pollyanne a brush while you're getting changed?' I enquired.

'If you want to, that would be a great help, thanks.' He disappeared off to find a changing room among the rabbit warren of corridors, rooms and offices underneath the stage.

I climbed into Pollyanne's pen and took to brushing her. She responded immediately, leaving her hay net and turning to face the stage, ears pricked.

Kay laughed, 'She knows exactly what's going on, don't you think?'

'She certainly does – quite the performer, isn't she?' I replied.

'I have to say I deal with all sorts of animals in my line of work and Pollyanne is one of my favourites, she's such a character. I'm sure John told you about the night when Radio Three were here recording *Pagliacci* with Plácido Domingo, and Pollyanne let out an almighty bray during a duet. John was mortified, but everyone else thought it was hilarious.'

'He did tell me, but I didn't realize it was when the BBC were recording the performance.'

'Oh yeah. After that people started queuing up outside the stage doors to get hoof prints of Pollyanne in their programmes, it was unbelievable. John took it all in his stride, as you'd expect.'

'How funny,' I mused. 'Quite the celebrity.'

'Who is?' John said, suddenly reappearing, now dressed as a simple Spanish peasant farmer in old boots, chaps, flannel trousers, white shirt and grey jacket.

'Pollyanne,' Kay responded. 'I was just telling Jon about how people used to queue up for her autograph.'

'Oh yes,' John chortled. 'Took me quite by surprise the first time, but we soon got pretty good at it. Her hoof oil worked brilliantly as ink.'

'You couldn't make it up,' I chuckled.

'Well, what do you think?' John asked. 'Do I pass as a Spanish peasant?'

'You certainly look quite the part. So, what *is* your role?' I said, realizing for the first time that I didn't actually know the story.

'Well in Act One it's a street scene and we appear on stage, with Pollyanne wearing a pair of pannier baskets filled with old-fashioned wine flagons, and I saunter around the stage offering them to villagers. Then in Act Three we walk onto the remnant of a battlefield. This time the pannier baskets are full of ammunition, and I sell them, along with Pollyanne, to some gypsies who walk off with her.'

'I can't wait to see it,' I said.

'Come on then, Pollyanne, time to put your outfit on.'

The wings were all starting to fill with the performers, many of whom were keen to greet Pollyanne, while the bustle of the audience taking their seats was now clearly audible on the other side of the curtain. The stage caller wandered around, announcing, 'Ten minutes.'

I felt an eager anticipation, but the routine of just another day in the office was evident among the cast, who were nonchalantly playing on their phones or chatting away. Pollyanne was now wearing her panniers over a very cleverly designed harness that had a subtle sack at the back to catch any droppings, should an accident happen on stage – although in nine years it never had. John donned his simple wide-brimmed hat and put his pipe in his mouth.

'Five minutes to curtain up, take your positions and all quiet back stage, thank you.'

Quietly and efficiently, phones were put away and various cast members took to the stage while others got into position in the wings ready for their cue, as relaxed as ever. I marvelled at how slick and professional it was, but then this was the Royal Opera House, so I guess it had to be.

The orchestra started, the curtain went up and as the opera began I snuck forward to watch from the wings at the front of the stage. The auditorium was packed, with every single one of the 2,256 seats taken. I felt nervous just standing there watching the performance, and I wasn't even on stage. I was just feet away from the limelight, it would be so easy to just walk out onto the stage, wave or take a bow. It was the same dizzy sort of feeling you get when you're standing at the top of a tall building and imagine jumping off. After a few minutes I started getting used to my hidden vantage point, enjoying the unique privilege of the opportunity. Before long Pollyanne and John came on for Act One and then in no time they were back off stage, having delivered, as far as I could tell, another faultless performance. I wandered back over to join them. John took no time in removing Pollyanne's costume to give her a brief rest, as they wouldn't be needed for the rest of the first half. Pollyanne, so familiar with the routine, settled back into her hay net.

At the end of Act Two the screen came down to signal the interval. The hive of activity from the audience drowned out any noise that we made and so we were able to start talking normally again.

'Time for a coffee, I reckon. Would you like one?' John asked. 'If you stay with Pollyanne, I'll pop and get one.'

'Sure, thanks.'

John disappeared with most of the cast as they headed to the dressing rooms. A few people stayed to engage with Pollyanne, who turned to greet her admirers. She never seemed to tire of the attention. The stagehands busied themselves on stage and in the wings as they altered the set for the second half.

John soon returned with coffees.

'Enjoying it so far?' he asked as he handed me one.

'The whole experience is amazing. I still can't quite believe I'm backstage at the Royal Opera House,' I confessed. 'It's all a bit surreal.'

'You have to go on stage after the performance, when everyone has gone. It's incredible to look out at all the seats. It's only then that you realize quite how special this place is.'

'I'll be sure to do that.'

Coffees finished, John set about getting Pollyanne ready again, and the cast started filtering back, several in new costumes.

'Five minutes to curtain up for the second half, positions please.'

Once again the cast swiftly took their places and minutes later the orchestra erupted in its full glory. Up went the curtain, and the second half was under way.

Again I watched parts of it from the wings, although I found myself tiring of the limited view. If there were any tickets left for any of the performances, I vowed to come back and see it properly. As the opera reached it climax, I wandered down the wing to the back of the stage where Samantha was holding Louis with Gábor Bretz, who played Escamillo, already mounted up to ride on stage for the grand finale.

As the final notes died away, the audience erupted in delight at the evening's entertainment. The cast took their repeated bows and then the curtain descended and all was over. Immediately a fever of activity broke out behind the curtain as the stagehands started striking the set. *Carmen* was not on again till Saturday, and in the meantime The Royal Ballet would be performing *Romeo and Juliet*, so things had to be dismantled for the stages to be switched around. I watched in amazement at the efficiency of the operation. After about twenty minutes of organized chaos the stage was completely empty, revealing quite how vast the space actually was. The curtain then rose to reveal the now empty auditorium, I tentatively left my seat by Pollyanne's pen and headed to the front of the stage, looking out across the stalls, the grand tier, balcony and amphitheatre. John was right: it truly was breathtaking. I thought of the catalogue of world-famous ballerinas and opera singers who had performed on this very stage. And then I wondered how many vets had stood where I was standing.

# Donkeys: fast facts

*Equus africanus asinus*: The donkey

**Distribution:** There are 185 different breeds of donkey across the world, but the greatest populations are found in Africa, Asia and Latin America. They all originate from the now endangered African wild ass, which is found in Egypt, Sudan, Ethiopia and Somalia.

**Names:** An adult male is called a 'jack', a female a 'jenny', and the young a 'foal'. A male donkey can be crossed with a female horse to produce a mule, and a male horse can be crossed with a female donkey to produce a hinny. A group of donkeys is called a 'drove'.

**Life span:** About 30–50 years.

**Habitat:** Their natural aptitude is for arid or semi-arid climates, but their resilience and usefulness as a working animal means they have adapted to survive in most environments.

**Diet:** They are grazers, naturally feeding on grass and scrub and although, like the horse their food is broken down by microbial action in the hind gut, their digestive system is more efficient, allowing them to survive on a much poorer-quality diet.

**Gestation:** 11–14 months.

**Weight:** Foals weigh 8–16 kg, growing to 80–480 kg as adults, depending on the breed.

**Growth:** Although a jenny can come into heat as soon as 9 days after a foal is born, she won't naturally mate until the foal is weaned at about 6 months. Jacks reach puberty at about 10 months, and jennys at about 2 years, but neither are fully grown until about 3 years.

**Body temperature:** 36.2–37.8 °C.

**Interesting fact:** The donkey has been used as a working animal for over 5,000 years and, after human labour, they are the cheapest form of agricultural power.

**Conservation:** There are an estimated 40 million donkeys worldwide, about 96 per cent of them in undeveloped countries. In 2006, 27 per cent of the global population of donkeys lived in China but this has now reduced to 7.5 per cent, following growing demand for donkey meat and donkey-hide gelatin, 'ejiao', which can sell for about £300 per kg. This has led to donkeys being traded from Africa where they are often kept in appalling conditions. Brooke is an incredible equine charity that seeks to relieve the suffering of donkeys and mules all across the third world: **www.thebrooke.org**. The Island Farm Donkey Sanctuary also does a wonderful job in caring for neglected donkeys within the UK: **www.donkeyrescue.co.uk**.

# 12

# FERRET

*'Ferrets, they are the most lovely noble darlings in the world.'*

D. H. Lawrence

I 've just booked you an emergency,' Hazel said, popping her head round the door of my consulting room. 'It's a ferret. Apparently he's behaving very strangely, and the owners are worried and are bringing him straight down.'

'OK, thanks,' I replied, wiping down the table between patients. It was not an unusual scenario to have an emergency in the middle of a consulting list; it was all part of the job. If you were fully booked then you prioritized it. There was no A&E facility, so sometimes it meant other clients had to wait, but most understood, taking the view that if it was their animal they would want the vet to see it first. With this particular emergency it looked like I would be lucky. I had half an hour's gap after my next patient so hopefully I wouldn't get too behind, and with that thought I cast the emergency out of my mind and walked out into the waiting room.

'Sam White?' I enquired. The only animal in the room was a boisterous and excited, slightly rotund chocolate Labrador accompanied by a man in his thirties dressed in jeans, shirt and puffer jacket and a boy of about six who was dressed as a mini version of his dad.

'Come on, Jack, we've got to take Sam for his injections to stop him getting ill.'

'Can I take him, Daddy?' Jack asked, pestering his father to let him hold Sam's lead.

'I'll take Sam, and you can take me,' suggested his dad.

'So Sam is here for his booster and general check-up, is that right?' I asked when we were all in the consulting room.

'Yeah, that's it,' replied Mr White.

'Great, so how is he doing? Do you have any particular worries or concerns?'

'Not really, he's generally great. We want to get some weight off him, but a certain person enjoys sharing his dinner with him!'

I sympathized. It wasn't the first time I'd heard something similar and looking at Jack, his arms draped around Sam's neck, loudly whispering, 'It's OK, Sammy, the doctor is going to make you not get sick,' I could see they had a very close bond.

I picked up my stethoscope and bent down to introduce myself to Sam and start my examination. He responded in excited exuberance, leaping forward, tail wagging furiously, and licked my face. Seeing this, Jack immediately started giggling uncontrollably. It was amusing, sure, but not *that* funny, I thought, but Jack was laughing hysterically until he finally burst out: 'Sam just licked your face after he licked his willy!'

It probably wasn't the first time I'd been licked in the face by a dog that had just been cleaning itself, but to have it pointed out by a rather too observant and vocal child was a new one on me.

'Jack, calm down,' said his father, in a failed attempt to stifle his chuckle.

Jack slapped his hands across his mouth as a reflex attempt at politeness, but realizing that Daddy thought it was amusing too, knew he wasn't really in trouble and so the chuckling continued.

'I do apologize for my son,' the father said.

'No, please don't worry, it was very . . . funny,' I replied.

The rest of the consultation proceeded uneventfully, but haunted by the child's comment, I took a moment to wash my face after they had gone. As I was drying off, I heard the doorbell signalling the arrival of the sick ferret.

I heard them at the front desk, and then in a whirlwind a young couple burst through into my consulting room, the female member of the party clutching a towel, which presumably contained the ferret, in her arms.

'Please, sir, you must do something, please, there's something wrong with Freddie, I think he might be dying.'

She placed the towel on the table.

Reeling from the sudden invasion, I took a moment to regain my composure and then carefully unwrapped the towel to reveal a fairly recumbent large male sable ferret. The disturbance caused him to twitch involuntarily and then lift his head trying to stand. As soon as he found his feet, his head started gently swaying from side to side, so uncontrollably and to such a degree that when he tried to walk he lost his balance and fell over, face planting into the towel. Determined, he attempted it again with the same outcome, and then a third time. It was distressing to watch.

'How long has he been like this?' I asked. I had a moderate amount of knowledge about ferrets, but I had never seen anything like this before. The couple looked at each other, and then the man answered.

'We just found him like it, he was fine this morning.' He looked to his partner for confirmation.

'Yeah, that's right,' she said quickly. Their behaviour was odd, and I couldn't quite work it out. 'Is he going to be all right? Please, do whatever you need to, he's our baby.'

'I can't say for sure, I've never quite seen anything like this before in a ferret.' Then, thinking aloud, I processed the sight before my eyes. 'It's odd, very odd, such an acute onset . . . maybe he's ingested something, like some sort of toxin?' As soon as I said it, it suddenly seemed to make more sense. 'Does he live in a cage or does he just roam round the house?'

They looked at each other again, and then he answered. 'Yeah, he has a cage that he's in at night or when we're out, but when we're home we just let him loose. He's very sociable so tends to stay in the same room as us, so we usually know what he's got up to.' This answer seemed to roll off his tongue more fluently, and this time he didn't seek his girl-friend's approval. They were hiding something, I was sure of it, but what?

'So has he been out today and did you see him eat anything he shouldn't have?' I asked.

'Um, well . . .' he began.

'Is he going to be all right?' she interrupted.

Yes, there was definitely something odd here, I thought. A toxic ingestion seemed to fit the bill, but what? Chocolate could be a possibility, but he seemed too sedated for that. Grapes would cause an acute kidney failure and he would be sick rather than sedated. Besides, if it was something like that, why were they being so cagey? What could it be? It was almost as though he was drunk. I needed to probe a bit more.

'I'm honestly not sure. If I knew what he had eaten, then it would give me a better idea. Can you think what it might be?'

'Um, well . . .' he said again.

'Steve, you've got to tell him. Just tell him, he needs to know, and if Freddie dies it will all be your fault,' she exclaimed.

'Um, well, what it is, right . . .' he began, 'I went round to my mates, right, to play some computer games, right, and, um . . . I took Freddie with me, cos Jess was out and I didn't want to leave him on his own. Anyway, we was playing Call of Duty and Freddie got into my mate's rucksack which he had just left on the floor—'

'He's eaten marijuana,' Jess exploded then, turning to Steve and unleashing a tirade. 'I can't believe you left your weed in your rucksack on the floor while you and Mike played your stupid computer games, he was bound to get to it, you *idiot*!'

'JESS!' Steve cut in, scared that she was giving away too much information. 'It was my mate's dope, right?' he said with conviction, looking at Jess for backup, 'I didn't know it was there, did I?'

'I don't care, I'm not covering for you anymore. You let him eat your weed, you're an idiot, a complete and utter idiot! Stupid man, you deserve whatever trouble you get – I don't know what I see in you, and if Freddie dies I don't know what I'll do.'

Now everything made sense. I understood it all. This ferret in front of me was stoned, completely high! It was certainly a novel case for me. I remembered learning in vet school about the effects of cannabis on dogs, but not ferrets, though, logically, the symptoms and treatment should be similar. The key question that would determine his prognosis was how much had he consumed. If the taste hadn't matched the intriguing smell and he had just had a nibble, then all would be good; he might sleep for a while, but should make a full recovery. If on the other hand he had properly tucked into the marijuana, then it would undoubtedly prove to be his last meal.

The domestic argument that had erupted in front of me was still in full swing.

'Look, I'm not going to report you,' I interjected, 'I just need to know exactly how much he's eaten and in what form, so I'll know what his prognosis is and what we need to do.'

'Well, Steve?' Jess said, turning to him accusingly. 'How much was left from your Saturday night with the lads?'

'Don't play innocent, Jess, you had some too.' Clearly Steve didn't entirely trust me and now if he was going down he'd make sure to take Jess with him.

'STEVE, just tell him!'

'All right, all right. I don't reckon he had much. I heard the rustling in the rucksack, didn't think much of it, and then remembered the grass, so I rushed to my bag and grabbed him out. He had some on his nose, but there didn't look like much had gone from the pouch. I don't think he was in there long at all.'

'OK, well, that's good. If you're right then his prognosis should be pretty good, but he'll need supportive care until the effects wear off. We'll need to put him on a drip, keep him warm and monitor him.'

'So he'll be OK, then?' Steve asked, starting to sound relieved.

'Well, I can't be completely sure, I've never dealt with this scenario before, but I know it is rarely fatal in dogs and it obviously depends on how much he's eaten.'

'It really wasn't very much, I'm sure of it,' Steve said, sensing that if Jess could be reassured that Freddie was going to be OK, then his imminent chastisement would be shorter lived.

'Thank you, sir,' said Jess now. 'Just do whatever you need to for Freddie, he's so precious to us.'

I printed out a consent form and discussed the cost of treatment. This was one of those occasions when the financial penalty could serve as an additional deterrent against a repeat episode in the future.

'You can pay for it instead of your next stash,' Jess said to Steve as she signed the consent form.

'I'll take him through and start his treatment. I'll call you later with an update, but as I say, I reckon he'll probably be here for a couple of days.' I scooped up the bundle from the table. Jess leaned over and kissed Freddie on his head, which was just protruding from the towel.

'This man is going to make you better, Freddie,' she said, then, turning to me, 'Thank you, sir, please look after him, I know he's in the best place.'

'We'll do everything we can,' I reassured her, and headed out into the prep room as Jess and Steve left, no doubt to continue their exchange in the car home.

Heather was busying herself repackaging surgical kits to go into the autoclave for sterilization. She looked up with a slightly quizzical expression when she saw the bundle in my arms.

'Is that the ferret?' she enquired. 'What's wrong with it? What are we doing to it?'

'You'll never guess.'

'What?' Heather asked as she cleared away, making a space on the table for me to put him down.

'He's stoned! Got into the owner's cannabis supplies.'

'You're joking.' Heather responded and burst out laughing, but then as I opened the towel and she saw his disorientated, ataxic stagger, added, 'Poor little fella, what are his chances?'

'Well, they don't think he's eaten very much so they should be pretty good. Dogs tend to do OK, but I've never heard of a ferret eating marijuana before. We'll just have to see. He'll probably be out of it for a day or two.'

'What an idiot for leaving it lying around where the ferret could get at it.'

I explained what had happened. 'Naturally he thought the bag was a good hiding place and then couldn't resist the intriguing smell!'

'Unbelievable. So what's the plan?'

'Drip, put him somewhere dark, warm and quiet to minimize any stimulation, then it's just wait and see.'

'OK, he can go in a cat kennel with a heat mat. We haven't got any cats in, so it'll be quiet and I'll put a towel in front of his cage.' She started getting things together.

'Perfect, thanks.'

'Have you got anyone waiting?' she added.

I double-checked the computer screen in the corner of the room. 'Next one is in ten minutes.'

'OK. Yellow intravenous catheter, I assume? Hartmann's or saline?'

'Yeah, yellow and Hartmann's, 250 ml.' The catheter colour indicated size: generally speaking, pink or green was for dogs, blue was for cats, and yellow for kittens, small puppies and, in this case, ferrets.

With all the equipment laid out and the drip line set up, Heather held Freddie and extended his front left leg which I clipped and cleaned before gently inserting the intravenous catheter. In a normal awake ferret this procedure would have been a virtual impossibility without being savaged multiple times, but Freddie put up little resistance. I connected the Y-piece, then taped and bandaged it in place.

'Did you weigh him? What fluid rate do you want?'

'No, sorry. Maintenance should be fine, he's not dehydrated, but won't be able to drink anything until he recovers.' A maintenance rate was an animal's daily fluid requirement. Under normal circumstances, for a small animal like a ferret it was estimated to be 60 ml per kg of body weight per day.

'OK, there are scales in the cat ward so let's take him through and then I can set up his cage,' said Heather, picking up Freddie who was still in his towel bundle. I grabbed the drip stand with the bag of fluids connected to the drip line, which ran through a pump that could accurately control how much fluid was administered per hour, and we headed into the cat ward next door.

With Freddie settled in a darkened cage, complete with a heat mat, several towels for padding to stop him inadvertently banging against the walls in his stoned stupor, and connected up to fluids, I returned to finish my consulting list.

The rest of my afternoon cases were less unusual – an itchy dog, a hamster with a lump, a couple of dog vaccinations, a cat with a flea allergy and an egg-bound chicken – and with these completed, I was able to return to check on Freddie. I crept into the cat ward trying not to make a sound for fear of overstimulating him. Tiptoeing up to his kennel, I gently drew back the towel to assess him. I could hear what sounded almost like a high-pitched wheeze. It took a moment for my eyes to adjust to the dark, but when they did, I could see Freddie lying on his front, face planted into the towel, nose squished to one side, legs sprawled out, and I realized the noise I was hearing was him snoring. He looked very sweet, but was completely and utterly out of it, in a comatose stupor.

And there he stayed for the next two days, barely moving, snoring soundly, occasionally rousing slightly to the sound of a cage door opening as cat patients came and went, or in an attempt to acknowledge his owners when they came to visit him: seemingly content, in some weird, chilled-out drug-induced ferret dream.

I arrived at work on the morning of the third day to news from the night duty nurse that he seemed to be waking from this prolonged doze. I wandered in to check on him and indeed he was, wide awake and exploring his cage for an escape route.

'Morning, Freddie, did you have a good siesta?'

'Should I offer him some food?' Julie asked.

'Yeah, that would be good, he certainly seems awake enough to eat.'

'What shall I offer him?'

'Cat food would be best, a pouch of something.'

Julie returned moments later with a small bowl of food. As she opened the cage door, Freddie's reaction was extraordinary. Even before she had placed the bowl down, he virtually launched himself across the cage, face planting in the bowl and devouring every morsel in seconds and then frantically circling the cage looking for more.

'I think he's hungry,' Julie commented drily.

'I presume that's what they call the munchies.'

'Hilarious. Shall I offer him some more?'

'Yeah, why not, let's go with the same amount again.' This time Freddie was climbing the cage door in eager and obsessive anticipation of a further food source when Julie returned. It was hysterical to watch him once again, with no decorum or delicacy, immerse himself in the bowl of food, snorting as he devoured it.

'I think he's feeling better, don't you?' I said.

'I reckon so.'

We disconnected his fluid line before it fell victim to his hunger pangs, and then I called the owners.

'Good news. Freddie has woken up and seems completely fine, so you can come and pick him up. Oh, and I must thank you for adding to my education. I had never really experienced the concept of the munchies before, but it's safe to say that ferrets experience them too.'

# Ferrets: fast facts

*Mustela putorius furo*: The ferret

**Distribution:** The ferret is the domesticated form of the European polecat, which is found across mainland Europe and much of Russia.

**Names:** A male is called a 'hob', a female a 'jill', and the young a 'kit'. A vasectomized male is called a 'hoblet' and a group of ferrets is known as a 'business'.

**Life span:** About 6–10 years.

**Habitat:** In the wild they are found predominantly in forests, but will be found anywhere that a food source of mice, rats, small birds, reptiles or amphibians exists.

**Diet:** Ferrets are crepuscular and obligate carnivores, consuming the whole of small prey including bones, feathers and fur. They lack a caecum so are unable to digest any plant matter.

**Gestation:** 42 days, with a litter of 3–7 kits.

**Weight:** 10 grams at birth, reaching 0.7–2 kg as adults.

**Growth:** Kits are born with their eyes and ears closed and completely helpless. At 5 weeks their eyes open and they wean, at 3 months they are independent, at 4 months they are both grown, but neither hobs or jills reach sexual maturity until about 7 months.

**Body temperature:** 37.2–40 °C.

**Interesting fact:** Jill ferrets are induced ovulates, meaning they will only ovulate when mated. A failure to mate causes a prolonged oestrus and the subsequent high level of circulating oestrogen causes a life-threatening aplastic anaemia. For these reasons, a male may be vasectomized to allow mating and thus ovulation to occur without breeding.

**Conservation:** Ferrets are abundant in number across the developed world, being kept as pets or in rural settings for 'ferreting' which involves sending them down rabbit holes to flush out the inhabitants into nets. However, their wild cousin, the black-footed ferret, is categorized by the IUCN as endangered. They were declared extinct in the wild in 1987, but a captive breeding programme launched by the United States Fish and Wildlife Service has allowed them to gradually be reintroduced into 8 western states. Now there are over 1,000 wild-born individuals across 18 populations. See: **www.blackfootedferret.org**.

# 13

# GIANT PANDA

*'Summit meetings tend to be like panda matings. The
expectations are always high, and the results usually
disappointing.'*

Robert Orben

As my driver negotiated his car through the bustling streets
of Chongqing, I gazed out the window, mesmerized by
the morning routine unfolding before me. A frail old
lady wearing the iconic Asian rice hat, carrying two baskets
of fruit on a bamboo shoulder pole. A motorcyclist weaving in
between the traffic, visor raised, cigarette protruding, enjoying
his smoke as he rode. The immaculately dressed schoolchildren
proudly carrying their oversized rucksacks, each emblazoned
with the latest Chinese cartoon character. A cyclist whose
mouth and nose were obscured by a surgical mask in hopes
of minimizing smog inhalation. A businessman impeccably
dressed in his tailored suit, savouring the last morsels of his
fried duck beak before entering the office to start his day.

It was my first visit to China, and even though I was now eight days into my trip, these vivid daily scenes were still intriguing. I had visited many different countries, but never felt as much of an outsider as I did here. For me, this experience was the very definition of culture shock. People were still people, of course, children had to be educated, adults had to work, food had to be sourced and money had to be earned, but within those bounds everything was so unfamiliar, so different, so new. It was like being a child again, having to learn how to interact with people, recognize social cues and understand table manners. Then there was the food. Always game for new experiences, and having been brought up to eat whatever was put before me, I had resolved to do that on this trip. So far, I had eaten snake, chicken's feet, cow's rumen, sheep's abomasum, pig's caecum, eel, and pig brain. It had become a game for the Chinese colleagues I was working with to try to find a dish that I wouldn't eat or would make me heave. So far they had failed, but I was starting to long for a pizza, fish and chips, or bangers and mash.

It was surreal to think that just two weeks before I had been going about my usual, daily work in the rolling Cotswold hills, and now here I was among a multitude of people who could no more understand the world that I came from than I could theirs.

We turned off to negotiate a narrow street, which, even at 7.30 in the morning was bustling. Every shop was some form of eatery, with the kitchen spilling out into the street. Old rusty bath tubs full of tilapia fish, cages of chickens or rabbits, huge woks of vegetables and cauldrons of bubbling soup all cluttered the pavement. The driver parked and ushered me into one of these shops for a breakfast of spicy noodle soup. This dish would have felt so alien to me even a week before, but now it was part of my daily routine. After an animated exchange between the establishment's owner and my driver, we each took our seats in an all-in-one plastic table and chair set that reminded me of my primary school dining-hall furniture. No sooner were we seated than the familiar bowl was thrust in front of us. We slurped on our noodles, exchanging appreciative grins and thumbs up as he didn't speak any English and I only had a handful of Mandarin words that I was using to exhaustion. Yet despite this complete language barrier we had struck up a novel friendship where facial expressions and monosyllabic words covered the varied breadth of an entire dictionary. It's only when communication is inhibited that you truly realize the power of body language.

Back in the car we continued our journey to Chongqing Zoo. It was my fifth and final day there. The primary reason for my visit to China and Chongqing was to meet Professor Zhibiao Wang and his team at Haifu Medical Technology. Professor Wang and his team are one of the few companies in the world developing a novel medical technology called 'focused ultrasound'. At high intensity, an ultrasound beam emitted from a transducer outside the body can be focused on tissue within the body. At the focal point of the beam, temperatures in excess of 80 degrees centigrade can be achieved, meaning that the tissue in the focal area is destroyed. This technology already had global recognition as a successful treatment option for some uterine fibroids and prostate cancers. Now many of the best medical facilities in the world, including my father's department in Oxford, were researching its use for treating other cancers and conditions.

While I had done my final year's research project at vet school exploring the potential applications of high intensity focused ultrasound (HIFU) in the veterinary profession, my interest now lay with the low intensity focused ultrasound (LIFU) machine that Haifu had developed. With osteoarthritis being one of the commonest causes of chronic pain and discomfort in geriatric animals, there is a real need for more treatment options. I've seen far too many heartbroken owners say goodbye to their beloved family pet because of crippling arthritis; although the animal's mental faculties remain as acute as ever, they become unable to stand, with a downward spiral of joint pain leading to decreased exercise which in turn leads to muscle wastage and weakness. Medications and complementary therapy can slow the progression quite dramatically, but when quality of life is brought into question, euthanasia often becomes the kindest option.

Evidence of the clinical benefit of therapeutic ultrasound in a variety of musculoskeletal conditions dates back to the late 1940s, and I was keen to see if the new machine Haifu had developed could help treat geriatric animals. The ultrasound waves cause an increased blood flow to the area, which can decrease pain by reducing swelling and gently massaging muscles. To me the technology offered a wide range of potential benefits for dogs, horses and other animals and I was keen to learn more about it.

Professor Wang had generously invited me to accompany my father on a trip to Chongqing to discuss the role of LIFU in veterinary medicine. China had always been somewhere I had longed to visit, unashamedly with the sole desire to learn about, work with and maybe even treat giant pandas. So when the invitation came I brazenly asked if it would be possible to link up with the team at the Chendu Research Base of Giant Panda Breeding during my stay. Unfortunately, that wasn't possible, but after a few further phone calls, they came up trumps with an alternative. I was offered the opportunity to spend five days at Chongqing Zoo with Dr Wu, the zoo's senior vet, and Dr Tang, its giant panda specialist. With fifteen giant pandas, Chongqing Zoo has the fourth largest collection in the world and the largest outside the research centres in Sichuan province.

So here I was, by luck and good fortune, yet again achieving a dream. As I made my way through the main entrance, heading for the zoo's main attraction, I passed the communities of senior citizens in their silk pyjamas engaged in their morning t'ai chi or badminton practice. It seemed they had permission to use the zoo for these purposes before the gates opened each day. It was relaxing, calming and serene, a complete juxtaposition from the morning melee I had come from on the other side of the gates. It was incredible to find a place of such peace and tranquillity in a sprawling city of 10 million inhabitants, but it would take more than that to keep me sane in a metropolis such as Chongqing. I am not a city person; far from it. After a few days in a city I feel like a caged animal; I need space and I need nature, which is why I had loved Africa so much.

Before heading up the steps and into the main panda enclosure where I had arranged to meet Dr Tang, I took a few moments to greet and observe Xi-Xi enjoying her breakfast of bamboo shoots in her pen, away from the others. At thirty-one years old, she was the oldest giant panda at the zoo and one of the oldest in the world. Although a bamboo's rich shoots are a giant panda's preferred part of that plant, they are also the most expensive, so in most cases their consumption was restricted to treats as opposed to the stalks and leaves, which made up the bulk of their diet. However, like many aged animals, dental deterioration makes chewing difficult, and so at her grand age, Xi-Xi was afforded the luxury of shoots three times daily. It was captivating to watch her place a handful of shoots onto her belly, then proceed to pick one up in each hand, systematically devour three-quarters of each shoot, discard the rest and move on to the next. All she needed was a white vest, baseball cap and open beer can and she could have been Onslow from *Keeping Up Appearances*. And that strange resemblance was exactly the point. Giant pandas are arguably the most iconic and best loved animals in the world. Their rapid decline, to the brink of extinction, in the second half of the twentieth century touched the world in a way that many other endangered species have not. And why? Probably because the cubs are particularly cute, and because the adults are so eerily human in their mannerisms that they resemble the slob in all of us. Whenever we watch them, it's as if we're waiting for the person wearing the costume to remove the head and mop their sweaty brow before walking off for a coffee and cigarette.

Over the last four days, as I had sat in Dr Tang's office overlooking the main enclosures where You-You, Mi-Mi, Ling-Ling and Curiosity sat completely engrossed in systematically devouring their bamboo, I had found myself utterly captivated. It was effortless to idle away endless hours transfixed by their mundane daily routine of eat, sleep, sleep, eat, eat a bit more, sleep a bit more ... and then maybe find a new location for a bit more eating and sleeping.

I entered the door to the private quarters which housed the feeding kitchen, the staff area and Dr Tang's office. Dr Tang and Dr Wu were having an animated conversation as they peered at a monitor. The monitor in question was relaying footage of a mother with her six-week-old cub from a CCTV camera located in a hidden enclosure a few hundred metres away. Panda cubs are born weighing a mere 150 grams, pink and hairless, resembling a tiny piglet more than a giant panda.

But now at six weeks old, the cub had a full, distinctive black-and-white coat and weighed about 1.5 kg.

I had arrived at the zoo excited by the prospect of encountering and working with giant pandas at close quarters. To then discover that they had a month-old panda cub, the first panda to be born at the zoo in five years, was thrilling beyond words. The mother was very attentive and caring, spending most of the day with the cub nestled tightly in her chest. An adult female panda will weigh about 90 kg, and such was the discrepancy in size, the cub was often obscured from view, hidden under the mother's arms. As I gazed at the screen I would find myself ignorantly panicking, wondering if I should alert Dr Tang that the cub seemed to be missing or not moving. Then suddenly a tiny face would wriggle to the surface and try to squirm free from Mum to explore their straw bed. She would oblige for a few seconds, and then effortlessly lean forward and scoop her tiny charge back into her arms. It was wonderful to see the natural instinct of motherhood playing out. The only time when Mum would leave her cub was when one of her three daily meals of bamboo was brought into her enclosure. During this time she would crawl out of her nest and then gently place her cub face down on the straw bed before turning her attention to the 40 kg of her daily bamboo requirements. During these periods it was possible to get a good view of the little cub aimlessly writhing around on his bed, exploring what was, at that point, the limits of his universe. Just like a baby on a play mat, it was an image that would resonate with any parent.

Since the day the cub was born, Dr Tang and his team had been on a night-shift rota, each taking it in turns to sleep in the office, waking every two hours throughout the night to document mother and cub's behaviour and to keep a close eye on the latter's progress and health. The previous night had been Dr Tang's shift. Since the early hours of the morning he had been concerned that the cub had been sporadically coughing through the night and was worried that this could be the start of a chest infection or even pneumonia. The subject of the discussion between Dr Wu and Dr Tang that I had walked in on was whether the cough was serious enough at this stage to warrant the stress to mother and cub of removing the cub to examine him. As this was explained to me, I joined them, studying the monitor intently. The cough was there, no doubt – a distinctive soft dry puff of a cough. Instinctively my veterinary training kicked in. I had heard thousands of coughs from many different animals. At this stage the cub seemed to have a dry 'non-productive' cough, making pneumonia unlikely, but that was not to say it wouldn't progress. He was also very bright and behaving as normally as you would expect of any helpless crawling baby. So the dilemma continued: should we investigate at this stage while the cub was well, or would that cause unnecessary stress? Alternatively, should we just wait and see, and then risk the situation progressing and the cub becoming quite ill? I found myself in a slightly different dilemma: I obviously wanted the best for the cub, but who wouldn't want the opportunity to hold, examine and treat a six-week-old panda cub?

Having been briefed on the situation through my translator, I was now included as a colleague and an equal in the discussion between Dr Tang and Dr Wu, who asked my opinion, based on my experience with other animals I had treated with pneumonia and chest infections. Trying not to let my personal wishes cloud my judgement, I thought it through. What would I do if it were a calf or a lamb? The answer was, of course, that I would examine it. Until we had taken its temperature and listened to its chest, we would only really be speculating. I asked how stressful the separation between mother and cub would be, and whether feeding time might give us our best window. We concluded the stress could be managed and mini-mized. The same keeper had been feeding the mother every day since the cub was born. If he fed her in the outer part of the enclosure, she might leave the cub for a few minutes in favour of breakfast, allowing the door between the two areas to be closed and the cub to then be moved around the corner and out of sight to where we would be waiting. It was important for us to be invisible to the mother, since too many strange people would make her realize that something was up, making her, and therefore her cub, more nervous and stressed out. Out of sight of the mother, we would be free to carry out our exami-nation before returning him to his enclosure. So it was settled: we were going to examine the six-week-old cub. I maintained an air of complete professionalism, but inside I was jumping up and down like a gleeful child waiting to enter a sweet shop.

With the decision made, the office turned into a hive of activ-ity. Dr Wu radioed the keeper who was responsible for mother and cub. For the last six weeks they had been his only responsi-bility, to reduce the risk of inadvertently spreading disease from one of the other giant pandas to the cub, whose immune system was still quite 'naïve', reliant as he was on ingesting antibodies through his mother's milk. Dr Wu then turned to me to enquire, for reasons of biosecurity, whether my clothes were clean that morning or whether I had worn them on other days that I had been working with the pandas. Fortunately, they were indeed clean on that day and as yet I hadn't come into contact with any animals. The question briefly conjured up the memory of my grandmother demanding that I strip down to my boxers before I was allowed through the front door every night when I stayed with her for my lambing placement as a first-year veterinary student. Presumably the zoo would have had a dis-posable suit for me to wear on this occasion rather than having me perform the examination in my underwear!

Twenty minutes later we made our way across the public area of the panda enclosures, towards an old brick building which the unknowing public would doubtless assume was derelict and uninhabited. Dr Wu unlocked the outer gate. As we approached, a keeper opened the door and started fervently addressing Dr Tang in a whisper. It was only when he stopped to take a breath that Dr Tang was able to introduce my translator Yersina and myself as the additional members of the party. He paused briefly to greet us before continuing, as Dr Wu, who had been relocking the outer gate, now joined us in the building and an animated three-way conversation ensued. The energy that they were putting into the conversation made it seem as though some catastrophe had unfolded in the five minutes since we had left the office and its monitor, but as Yersina explained, they were simply debating where best to put the bamboo shoots for Mum in the outer enclosure. It was yet another cultural difference: I could not discern any correlation between the intensity of a conversation and its relative importance.

The building consisted of three rectangular enclosures, each about 3 metres wide by 6 metres long, separated by a 2-metre-wide passage that allowed access to each individual enclosure through a large, lockable sliding door. There was also access to the outer enclosure from the passage. Each enclosure and door was constructed of 2-inch, floor-to-ceiling wrought-iron bars, which were a rusty brown in colour, with a polished smooth finish from years of repeated cleaning. In truth the building was damp and dingy, resembling a medieval dungeon – not my idea of luxury accommodation – but with a large bed of straw it must have felt like the perfect cave and den for the panda.

With the protocol decided we then hung back out of sight in the corridor while Xang, the keeper, chose four lush green bamboo branches, each about 10 feet long, from a pile of twenty or so that lay in the corridor, and then proceeded through the passage and into the outside enclosure. We heard the heavy clanking sound of the outer passage door being closed and locked, and then the sound of the door from the mother's cage being opened, allowing her access to the outside where her breakfast awaited her. She was clearly hungry for a feed because it wasn't long before we could hear the door sliding shut again and the lock snapping to. The mother was now secured outside and Xang then opened the door into the enclosure and moments later appeared holding a little black-and-white ball of fur squirming in his hands.

Xang laid the cub on its back on the electronic scales so as to document his weight: 1.25 kg, an 800 per cent increase on his birth weight of 157 grams. With the data recorded, Dr Tang then asked me to perform my clinical examination while he took the cub's temperature, placing the thermometer under the panda's armpit. It beeped at 36.9 °C: normal. I crouched over the cub, who raised his tiny head as I came into view. Struggling to focus on me through his bleary eyes, he had obviously just been woken from a postprandial siesta, but even when fully awake, at six weeks old his eyesight was still developing and I would have just been a blurry shadow to him. It was magical. Every mannerism and movement resembled that of a helpless human baby. He would wriggle on his back for a moment, his tiny paws reaching out to grab thin air, and then, after a great yawn and a couple of lip smackings, his eyes would close and he would be momentarily stilled, before the whole sequence was repeated. I gently placed my stethoscope on his chest and the cold of the instrument induced a sudden jolting movement followed by a small shrill bark. It was cuteness personified.

His chest was clear; all lung fields sounded completely normal, he had a little bit of mucous nasal discharge, but not the green snotty kind that might indicate an infection. He seemed very healthy. So what was the origin of the cough? I discussed my findings with both Dr Tang and Dr Wu who confirmed my observations. We concluded that, although the cough may have been insignificant, the dampness of the inside building was certainly a contributing factor. It also enhanced the risk of fungal spores in the environment. The agreed solution was an air-conditioning unit, which would help control the temperature and dry the atmosphere to reduce these problems.

While Dr Wu radioed through to the maintenance department, I soaked up my last few moments with the cub before Xang gathered it in his arms as delicately as a mother would her child and returned it to the straw bed in its enclosure. We heard the clunk of the enclosure door being shut and locked and then the sliding open of the outside door; mother and cub could now be reunited. As we exited the building we could see that the mother was still relishing her breakfast, oblivious to the intensely attentive assessment that had just been levelled at her baby.

Back in the staff quarters, as I sat drinking my cup of tea, I was lost in thought, processing what I had just experienced. The cub was one of only thirty-five giant panda cubs to be born in the entire world that year, and I had been holding it, examining it, and offering my professional opinion on its well-being. It was a truly unforgettable experience and an utter privilege. It was also a dream come true.

# Giant pandas: fast facts

*Ailuropoda melanoleuca*: The giant panda

**Distribution:** Restricted to a few mountain ranges in central China, mainly in Sichuan province, but also in Shaanxi and Gansu.

**Names:** A male is called a 'boar', a female a 'sow', and the young a 'cub'. A group of pandas is called an 'embarrassment'.

**Life span:** About 15–20 years in the wild, and up to 35 years in captivity.

**Habitat:** Temperate bamboo, broadleaf and coniferous forests between elevations of 4,000 and 13,000 feet. Farming and deforestation has driven them out of the lowland areas where they also once lived.

**Diet:** Almost exclusively bamboo, with only about 1 per cent consisting of other plants, fruits or meats. Bamboo has such poor nutritional value, however, pandas need to spend 14 hours a day eating up to 40 kg of bamboo to meet their daily energy requirements.

**Gestation:** 95–160 days (due to the varied delay in implantation of the embryo in the uterine wall, a condition called 'embryonic diapause').

**Weight:** Cubs weigh about 150 grams when born, 1/800th of the weight of their mother, making them proportionally the smallest baby of any mammal. Adults weigh 60–110 kg.

**Growth:** They are born completely helpless with their eyes and ears closed and only sparse hair covering their pink bodies. They grow quickly, will wean at 1 year, leaving their mother at 2 years, when fully grown. Females are sexually mature from 6 years, and males from 7 years.

**Body temperature:** 36.5–37.5 °C.

**Interesting fact:** Breeding giant pandas in captivity has been notoriously difficult because they only come into season once a year and then for only 2–4 days and both sexes are selective on the partner they choose. If pregnancy is achieved there is a 50 per cent chance of twins, who for decades had a poor chance of survival, but with the technique of interchanging cubs between the mother every few hours for the first few months, she is fooled into thinking she is only rearing a single cub and survival rates is now over 90 per cent.

**Conservation:** In September 2016, the IUCN reclassified the giant panda as 'vulnerable' after 32 years on the endangered list, making it one of the great success stories of twentieth-century conservation. There are now nearly 1,900 in the wild and about 300 in captivity, distributed across the world. This success is largely down to the efforts of the Chinese government in striving to protect and secure natural habitats, such as the Wolong National Nature Reserve, as well as the work of the Chengdu Research Base of Giant Panda Breeding. The giant panda is China's national animal and all of them in the world technically belong to China. See: **www.worldwildlife. org/species/giant-panda**.

# 14

# PIG

*'In each human heart are a tiger, a pig, an ass and a nightingale. Diversity of character is due to their unequal activity.'*

Ambrose Bierce

Adrian was out of town visiting one of his pig clients in Norfolk. As a pig specialist, he travelled the length and breadth of the country to see clients, but this often meant if a client needed an imminent visit and he wasn't available then he would request someone more local to attend. One such regular request was to perform a post-mortem examination (or 'PM'). Pig farms usually have such large numbers of livestock that disease spreading through the herd causing high morbidity or mortality is a constant worry. For this reason most pig units employ very strict biosecurity protocols; showering and changing clothes before entering a facility are not uncommon procedures and visitors to these units are required to have a period of between twenty-four and forty-eight hours without any contact with pigs before entering.

So if there is a sudden, unexplained death of a pig, a farmer is usually keen to find out the cause so that they can respond appropriately. If an infectious disease is responsible, then shutting down the farm, quarantining a group, and treating or vaccinating them will help prevent the disease spreading. The sooner the farmer can implement such policies the better the outcome will be.

In herd, flock or group animal management, a post-mortem is a vital part of the armoury, key to determining why an animal has died and giving information about a wider problem in a population of animals, for example a heavy worm burden, nutritional deficiencies or an infection.

'Jon, it's Adrian,' came the voice down the phone. 'You wouldn't happen to have some time this morning to do a post-mortem for me, would you? Jane said you might be free late morning.'

'I'm just on my way to Blackman's now to see a downer cow, but then I'm free till the afternoon.'

'Great. I'm up in Norfolk just now, but Graham Bartlett has a post-farrowing sow that he found dead this morning and wants her checked out. It doesn't sound like anything too suspicious, but I said I'd get someone to pop along and check her out. Is that all right?'

'Yeah, sure. Remind me where Graham's farm is?'

'Jane will give you directions. It's a big unit, but Graham said he'll bring the sow to the outside of the buildings so that you don't have to shower in. You go down the long driveway towards the buildings, you'll see some large feed hoppers on your left-hand side and the sow will be by them. If you give him a call when you're on your way, then he'll meet you there. I'd take the usual samples – lung, liver, kidney, spleen, heart, jejunum, ileum, colon, caecal fluid and mesenteric lymph nodes should cover it – and send them off to IDEXX . . .'

IDEXX is a prominent multinational company whose laboratories specialize in veterinary diagnostics.

'Oh,' he added, 'you haven't been near any pigs for two days, have you?'

'No, don't worry, the last pig I saw was a couple of weeks ago.'

'OK, great. Just had to check. Thanks, Jon.'

I must confess, the call didn't thrill me. Post-mortems are never fun, though of course they're an essential part of the job, but naturally I much preferred dealing with live animals rather than dead ones. Occasionally you would find some really interesting pathology, but often it was a lot of fumbling around inside a cold, odorous carcass examining organs and taking samples, with no obvious visual pathology, and hoping the lab might shed light on the cause of death. On top of this, it was a client I hadn't been to before. Adrian was obviously their preferred vet, so Graham would be disappointed not to see him. I was sure he'd be understanding and accepting, but Adrian would be the benchmark against which I would be compared.

I temporarily put the call out of my mind and headed to Mr Blackman's cow. It was a fairly uneventful visit. The cow had milk fever, a condition that mainly happens around calving time in old dairy cows, although any cow can be affected. A huge increase in milk production around this time drains calcium from the blood and the cows are unable to replace it quickly enough. The cow therefore has much less calcium for her own bodily requirements such as muscle contractions. In its mild form the cow is simply unable to stand, but if left untreated it can be fatal. Fortunately, this cow was on the milder end and after I slowly injected 400 ml of calcium borogluconate into her vein, she was up and walking around as normal. It's always very satisfying when a simple treatment gives such a dramatic response that you feel like a miracle worker. So with my mood bolstered by that visit I rang Jane to let her know I'd finished the call, received her directions to Mr Bartlett's farm, and set off.

The sat nav reckoned it was twenty minutes away. As I drove, I mentally rehearsed the samples I would be taking and went through a checklist to ensure that I had everything I might need. Large scalpel blades, plenty of pots and a pair of arm-length gloves should cover it, and these were all knocking around somewhere in my car, the only immediate problem being tracking them down.

The farm was down a long straight, concreted driveway that ran between two large open ploughed fields. As I approached the entrance into the farmyard a large sign greeted me:

STOP! THIS IS A BIOSECURE AREA.
NO UNAUTHORIZED ENTRY.
ALL VISITORS MUST REPORT TO RECEPTION.

The reception was off to the right, tacked onto the first in a row of large, green, corrugated aluminium-sheeted buildings, obviously where the pigs were housed. Each building had a large 40-foot-tall feed hopper at the end of it, from which a pipe fed into the building. Off to the left of the farm entrance were three concrete silage 'clamps', the first of which was the general rubbish dump, and the next two apparently used as the unit car park. In front of the first clamp stood a yellow Matbro telehandler, a sort of forklift tractor, with a grain bucket attached. As I drove into the farm looking for somewhere to park, I caught sight of four pig's trotters sticking out of the grain bucket. So this was obviously the sow I had to post-mortem. I pulled up alongside.

As I put on my wellingtons and waterproofs by the boot of my car, a broad-set man in his mid-forties, in the classic farmer's garb of green wellingtons, blue jeans, checked shirt and green gilet, came towards me.

'Jon, I presume? I'm Graham.'

We shook hands.

'Nice to meet you.'

'Thanks for coming. Adrian doesn't think it's too much to worry about, but I'd rather be safe than sorry.'

'Sure, I completely understand. I presume this is her,' I said pointing to the grain bucket.

'Yeah. You all right to do it in there? I just thought it would be less mess and easier to clean up.'

'Yup, no problem.' Having grabbed the various items I needed, we walked over to the front of the Matbro. The deceased was a full-grown Large White–Landrace cross-breed that must have weighted about 250 kg. Her twelve udders were all engorged with milk, indicating that she had been feeding piglets, which made her sudden death all the sadder. Having put on my arm-length gloves, followed by a pair of latex gloves, I started examining the carcass. On first inspection there were no obvious clues; no discharges from her mouth or nose, no diarrhoea; she had some blood around her back end, but she was otherwise in good bodily condition.

'When did she farrow and was she fine yesterday?' I asked.

'Farrowed two days ago, her third litter, and yeah, she seemed to be feeding all twelve piglets no problem. No clues of illness or any suggestion we'd find her in this state this morning.'

'There certainly isn't anything obvious externally. Let's open her up and have more of a look.' I picked up my large scalpel and started cutting from the umbilicus, forward to the sternum and backwards to the pubis. As I cut through skin, muscle, and then into the abdominal cavity, gas-filled intestines started spilling out. Pushing them out of the way I orientated myself. The liver was an easy place to start. It looked fairly normal, and so did the spleen, so I pushed the intestines to one side and located the stomach, then dug deeper and found the kidneys. Everything looked normal.

'Don't you make a bigger incision than that?' Graham commented, leaning over my shoulder. 'Adrian cuts from the chin to the butt and just opens them right up.'

He had a point. I was used to doing PMs on lambs, where the focus was generally the abdominal cavity, looking for a worm burden or clostridial disease. You could cut through the diaphragm and check out the lungs for signs of pneumonia, but if it required anything more thorough than that, I would normally advise the farmer to take the carcass to the local veterinary laboratory where they could perform a complete PM. But Graham was right: I should open her up fully, especially if that's what Adrian did. The only problem was that I didn't have the right equipment to cut through the ribs.

'I'll open the thorax in a bit. You, er . . . you wouldn't have a saw I could use, though, would you? I'm afraid I don't have one with me.'

Graham gave an audible snort of indignation. 'There might be one in the back of the Land Rover,' he said, returning moments later with a rusty hacksaw. 'This do?'

'Perfect, thanks,' I said, taking it from him rather gingerly. I was now feeling a little flustered, so I broke away from my inspection of the jejunum and started sawing through the sternum to open up the thorax and examine the heart and lungs. In such a big sow it was fairly hard physical work, but after a few minutes I was cracking open the completely normal-looking chest. The lungs and heart all looked very healthy, with no evidence of pneumonia, no pleural effusion, so I felt for the mediastinal lymph nodes, which were also normal. I moved back down the abdomen, ready to finish my visual inspection and then start cutting into the organs to take samples. I reached the back of the abdomen and as I fumbled below the intestines I pulled up a section of colon. It was thickened and very engorged, inflamed and bloody.

'Hmm, this doesn't look too healthy,' I commented, turning to Graham.

'What is that?'

'Colon. Looks quite haemorrhagic.'

'What are you thinking?'

'Well ... haemorrhagic colitis can be caused by swine dysentery.'

'Seriously? Isn't she a bit old for that? She hasn't had diarrhoea.'

'It is usually a disease of piglets, but it can occasionally affect sows. But I agree, it doesn't make much sense. Maybe she developed a severe septicaemia and with her immune system being suppressed post farrowing it really hit her?'

'Well, if it's swine dysentery, this could be trouble. Can you take some samples and get them sent off today? We need to get on top of this ASAP.'

'Sure. It'll go off to IDEXX today and I'll put an urgent request on it.'

I then set about cutting out a section of colon, putting it into one of my formalin pots, repeating the process with the jejunum and ileum before moving on to take samples from the liver, kidneys, spleen and lung. I then removed the heart and opened it. There was no evidence of muscle enlargement, but I took a sample from that, too. Everything seemed completely normal except for the colon.

With all my samples taken, I turned to Graham. 'Do you need me to stitch her up?'

'No, don't worry about that. Just get those samples sorted and sent off.'

I removed my gloves and then labelled the pots before gathering everything together and washing myself off at a tap next to the reception building.

Cleaned down and with everything loaded up, I climbed into the car to head off.

'I'll call Adrian and let him know what I've found. One of us will be in touch in the next day or two, but in the meantime I'd isolate any other sows that were in the same group as her.'

He thanked me, and I drove out of the farm, back down the long driveway. The sooner I called Adrian the better, I thought.

'Let me guess,' he said. 'You didn't find anything?'

'Well, actually, I did. I mean, most of it was completely unremarkable, but the colon was severely haemorrhagic and inflamed.'

'Seriously? That's not good. Had she been scouring?'

'No, literally nothing. I mean, there was a bit of blood around her back-end, and she farrowed two days ago, but otherwise everything else was normal.'

'Hmm . . . Odd for it to be swine dysentery. Did he say how the piglets were doing?'

'Yeah, the piglets are all fine.'

'Interesting. Well, I assume you took some samples, so get those sent off as urgent and I'll give Graham a call and have a chat with him.'

'Will do.'

'Thanks, Jon. It seems it was just as well we did that post-mortem.'

I drove back to the practice, checked with Jane that there weren't any pressing calls and set about filling in the lab submission form and sealing up the pots, which I left in the out -tray for the duty nurse to package up and send off to IDEXX.

Adrian telephoned two days later. 'Have you seen the IDEXX results on Graham's sow? They're back.' There was a tone in his voice that I couldn't quite decipher.

'No, I haven't. What did they say? Is it good news?'

'Um, well, I'll email it over to you. I think you should have a look. Why don't you give me a call back when you've read it?'

He hung up. What was that all about? He seemed in a very good mood, almost as if he'd been trying not to laugh.

Moments later my phone pinged with an incoming email. It was the test results from Adrian. I opened the attachment.

'*IDEXX Laboratories Test Report,*' I read. '*Owner: Bartlett. Patient: sow. Age: adult. Partial report. Samples submitted: lung, heart, liver, spleen, kidneys, jejunum, ileum, colon. History: sudden death of a two-day post-farrowing sow. Histopathology . . .*' I skimmed through the usual preamble, and then moved down. '*Diagnosis: This was an unusual and somewhat confusing submission. Eight sample pots were submitted, all clearly labelled to identify them. Our attention was drawn to the sample labelled "Colon" and the concern raised on the submission form that this was inflamed, haemorrhagic tissue suggestive of swine dysentery. You can imagine our confusion, then, when on histological examination we confirmed that the colon sample submitted was in fact normal, healthy uterus, consistent with two days post farrowing.*'

I put my hands to my head in sheer disbelief. The section of tissue I had found, and then confidently shown to the farmer as a piece of severely inflamed, bloody gut was not gut at all, it was the uterus; and furthermore it was exactly as the uterus should look two days after producing a litter of twelve piglets.

'*The rest of the results are pending*,' the report went on, '*but if you would like to discuss this case further, then please don't hesitate to call to speak to one of our pathologists.*' Somehow I didn't think that was a phone call I would be making any time soon. I imagined the pathologist had had a great laugh constructing that report over their tea break. I wonder if they had a wall in their staff room for their funniest submissions. If so, this one would have been pinned in the middle. How utterly, humilatingly embarrassing! After five years of vet school, and I couldn't distinguish between a sow's intestinal tract and her uterus. So *that* explained Adrian's tone of voice on the phone. Well, at least he'd seemed amused rather than angry – though that also meant there was no way he'd be keeping this one quiet. I rang him back.

'So . . . not swine dysentery then,' he said, laughing. 'That's good.'

'I'm really sorry, Adrian. I can't believe I did that.'

'I love the line "*You can imagine our confusion* . . .". That's pure brilliance, Jon! It's the best lab report I've ever seen . . . I think we should get it framed and hang it up in the office. It's really made my day.'

'So . . . do you want me to ring Graham Bartlett and let him know?' I said eventually.

'Don't worry, Jon,' he replied, more serious for a moment, immediately understanding my position. 'I'll call him. I might omit the fact that you sampled the uterus instead of the colon, though. I'll just tell him it's nothing to worry about and that you were a tiny bit enthusiastic with your diagnosis. He'll be so relieved to know it's not swine dysentery he probably won't ask too many more questions.'

'That's good of you, Adrian, thank you,' I said, the relief flooding through me. 'And once again, I'm *so* sorry . . .'

'Honestly, there's no harm done, and you've given us all something to laugh about. These things happen . . . Not that, to the best of my recollection, I've ever confused the reproductive tract for gut, but we all make mistakes, so don't stress it. It'll be a good story for the Christmas party.'

I groaned. The practice's Christmas party was only a few weeks away, and with the staff from all the different branches attending, with wives, husbands and partners in tow, there'd be over a hundred guests. Hopefully he'd have forgotten all about it by then.

In fact, he didn't, and at the end of the Christmas meal, and after a few awards had been handed out to various people, Adrian took enormous pleasure in reading out loud the full IDEXX pathology report to the assembled throng, before presenting me with a step-by-step guide entitled 'Five Easy Ways to Distinguish between the Gastrointestinal Tract and the Reproductive Tract'.

Riding one of my grandparents' donkeys, aged 7. Noddy, Tizzy and Carole gave me a real love for these wonderful animals from a young age.

A selfie with my famous friend Pollyanne.

This Simmental calf suffered a broken leg after his mother accidentally trod on him, but a month in a cast ensured the bone could heal fully.

IMAGE COURTESY ALL THINGS WILD

Not the famous ferret Freddie, but still equally cute.

Large White sows can weigh up to 300 kg so need to be respected, particularly when they are nursing a litter.

At 4.6 metres long and weighing over 700 kg, this fella (an African Nile crocodile, which we were relocating) was seriously intimidating up close.

Conducting my clinical examination on a panda cub.

She took some persuading, but the bamboo shoots convinced giant panda Xi-Xi to pose for a photo with me.

My first encounter with a grey kangaroo was out in Australia. Little did I know then that I would be chasing one around a vet practice one day!

Final checks before taking off to dart some zebras.

Relieved and happy, posing with one of the male zebras I successfully darted.

Shane the sugar glider being positioned for surgery, pom-poms clearly on display, moments before the incident happened!

A Blue wildebeest, like any wild animal, is much less intimidating when it's asleep. This one was from another capture.

Aerial view of the large tarpaulin enclosure, funnelling down towards the truck. Several of the curtains are closed, separating off the different sections.

Max and Mungo, my faithful companions.

# Pigs: fast facts

*Sus domesticus*: The domestic pig

**Distribution:** Considered a sub-species of the wild boar which is originally native to much of Eurasia, North Africa and the Greater Sunda Islands, it is now distributed more globally.

**Names:** A male is called a 'boar', a castrated male a 'barrow', an adult female a 'sow', a female under a year that has not bred a 'gilt', and the young a 'piglet'. A group of pigs is called a 'sounder'.

**Life span:** About 15–20 years.

**Habitat:** The wild boar's natural habitat is a deciduous forest, but the domestic pig tends to either live in concrete sties or muddy paddocks.

**Diet:** Pigs are omnivores, which means they consume both plants and animals. In the wild they are foragers, eating leaves, roots, fruits, flowers, insects and fish. As livestock they are fed predominantly on corn and soybean meal.

**Gestation:** 116 days, giving birth to up to 15 piglets.

**Weight:** About 1.3 kg at birth, reaching 140–300 kg as adults.

**Growth:** A piglet would naturally wean at about 8 weeks as the sow's milk production declines. Commercially, a piglet will be weaned at about 3 weeks when it reaches a weight of around 6.5 kg. They reach sexual maturity between 3 and 12 months, but are not fully grown till 2–3 years of age. A gilt will be bred at about 6 months, and a boar used from 8 months.

Pigs will be slaughtered for meat anywhere between 4 and 12 months.

**Body temperature:** 38.6–39.2 °C.

**Interesting facts:** Pigs have very few sweat glands and thus regulate their body temperature by wallowing in mud and using it as a sunscreen. Their most developed sense is that of smell, which is why they have been trained to locate truffles underground.

**Conservation:** It is estimated that there about 2 billion pigs in the world, over half of them in China. There are 17 different species within the genus *Sus* and several hundred different breeds of domestic pig. One of the biggest welfare concerns surrounding pigs is the use of farrowing crates that are designed to prevent a sow accidentally squashing her piglets. A metal cage on a bare concrete floor, these crates are often so narrow that a sow struggles to stand up and lie down and is unable to turn around. In many systems where farrowing crates are used, sows are kept in them for most of their lives, unable to express such normal behaviour as foraging, exercising and socializing. Charities such as World Animal Protection work tirelessly with one simple goal: to create a world where animals are free of suffering. See: **www.worldanimalprotection.org.uk**.

# 15

# IGUANA

*'Being turned into a lizard can really mess up your day.'*

Rick Riordan

'I've got a client on the phone,' Jenny the receptionist said as she bustled into the prep room. 'She wants to talk to a vet about her green iguana – didn't say what it was about, but she sounded quite panicky. I thought it was one for you. She's on line two.'

'OK, thanks,' I said, picking up the prep-room phone.

'Hello, this is Jon, one of the vets. How can I help?'

'Hi, thanks, um, so . . . how long does it take for something to pass through an iguana?'

'I beg your pardon?' I said, somewhat bemused.

'You know . . . If an iguana ate something, how long would it take to come out the other end?'

'Oh, I see . . . Well, it very much depends on the animal's size, the environmental temperature, what they've eaten – a whole number of factors. But I would say anything between a day and a half to four days.'

There was a momentary silence on the other end of the line as the lady herself digested what I had just said.

'And . . . how can you tell if an animal like an iguana has eaten something?'

'Well, X-raying the animal is usually the best way. Not everything will show up, but if it's radio dense it will be obvious. Otherwise you look for clues like gas build-up from a blockage, things like that,' I replied. 'Can I ask what this is all about?'

It was if she hadn't heard my question. 'What do you mean, "radio dense"?'

'Sorry, I mean *heavy* things, something like metal, things that are very dense. For example, bones show up white. The heavier it is, the more obvious it will be on an X-ray,' I explained. 'Why, what do you think your iguana may have eaten?'

There was another brief silence. Then she blurted out, 'Rich is going to kill me!' before answering my question. ' I think my green iguana has, um, just eaten my engagement ring.'

It was my turn to process what I had just heard.

'Ah . . . I see the problem.'

'I was doing the washing-up so I took off my engagement ring and put it on the side – Gary was just sunbathing by the window as he usually does. Anyway, there was a lot of washing-up cos I hadn't done dinner from last night, and when I'd finished I went to put my ring back on and it had gone. I searched everywhere, but couldn't find it, and then I noticed Gary was sitting there, licking his lips. Rich is going to kill me. I gave him so much grief about making sure he only proposed when he had the right ring . . . he designed it and had it specially made. I've only had it three weeks. What can we do? I mean, I love Gary to pieces, but if he's eaten my engagement ring I'll, I'll . . .'

'Don't panic,' I said assertively, although I couldn't quite suppress a smile as I caught Sarah's face as she tidied away from the last patient. She'd obviously heard snippets of our conversation. 'I think it would be best if you brought him in. If we X-rayed Gary, the ring would show up very clearly. Is he behaving normally at the moment?'

'Yes, he's absolutely fine, but then he's only just eaten it. I called you as soon as I realized. If it's in there, what can we do? Will it pass through him normally? Or will you have to operate to remove it?'

'Usually with foreign bodies we don't operate unless it's causing an obvious blockage. How big is Gary, and how big is the ring?'

'Well it's a solitaire diamond ring on a white-gold band – it was just what I wanted. Rich is going to kill me,' she said again.

'And how big is Gary?'

'Oh yeah, he's my baby, I got him when he was about seven months, he's now two years old, so friendly, such a character . . .'

A two-year-old male, so he'd probably be about 3 feet long. If so, there was a chance the ring could pass through him without too much of a problem – though whether she'd want to wear it again was a different matter.

'It might be all right,' I said. 'I wouldn't want to operate unless I thought he needed it.'

'Oh, boy! So unless we do the X-ray, I might need to keep this a secret from my fiancé for four days?'

'At least if we X-ray him you'll know one way or another. I've got a couple of operations left to do today, but if you pop over with him I can always squeeze you in. It won't take long to do a quick X-ray.'

She told me she'd head over right away, and hung up.

Sarah and I exchanged glances.

'Did you catch most of that?' I enquired.

'Something about a green iguana eating her engagement ring?' she said, laughing. 'Do you think it has?'

'No idea, but she seems pretty convinced. I guess we'll know soon enough.'

'Hey! You realize if it has, you could enter into the Annual Veterinary X-ray Contest?'

'The what?' I asked.

'It's an annual competition that's held in America for the most bizarre X-rays of things animals have swallowed. I saw something about it in the paper. Last year's winner was a dog that ate nine billiard balls!'

'Seriously? No, I've never heard of it . . . I once treated a dog that had eaten a child's rubber duck. You could see it perfectly silhouetted on the X-ray. I did check to see if the dog squeaked after we had anaesthetized him, but he didn't.'

'Amazing. Well, this could be another good one for you.'

'OK, Sarah, so here's the million-dollar question: say this iguana *has* eaten the engagement ring, say it passes through intact, no harm done, and say your fiancé had had it individually made. Would *you* ever wear it again after it had transited through your iguana's intestinal tract?'

'I guess I'd want it professionally cleaned first . . . but of course! You'd have to, wouldn't you? I mean, it's your *engagement ring*, right?'

'That's true. I suppose it's better than that really expensive coffee, kopi luwak it's called, which passes through the digestive tract of a civet.'

'What?'

'Yup. Cat-poop coffee – it's the most expensive in the world. In Indonesia people go round collecting civet scat, searching through it for the coffee beans, which are then washed, dried, roasted and ground. You brew it like any other coffee, but it costs about a hundred dollars for a single cup.'

'You're joking? People actually pay vast amounts of money to drink a solution of cat poo? They should come and work here for a day – that'd put them off.'

'Apparently the digestive process gives it a unique flavour. You have to drink it without milk or sugar so that you appreciate the full flavour!'

'You seem to know a lot about it, Jon? Your usual morning coffee is it?'

'Didn't you ever see *The Bucket List*, that film with Jack Nicholson and Morgan Freeman? It was the only coffee Jack Nicholson's character would drink. It's a bizarre one, that's for sure.'

'Well, you learn something new every day. Shall I put the kettle on while we wait?'

'Miss Rogers is here with Gary,' said Sarah, raising an eyebrow, adding in a whisper, 'Good luck.'

I headed through into the waiting room. Miss Rogers was a young lady in her mid-twenties, at a guess, with black hair, black make-up and multiple piercings. She wore a heavy black overcoat from the collar of which Gary's head could be seen poking out.

'Miss Rogers? Please come through,' I said, leading her into my consulting room. She half unbuttoned her coat and lifted Gary out, placing him on the table. 'And this must be Gary, I presume, the naughty boy. Goodness, though, isn't he handsome?'

It wasn't just a line; he truly was a stunning specimen. I was pleased to see that I'd been right in my estimates. He was about 3 feet long, of an iridescent green colour with a large dewlap, the set of dorsal spines along his back indicating he had reached sexual maturity. He lay on the table, head up and erect, as though fully confident of his own magnificent beauty.

'Yes, this is my baby,' said his owner, 'but I'm *so* cross with him, he's going to get me in *so* much trouble. Do you think he can have eaten it?'

'It's difficult to say. Green iguanas are herbivorous, but they're also renowned for having very good vision, and if the diamonds were glinting in the sunlight he might have thought it was a fly or something, and been intrigued. There's only one way to find out . . .'

'Yeah, I realize that. How long will it take, do you think? Does he need to be sedated or anything?'

'I can do it now. Usually they just lie there, much like he is now. Believe you me, if he has swallowed the ring it'll be fairly obvious.'

'Oh wow, that's great. Should I wait?'

'Yes please, it'll only take five minutes.'

'Thank you,' she said, and then, leaning over to Gary, 'This nice man is going to see if you have eaten my beautiful engagement ring, so be good to him.' She turned back to me. 'He's very friendly.'

I leant down and picked him up, one hand under his chest and the other supporting his tail. As his feet lost contact with the table they thrashed around, trying to gain traction against something. That something happened to be my forearm. His claws dug in, and I grimaced, swallowed hard and then tried to smile through the pain as I walked out of the room and into the prep room.

'Sarah, be a sport,' I said through clenched teeth, 'would you mind detaching this iguana from my forearm?'

By now his sharp claws had drawn blood. As Sarah tentatively unpicked the five claws of Gary's right front foot from my arm, I was able to place him onto the already positioned X-ray plate, where Sarah held him down, allowing me a chance to attend to my wound.

Meanwhile Gary, although content to pose on the consulting-room table, evidently did not feel the same way about the X-ray plate, and so when Sarah let go of him, he immediately shot off across the table, nearly nose-diving off the end. She managed to grab him just in time, but when she once again replaced him on the X-ray plate, he repeated his kamikaze bid for freedom, before once again being firmly stopped.

'Hmm,' said Sarah. 'Doctors don't have this problem of patients running off the X-ray table! What do you want to do?'

'This might work,' I said, after successfully patching up my arm. I grabbed a roll of the professional bandage-tape known as Vetrap and a bundle of cotton wool from the cupboard, then rolled the cotton wool into two small balls, which I gently placed one over each of Gary's eyes, holding them in place with a strip of Vetrap around his head, making sure that his air passages were free. It worked beautifully: when I replaced Gary on the X-ray plate he was transformed into a living statue.

'That's a neat trick,' Sarah commented.

'Yeah, one of the tricks I stored away from our brief lectures on reptiles at vet school.' Gary remained motionless as I adjusted the setting on the X-ray machine and we left the room. 'Well, Gary, let's see if you've enjoyed a very expensive breakfast, shall we? *X-rays!*' I shouted, to notify everyone, and clicked the button, before both of us hurried back.

Moments later, the beautiful image of a lizard skeleton appeared on the computer screen. I studied it for a moment, Sarah eagerly peering over my shoulder.

'Well . . .' I said. 'I don't know whether this is good news or bad news for Miss Rogers, but Gary does not appear to be the culprit in the strange case of her missing ring.'

'Good news for Gary, but that would have been an absolute classic X-ray.'

'Clearly, diamonds aren't a lizard's best feed.'

'Ha ha.'

Removing Gary's temporary headpiece, I picked him up, this time in a towel to avoid further lacerations, and carried him through to his impatient owner.

'Well?' she exclaimed as soon as she saw me. 'Did he eat it, was it him, is that where my ring's gone? Well?'

'I'm afraid I can't be sure what's happened to your engagement ring, Miss Rogers, but Gary most definitely didn't swallow it.'

'Really? Are you sure? How odd, I was sure it was him . . . Where on earth can it be?' She gently took the iguana from me, bringing his head up to hers. 'Oh, Gary, Mummy is so sorry . . . Did I blame you when it wasn't your fault? I'm sorry, but I'm sure you know what's happened to it. You need to tell me before Daddy gets home.' She turned back to me. 'Thank you so much. I'm so sorry to have wasted your time, but I'm very grateful for your help.'

After she left, I returned to the prep room, where Sarah was getting things ready for the next procedure.

'Well,' I said, 'you can't say this job is ever dull. Shall we get on with spaying that rabbit now?'

Half an hour later Jenny returned.

'I've got Miss Rogers on the phone again. She asked for you specifically, she's on line one.'

I picked up the phone. 'Hello, this is J—'

'I found it, Jon, I found it! It was under the cooker! I think Gary must have knocked it off with his tail or something.'

'Oh that's great news. I'm so pl—'

'Thank you so much for your help, Jon! I can't believe we went through all that, but I was just convinced Gary had eaten it. I'm so grateful to you – and so glad I won't have to wear a ring for the rest of my life that had been pooed out by a green iguana!'

# Iguanas: fast facts

*Iguana iguana*: The green iguana

**Distribution:** Originally found in Central and Southern America, from Southern Mexico to Central Brazil, the Dominican Republic, Paraguay, Bolivia and the Caribbean.

**Names:** A male is called a 'bull', a female a 'cow', and the young a 'hatching'. A group of iguanas is called a 'slaughter'.

**Life span:** 10–12 years.

**Habitat:** Iguanas are diurnal, arboreal rainforest dwellers, often found near water.

**Diet:** They are naturally herbivorous, eating leaves and some fruit in the wild; in captivity, kale, turnip, mustard or dandelion greens suffice.

**Incubation:** 90–120 days, laying anything from 20 to 71 eggs.

**Growth:** Hatchlings are about 3 inches long, weighing about 90 grams at birth, growing rapidly for the first 3 years when they reach sexual maturity. Growth then drops off dramatically, but they can continue to grow all their life and can reach up to 6 feet in length and weigh 9 kg.

**Body temperature:** Like all reptiles, green iguanas are 'poiki-lothermic', meaning they can't regulate their own body temperature. Their temperature gradient in captivity should be 26.6–34.9 °C.

**Interesting facts:** In the aftermath of Hurricane Luis in 1995, several uprooted trees drifted over 200 miles across the

Caribbean from Guadeloupe to Anguilla. These trees were found to be carrying about a dozen green iguanas, which subsequently started to colonize the island. Releases, either deliberate or accidental, from the pet trade have led to their classification as an invasive species in Texas, Florida and Hawaii.

**Conservation:** They are the most popular reptile pet in the USA despite being quite difficult to properly care for, and vast numbers will die within their first year. Their global population is unknown, but about 800,000 were imported into the USA in 1995. They are not considered an endangered species by the IUCN, but they are listed in the Convention on International Trade in Endangered Species of Wild Flora and Fauna, which recommends control of their trade. The major concern is the diminishing of wild populations to furnish the pet trade, and the massive welfare issues involved in it. Trade in wildlife is the second largest illegal trade in the world after drugs, with an estimated value of $323 billion in global imports of all animals in 2009. TRAFFIC is a global wildlife-trade-monitoring network that works in the context of biodiversity, conservation and sustainable development. See: **www.traffic.org**.

# 16

# CROCODILE

*'An appeaser is one who feeds a crocodile, hoping it will
eat him last.'*

Winston Churchill

I spluttered and coughed, inhaling the unavoidable haze of
the copper-red dry African dust that filled the minibus
through the open window. I quickly closed it to minimize
the effect. It was 6 a.m. on a cold morning in August, and
we had just turned off the main road onto a dirt track that
appeared to end in a barren wilderness of South African bush.
The only clue that we might vaguely be heading in the direction of habitation was the dilapidated house postbox by the
side of the road. My companions in the back of the minibus
were abruptly woken as the change in terrain greatly increased
noise levels at the same time as dramatically decreasing the
comfort of our ride. Each pothole and small boulder caused
the whole vehicle to vibrate and judder violently as its suspen-
sion was tested to breaking point.

In true African style the dirt track seemed interminable,
with visibility being reduced substantially by the distinct dusty

haze we were generating. We had already been travelling for an hour and a half when we turned off the main road for our final destination, and that leg was rapidly beginning to seem a mere prelude to our journey as a whole. We had left the comfort of our lodges in pitch darkness heading north-west from Nelspruit on today's adventure to catch and relocate a 4.6-metre male Nile crocodile weighing in at about 700 kg.

As another beautiful blood-orange African sunrise began to evaporate the low-lying mist, a solitary whitewashed brick building emerged in the distance. As we drew ever closer, other components of the farm hove into view. There were half a dozen buildings, all uniform in shape, single-storey brick sheds with tin-sheeted roofs. Each structure was about 10 metres wide by 20 metres long. From previous visits to other crocodile farms, I knew these to be the enclosures where the hatchlings were kept in batches of several thousand, arranged by age from the egg to two years old. Then there were a dozen similar-sized concrete pits, each containing a dam of water and a basking area, which contained the three-to-five-year-olds, this time in batches by size of a few hundred. The final structure was one large enclosure, about the size of a football pitch, with two dams surrounded by a large, grassy embankment. It was within this enclosure that the breeding males and females were kept, 120 in total, all fully grown specimens, ranging from 3 to nearly 5 metres in length. The boundary to this enclosure was a 1-metre-high concrete wall surmounted by 50 cm of chain-link fence. The two large dams were separated by the feeding gangway, which protruded halfway into the enclosure. This gangway was accessed through a locked gate and was a continuation of the surrounding concrete wall, though without the chain-link fence on top. I imagined the carnage of feeding time as the workers threw meat at the sea of snapping jaws.

The one noticeable element to the adult enclosure was that it was very much designed to keep the crocodiles *in*, rather than to keep humans *out*. There was no electric fencing, no double fencing, no reinforced fencing, and no barbed wire; there was no security guard, and only a couple of dilapidated signs reading 'WARNING! CROCODILES! TRESPASSERS WILL BE EATEN!' If someone were ever stupid enough to climb over the fencing, then good luck to them – that was the implication. This was not a mass of health and safety regulations like you'd find in Britain, Europe or America. This was Africa: a healthy fear and common sense were safety enough.

From the 1950s to the early 1970s, crocodilians the world over were extensively exploited, predominantly for their skin to fuel the leather industry, leading many species to the brink of extinction, including the African Nile crocodile. In 1975 the Convention on International Trade in Endangered Species (CITES) was enacted to regulate the trade in wild species, and many countries, including South Africa, adopted legislation to protect crocodilians and increase their global numbers.

With demand for crocodile skin and meat still as high as ever, crocodile farming became a way to reduce pressure on the wild population from illegal poaching, while restocking those populations by releasing juvenile crocodiles into the wild. So successful has this proved that many crocodile species have been taken off the endangered list. The initiative has demonstrated how a voracious human desire for animal products can be sustained while also protecting the very species that fuels it. The success of this concept means that it is often cited as a model for protecting other species, such as the rhinoceros. It would be nice to think that demand for such products could be stemmed, but the reality is that once humanity gains a taste for something, it is extremely slow to surrender it, and for many species that are being unsustainably exploited for a product, time is sadly running out.

We disembarked from the minibus, taking a moment to stretch muscles stiffened by the drive. Derik, having driven separately, was already at the boot of his car getting his equipment together when the owner of the farm came to greet us. Piet was a tall, broad-set man in his early fifties, wearing khaki shorts, a checked short-sleeved cotton shirt and a camo baseball cap. Addressing Derik initially in Afrikaans, he then turned to greet us in the warm, welcoming and friendly way to which South Africa had accustomed us. He briefly described his crocodile farm, and the reason for the animal's relocation, then gratefully explained how necessary it was to have a team of people for this job. The crocodile in question was about fifty years old, and for many years had been the farm's primary breeding stock, so the owner was keen to bring in a new gene pool and was therefore selling him to another crocodile farm.

The first step in the process would be to lasso a rope around the crocodile's upper jaw. He would instinctively clamp down on this and start fighting the restraint. This was where our extra manpower was vital, since in a tug-of-war battle, 700 kg of prehistoric cunning would attempt to gain the predatory advantage by taking to the water, where the immense muscle power of his tail could be used to maximum effect. Conversely, our own objective was to keep him on land to maintain our modest advantage and allow Derik the opportunity to sedate him.

Crocodilian anaesthesia is still something of a mystery, since many drugs that work well in mammals, and are effective in other reptiles, are unpredictable or ineffectual in crocodiles.

The doses required are often so large it makes them impractical to use. The induction time is at least five times longer than in mammals, but then the drug persists in the circulation for days, and sometimes longer than the reversal agent, which means a crocodile can re-anaesthetize the day after a procedure, a phenomenon known as 'renarcotization'. So an owner can drain a dam of water on the day of a procedure, then refill it the following morning, only to find his crocodiles have drowned in the afternoon because they have renarcotized.

One class of drugs that does work effectively, and within predictable parameters, are the paralytic agents, the required doses of which are also practical and manageable. However, these drugs are solely muscle relaxants rather than anaesthetic agents, so are not suitable for any procedure that will cause pain, but are ideal for a job limited to an animal's capture, transport and release. Gallamine was the preferred drug, since it relaxes the skeletal muscles well, but has no effect on the muscles that control breathing, which therefore promised a safe working environment for us without endangering the crocodile's life. Furthermore, with the animal safely relocated, there would be no need to administer a reversal agent: the drug would wear off naturally after a few hours, and then the crocodile would be fully functional again.

Once injected, it would take about fifteen minutes for the Gallamine to take effect, and then we could claim control of the situation. The immense strength of the crocodile's masseter (chewing) muscles – giving him 3,700 psi-worth of crushing power through the arcade of his eighty teeth – would be tamed by the Gallamine and then rendered ineffective by tightly taping his jaw closed. The 700 kg of raw, unfathomable muscular power would become nothing more than a limpless weight, and so one of the animal kingdom's most effective killing machines would be temporarily tamed enough to be securely craned onto a truck, safely transported and subsequently released into his new home. That was the simple plan, anyway, though one, as with all wildlife work, fraught with a plethora of potential dangers.

As we strolled from the parked vehicles, equipped with all we would need for the task, we got our first detailed viewing of the adult enclosure. The dams were a murky brown colour, making it impossible to see what lay beneath, but a few crocodiles were visible just above the surface, though by far the majority of the inhabitants occupied the dusty, grassy bank, basking in the heat of the early morning sun. Stretched in every direction was a sea of the biggest crocodiles I had ever seen in my life, their dun, murky green bodies starkly contrasting against the sandy, rubicund soil on which they lay. Some were poised to enter the water, others were tucked against the concrete boundary wall; some had their mouths wide open, exposing every one of their gleaming white teeth, others had their jaws tightly closed; some faced the water, others the wall. The one thing that united them all was their absolutely motionless form, their glassy green eyes inert. It was easy to imagine that what I was seeing was a collection of statues, and yet, given even the slightest stimulus, their reaction would be lightning swift, and deadly.

It was then that the realization dawned on me that we would be deliberately entering this pen and wrestling with this 700-kg Nile crocodile, in an enclosure containing 119 other adults. To voluntarily put ourselves in such acute danger seemed utter madness, though I knew it was my ignorance of crocodilian behaviour that was elevating the danger factor in my mind. While accidents invariably happen when dealing with such dangerous animals, they are largely caused either by complacency or by ignorance of their behaviour. If we were to enter the enclosure, there was certainly a way to do it safely – but it still required an immense application of mind over matter.

One factor that would contribute to our safety was the chosen time of the capture. 'Poikilothermic' or cold-blooded creatures, as all reptiles are, rely on the heat of the sun to warm them up to regulate their metabolism, so any reptile is less active first thing in the morning than at the end of the day. That's why a dog is more likely to be bitten by a snake on its morning walk than the evening one: in the morning a snake will be slower to move away from an inquisitive approaching dog and thus more likely to strike out in defence than slither off in escape, as it will tend to do later in the day.

A second factor was the day that had been chosen for the relocation. Adult crocodiles will usually only feed once a week, and feeding time for these animals had been the previous day, so they would be relatively sluggish, given the vast amount of energy it takes them to digest their meal – though their reaction time would still beat ours hands down. More significantly, though, they would not be hungry, and so, provided we didn't interrupt their morning siesta, or accidently step on one, they would be content sunbathing rather than bother to chomp on the nearest passing leg.

This was all very well in theory, but looking across the enclosure, I could see no safe route through the sea of bodies that lined the ground, so someone would have to clear a path by gently encouraging them to move. I had no idea how easy that would be, but it was not a job for which I was going to volunteer.

One of the farm workers met us at the gate to the feeding gangway, unlocking it and ushering us through. Piet led the way, pointing to the bank on the far side of the dam, deep in conversation with Derik. Despite my frustrating ignorance of Afrikaans, it was clear that he was indicating the male crocodile we were there to move. As I focused in on the animal, it was almost as though he grew before my very eyes. While at first glance there seemed to be a uniformity to all the crocodiles in the enclosure, on closer inspection I noticed the wide range of their size and width. Without doubt, though, this boy was the biggest. Lying motionless, at an acute angle, facing away from the dam, jaws wide open, his teeth glinting in the morning sun, it was almost as though he were inviting us to catch him if we dared.

As Derik and Piet continued their conversation, another farm worker passed us by, carrying a 10-foot-long, 2-inch-wide black plastic pipe, then climbed over the gangway wall into the enclosure. He boldly proceeded to thrash the ground in front of any crocodile that lay in his path as he sought to create a safe passage to the crocodile in question from the gangway where we stood. I was convinced his method was a sure-fire way of ending up as an unexpected bonus meal. Remarkably, however, although they were none too happy for their morning basking to be so rudely interrupted – a displeasure they made perfectly clear in a series of wild snaps and hissing noises – they slowly moved away or took to the water. It was a remarkable insight into this man's knowledge and understanding of crocodilian behaviour. After about ten minutes a path had been cleared, which he then proceeded to patrol.

Meanwhile, Piet was preparing a lasso from a 20-foot piece of industrial strapping, which he lightly fastened to a 6-foot pole. Task completed, he and another worker followed the first over the metre-high wall into the enclosure. Piet took the lead, approaching his quarry from the side. Our crocodile remained completely motionless as he eyed the potential threat. Standing at what seemed an insanely close distance, and well within striking range, Piet stretched out the primitive and clumsy con-traption, attempting to lower it over the animal's upper jaw.

The crocodile was not so easily fooled, though, and as soon as he felt the contact of the lasso on his snout, snatched at it, ripping it from Piet's hands and casting it aside, and then turned to face the water, his jaws almost shut. As if it wasn't obvious enough that this was not part of the plan, Derik let out an Afrikaans expletive that even I could understand.

The situation was now delicately poised: at any moment the crocodile might take to the water, which would make catching him impossible. If that happened there were only two possible solutions: either to come back another day, or wait the three hours it took to drain the dam. In my experience, African wildlife work was full of wasted days, and a range of Plans B, C, D or Z. It was one of the reasons for the vast costs involved in operations like these. More than any domestic animal, wildlife requires immense patience.

With this particular job, even if we drained the dam, there was still no guarantee of success, since the crocodile might decide to stay where he was. If so, the human risk factor would be infinitely increased, since the algal slime at the bottom of these drained reservoirs would be treacherously slippery. To attempt to go into one in pursuit of an adult crocodile would be suicidal. I remembered a terrible story Cobus had once told me. He had been asked to remove 150 adult crocodiles from a farm by the owner's wife, after her husband was killed attempting to clean a dam. He'd done the job thousands of times before, but on this occasion he slipped, and fell in, as the dam was draining. By the time the water had gone, so had most of him. Maybe coming back another day was the better option . . .

Fortunately, having repositioned himself, the crocodile now settled, apparently quite content to stay on the bank, showing no interest in the water. We still needed to wait for him to reopen his mouth, though, to allow Piet another attempt at lassoing his upper jaw. Giving the crocodile a chance to settle, and after reconstructing the lasso, Piet stepped back to watch him at a distance of a few metres.

It was probably ten minutes before the crocodile relaxed enough to slowly open his jaw. Piet allowed him another few minutes before slowly approaching his head for the second time. This time starting with the loop well in front of the snout, he ensured he was lined up with the upper jaw, and then in a quick movement brought the lasso into and over the animal's mouth. The crocodile did the rest, snapping his jaw tightly shut and whipping his head and neck away from Piet in a movement that elicited all this creature's trademark force. And that movement was exactly what was required to cause the loop of strap to tighten around his upper jaw: 4.6 metres and 700 kg of prehistoric muscle power was now caught. And he knew it.

The jaw-snap and neck-jerk was just the start of the unleashing of his fury at this unwelcome restraint. He started thrashing from side to side, deploying the immense power of his tail to create a full body movement. Backwards and forwards, side to side he went; the speed and strength with which he continued was terrifying to watch, and it was all Piet could do to hold on. The two farm workers were quick to lend added manpower, but the three of them were still no match for this creature who now, clearly dissatisfied with the progress he was making, decided to take the fight to his preferred hunting ground, and dashed into the water.

That immense, formidable tail, which had been such a powerful lever on the ground, now instantly became a colossal rudder that allowed him to repeatedly barrel-roll, snapping and thrashing as he went, with such massive force it was a wonder the strap held. The dam of water, serene and motionless just moments before, was now a violent, churning, chaotic storm. The crocodile's power on land was exponentially increased in the water, so the task of maintaining any element of control over him was now utterly impossible.

With every roll, whip and thrash from the crocodile, the three men precariously holding on to the lasso, were dragged ever closer to the water's edge, and in a flash the situation could have become extremely dangerous: the slightest loss of concentration, the slightest slip, and Piet and the others would be plunged into those primal waters. This was the critical moment we had been briefed about earlier, and before we could even register a conscious thought or verbalize the action required, we all responded instinctively and in unison, momentarily oblivious to the 119 other dangers within the enclosure. Scaling the metre-high wall, we sprinted to join the tug-of-war, grabbing on to a section of strapping that lay on the ground behind the three men. Three became four – five – six – but the still the crocodile dominated the contest. Seven – then eight – then nine – and finally, with ten bodies pulling against the crocodile, we were able to stabilize and hold fast against him. Like playing a fish on the end of a line, it was now a case of letting him tire himself out, so he could eventually be pulled back out of the water.

The storm he generated in the water made it impossible to see him, but the relentless pull on the taut strap left us in no doubt as to his power. As seconds turned into minutes, it seemed like an eternity, and still he showed no signs of fatigue. The thought occurred to me that maybe we would tire first; how would *that* play out? I tried to shake the image out of my head.

After what must have been twenty minutes of us holding fast, heels dug into the grassy bank, sweat dripping from every brow, and fingers numb from holding the strap so tightly, we got our first sense of his ebbing strength as we felt a shift of momentum away from, rather than towards the dam. Over the course of a further few minutes, step by step, little by little, inch by inch, we found ourselves retreating from the dam edge, gradually pulling our enormous catch onto the shore.

Once landed, he seemed to have given up the fight entirely, but our job was still far from complete. With the rest of us still holding fast, Derik peeled off to grab his pole syringe and draw up the Gallamine to inject into the crocodile.

One of the characteristics of reptiles is the presence of scales, from the soft, slimy covering of a snake to the hard, bony shell of a tortoise. Crocodiles have a bit of a mixture, with softer tissue on their underside and hard bony plates or 'scutes' over their back and flanks. These scutes complicate the procedure of administering an injection, since they are so strong that a needle will simple break off or bend if it makes contact with too much force. It is therefore esssential to insert the needle between these scutes, allowing it to penetrate through this outer layer into the underlying muscle, for the drug to be safely delivered into the body. The best location to do this is at the base of the tail, just where it joins the body, where there is more of a gap between these bony plates, and a larger injection site to aim for. This is also the greatest area of concentrated muscle in the animal's body, and that is the tissue we want the drug to enter, since muscle has a rich blood supply, and thereby facilitates the speedy absorption of the drug.

Derik returned with the 6-foot pole syringe – a simple light metal pole with a heavy-duty plastic syringe and needle attached, allowing the safe injection of a dangerous animal from a pole-length away. He wasted no time injecting the Gallamine, the crocodile responding with a final, violent thrash of his tail – and then we settled down to wait for the fifteen minutes of the final countdown. The test to ensure the efficacy of the drug was to push down gently on the crocodile's upper jaw: if it had worked, the crocodile would struggle to reopen his mouth; if it hadn't ... We made sure to give the head end a wide berth.

After ten long minutes, Derik gently touched the crocodile's nose with a long stick: no response. Then, applying greater force, he tried to push the jaw shut – and in an instant the crocodile responded, snapping up at the stick and crunching it to a pulp. We obviously had longer to wait.

Five minutes later, the same graduated provocation from Derik met no response. Gingerly removing the stick from the top of the nose, he brought it to the front of the snout, gently tapping at the exposed gleaming canines: still nothing. The Gallamine was working, it seemed. A few of us relaxed our hold on the strap to ready ourselves for the final phase. What we needed to do now was loop another lasso around both the top and bottom jaw, which we would then hold fast, and with the jaw tightly secured, Derik would tape the mouth shut with four or five rounds of industrial-strength gaffer tape. Even to approach the jaws of this monster crocodile required immense trust in the science and pharmacology of our profession. It is one thing to read about a drug in a book, to know how it works, what receptors it acts on, and the effect this causes in the body, but – believe me – to put yourself in harm's way on the basis of that knowledge requires colossal faith the first time you do it. This wasn't Derik's first time, and so without a moment's hesitation, as we held the animal down, he rapidly secured the lasso and applied the tape, circling the jaw multiple times to ensure its total restraint.

Now we were in complete control. Releasing the strap that had taken up our energies for over half an hour, our focus now became the securing of his legs so they wouldn't get damaged in the move, and then the larger task of lifting him onto a stretcher. The transport vehicle was a truck with a large crane attached. With the crocodile safely secured on the stretcher, we signalled to the truck driver to lower the crane, and within moments 700 kg of Nile crocodile were being hoisted through the air and lowered onto the truck. With the animal safely contained, the driver set off on the two-hour journey to his new home, and, after bidding Piet and his team farewell, we followed him on his way in our minibus.

We successfully and very easily offloaded him at his destination, the Gallamine still flooding his system to give the necessary muscular relaxation to allow us to work safely. It would be another few hours before the effects wore off, and then it would be time for him to explore his new environment. As we drove away, I felt it would take far longer for me to process the amazing experience I had gone through that day. It was another successful job well done, but I felt completely wrung out, both physically and emotionally. I had definitely stepped out of my comfort zone with this one. I had certainly learnt a lot about crocodiles' behaviour, and how to interact with them, but I tried not to think about the range of possible disasters that had all been averted – rather too narrowly, I couldn't help but think.

I still can't quite decide if the day had gone so well because of luck or skill.

# Crocodiles: fast facts

*Crocodylus niloticus*: The Nile crocodile

**Distribution:** Widespread throughout sub-Saharan Africa.

**Names:** A male is called a 'bull', a female a 'cow', and the young a 'hatchling'. A group of crocodiles is called a 'float'.

**Life span:** 70–100 years.

**Habitat:** It is the largest freshwater predator in Africa, inhabiting freshwater lakes, rivers, freshwater swamps, coastal estuaries and mangrove swamps.

**Diet:** Their staple diet is fish, but they will scavenge carrion and as ambush predators will attack anything unfortunate enough to cross their path, including wildebeest crossing the Mara river during their 'great migration'. Adults can survive a year without eating.

**Incubation:** 90 days, laying 25–80 eggs over a 2-month period.

**Weight:** About 11 inches long, weighing about 70 grams, on hatching, reaching 2–5 metres and weighing anything from 220 and 700 kg as adults.

**Growth:** Hatchlings grow to about 1.2 metres by 2 years, when they naturally leave the nest. By 4 years they are about 2 metres long and at this size they are much less susceptible to predation or cannibalization. They reach sexual maturity at 12–16 years, depending on their health, size and weight, and will continue to grow through their life.

**Body temperature:** Like all reptiles, crocodiles are 'poikilo-thermic'. Their ideal temperature range for basking, allowing optimum performance in the water, is between 18.8 and 29.2 °C.

**Interesting fact:** The Nile crocodile has temperature-dependent sex determination: if the average temperature during the middle third of their incubation period falls outside the range 31.7–34.5 °C, their offspring will be female, if within, male.

**Conservation:** In 1971 all 23 species of crocodilians were considered 'endangered' or 'threatened', leading to the foundation of the Crocodile Specialist Group (CSG). Crocodile numbers have since undergone the most dramatic improvement in conservation status of any group of vertebrates, with 7 species remaining endangered, 8 no longer considered endangered, and the remainder sufficiently abundant to support well-regulated annual egg harvests. The key to this success is the cooperation of companies involved in every facet of the international reptile skin and leather trade. Today the crocodilian skin industry views conservation as an investment in the future, with many companies contributing to conservation projects and actively curtailing illegal trade. While the work of the CSG has been extraordinary, they continue to strive to bring all crocodile species off the endangered list. See: **www.iucncsg.org**.

# 17

# KANGAROO

*'I have no fear of losing my life – if I have to save a koala or a crocodile or a kangaroo or a snake, mate, I will save it.'*

Steve Irwin

t had been one of those nights on call when sleep had eluded me, not due to insomnia, but a flurry of calls. It had started just as I was sitting down to a TV dinner at about 9 p.m. A limping cat was apparently loose in the local Tesco store, and no one could catch it. Two hours later, the hunt that had taken me down several food aisles and out into the store-room, now culminated in a stand-off under a Portakabin behind the back of the store. By this time the cat was far too stressed, agitated and scared to let me catch her without a fight. I attempted to crawl underneath the building to retrieve her while trying to avoid the hisses and swipes being aimed in my general direction, but failed miserably. I concluded that setting a trap would be our best hope. Once caught, her sore leg could be assessed and treated, before hopefully being reunited with her owner.

Then there had been Mrs Jones, who phoned at 2 a.m. about her itchy dog. Dermatologists happily admit that one of the reasons they choose that speciality is because skin problems are rarely an emergency, so you can understand my sense-of-humour failure on losing precious sleep to see a dog with fleas. Despite my gentle, drowsy attempts to persuade the owner that it could wait till the morning, she remained unconvinced and insisted I saw Bessie, her little West Highland White Terrier, in person. So I dutifully dragged myself out of bed on a cold November night to administer the most expensive flea treatment in history. Then, at 6 a.m. that morning, I received one of the most bizarre phone calls of my career.

'Hello, is that the vet's?' said the voice on the other end of the phone as I fumbled for my bedside light.

'Yes, this is Jon, the vet on call, how can I help you?' I said, trying not to sound as sleepy and bleary-eyed as I felt.

'Ah, good, thanks . . . Well, sir, it's my pufferfish, you see, he's floating around the top of his tank all . . . well, puffed up, but not like normal, like. He's on his side and I don't know what's wrong with him, but he's definitely not right.'

'Sorry, did you say your *pufferfish* isn't very well?' I asked.

'Yes, my pufferfish. He's in a really bad way, I think he might be on the way out. Can you take a look at him?'

Believe me, trying to sound intelligent, logical, knowledgeable at the same time as offering sane, wise advice at 6 a.m., when you've just been abruptly woken from a deep sleep is hard at the best of times, but when the subject matter involves one of the 8.7 million species that had bypassed our veterinary curriculum, I failed pretty miserably.

'Do you want a visit or will you bring him into the surgery?' I asked.

'Um . . . he's in a 6-foot tank, so I think you'd best come out to the house,' he replied, his tone reflecting the stupidity of my question.

'Ah, yes, of course,' I replied rather sheepishly. 'And whereabouts are you?'

'At home,' he said.

This was not going well.

'Sorry, I mean where do you live?'

'Oh, I see, West Brom, near the footie ground. Do you want the postcode?'

'That's great, thanks,' I said, noting it down. 'So did you just find him like this today?'

'Yeah, he's been fine. I mean, he puffs up when things startle him, but that's usual for 'em, but he's been doing it a lot more recently. I'm not sure he can control it like he used to – either that or he's just getting a bit jumpy in his old age. I've had him six years, so he's getting on for a puffer. Real character he is, though, I'll be sad to see him go, but I gotta do what's best for him, ain't I. I'm on earlies this week so went to feed them as usual when I woke up, and there he was, all puffed up and on his side, real sad to see.'

'I'm sorry to hear that. You got quite a few, then?'

'Oh yes, love 'em, such characters . . . Anyway, you gonna come out and see him or what? I mean, I doubt there's much that can be done, but I can't see him suffer, you know what I mean?'

'I'll be with you in about half an hour.'

I lay in bed for a moment processing the call. Was I really just about to go and see a pufferfish, somewhere near West Bromwich Albion's home ground? Even as I thought about it, it sounded completely absurd. But my client was genuinely concerned, so I dragged myself out of bed, dressed and set off.

Unfortunately, the pufferfish had indeed been beyond veterinary intervention, and so with the help of a bottle of euthanasia liquid, I had humanely decreased the global pufferfish population by one. Heading straight back to the practice, I made it by just after 8.30 a.m., feeling fairly awake and chipper, despite my sleep deprivation, though with the prospect of a whole day's consulting in front of me, I knew I would fade fast. It was going to have to be a multiple coffee and tea day.

I managed the first two hours without too much problem – the usual routines, with a couple of patients that needed admitting for some further investigation, blood tests, or to go on fluids, that sort of thing – but I was starting to flag, so welcomed the cup of tea that Lucy brought me at eleven in between patients. Taking a brief moment's respite to savour it, I scanned through the rest of the appointments on my morning list. The gap that had existed at 11.50 a.m. was now occupied by our client, Rich, from the local zoo. He was bringing in an eleven-month-old grey kangaroo joey called Kevin that had a snotty nasal discharge and runny eyes. A kangaroo with a cold: this was rapidly becoming one of the odder twenty-four hours of my career.

By the time Kevin's appointment came around, I was really struggling. After a long night on call, with little sleep or sustenance, and tired at the end of a full morning's consulting, I was all too conscious I wasn't functioning at my peak. I called Rich into the consulting room. He came in with a young assistant, the two of them sharing the load of a large animal-carrier, which only just squeezed through the consulting-room door.

Rich was in his late twenties, about 6 foot tall, of medium build, with long blond dreadlocks that he wore in a pony tail, and multiple facial piercings. He wore black cargo trousers and a green polo shirt emblazoned with the zoo's logo. He was the senior keeper, and as such I had dealt with him several times before and had grown to respect him immensely.

He had an intimate knowledge of the zoo's collection, always knowing an animal's age, as well as its medical history. He took great pleasure in researching and staying up to speed with all the latest ideas and thoughts on an animal's diet, enrichment and habitat. His special affinity, though, was for primates, and he had often come in with a little marmoset or tamarin on his shoulder.

'Morning, Jon,' he said cheerily now. 'You look terrible. Late night, was it?'

'Don't ask. I was on call last night – it was a long one. Anyway, nice to see you, Rich. How are things?'

'I wish I could say the same, but it's never nice to see you. Nothing personal, of course, but it always means one of ours is sick. Today it's this little fella, a joey we're rearing. We didn't realize his mum had had him until a couple of months ago, obviously he was hidden away in her pouch. Anyway, judging by the size of him, he's a foot tall, we reckon he's about eleven months old. He's seemed fine since we first spotted him, but Tim here –' he nodded at the young chap who had helped carry in the box – 'said that he noticed Kevin had a bit of a snotty nose yesterday. It seems much worse today and he isn't too interested in his breakfast.'

'That's right,' said Tim. 'He was fine in himself yesterday, but just seems a bit quieter today.'

'I wanted you to check him out before he got any worse,' continued Rich. 'He's a particular favourite now with the staff, you know, being a surprise and all – everyone's taken to him, the cheeky chappie that he is. Aren't you, Kevin?' he added, speaking to the crate. There was a thud from inside as Kevin stamped the floor in protest at his temporary incarceration.

'Fair enough,' I said. 'Well, let's have a look at him.' I bent down and began to open his cage, as I would with any other pet carrier a client had brought in.

This was an exhausted lapse of my exhausted thinking, however, and ran counter to all the usual protocols that Rich and I had established when dealing with zoo animals. My actions so surprised him that he was too slow to respond.

'Oh, careful Jon, he's a live wire, this one!' was all he could muster as I undid the latch on the box and gently opened the door, allowing Kevin a brief glimpse of freedom as he pushed his nose through the small gap. Then, with a massive spring, he powered himself forward. I was caught completely off guard, and in an instant Kevin the kangaroo had barged his way out the box before I had a chance to stop him.

If he had just stopped there, or if the back door of my consulting room, which led into the pharmacy, had been shut, then it wouldn't have been too much of an issue, but unfortunately neither of these was the case. Having been cooped up for half an hour, Kevin obviously decided he needed to stretch his legs, and in two hops he had disappeared into the pharmacy, from which, moments later, a catastrophic clattering emerged. I scrambled to my feet and hared after him, Rich and Tim close on my heels. Entering the pharmacy, we saw the trail of destruction that Kevin had wreaked through the corridor – boxes and bottles of drugs, bandage material, scissors, forceps and all the other equipment that had been neatly laid out on the pharmacy work surface now lay strewn all over the floor as we continued in our pursuit. The path Kevin was taking through the practice was now leading him into the prep room, and once again the door that could have helpfully blocked his progress stood open. Bounce, bounce, bounce – he was through the door and round the corner and into the prep room. Where complete and utter chaos ensued.

Two of my colleagues were busy preparing an anaesthetic procedure for the last operation of the morning. Hannah had just brought through the patient, a little dachshund who was having a lump removed, and was settling her on the table, where Gavin was just checking he had everything he needed. Meanwhile, in the corner of the room, Lucy and Jess were kneeling with one of the patients I had earlier admitted, a large German shepherd, into whose leg they were just about to insert a catheter to put him on intravenous fluids.

It was into this calm and busy scene that Kevin hopped, with me, Rich and Tim hot on his tail. The first reaction came from the German shepherd, who barked furiously and lunged forward, knocking Jess off balance, pushing Lucy to the side, and scattering their equipment everywhere. Fortunately, the German shepherd was restrained by a lead attached to a wall hook so his range was impeded, otherwise the chase would have been on and we would have met Kevin retreating towards us in panic. Instead, what happened was that Kevin was so startled by the sudden shock and aggression that greeted him that he hopped onto the prep-room table, which startled the daylights out of the dachshund, who now enthusiastically added her high-pitched yapping to the chorus of disapproval. Finding no safe haven, Kevin bounced onto the side work surface, where an array of surgical instruments lay drying on a towel, having been washed after use that morning. Slipping on the towel, Kevin sent the instruments flying in all directions, which of course panicked him still further.

This almighty commotion brought Jane running from reception. Bursting through the door, she held it wide open and, utterly speechless, her mouth wide open, eyes out on stalks, began to take in the chaotic scene – thus providing Kevin with the only means of escape at his disposal. Panicked by barking dogs, instruments falling all around him and feeling trapped, he hopped off the table and flew like a whirl-wind through the door into reception.

It was at this point that we got our lucky break: there were no clients waiting in reception, the front door was shut, and Kevin decided to hop past the counter towards it, inadvertently cornering himself. A moment of calm descended – though if a new client should happen to walk in at that moment, chaos would come again. With one bound, Kevin could have been out the front door and free, and I doubt we would ever have seen him again. I shuddered at the thought of having to explain myself to the staff of the zoo.

After a few minutes, though, Kevin stopped bouncing around, unsure where to go or what to do next, and simply stood in the middle of the room, assessing his unfamiliar environment.

At which point Rich took control. 'Tim,' he whispered. 'Pop back into the consulting room, will you, and get some of that fruit we put in the box with him.'

Moments later, Tim returned with a handful of mixed chopped-up fruit.

'Good lad,' Rich said, throwing the first piece in Kevin's direction. The incoming projectile caught Kevin's attention and he took a few steps to investigate it. The realization that it was food delighted him, and he picked it up, rapidly devoured it, then looked around for more. Rich threw a second piece, slowly creeping forward as he did so. 'Stay there,' he whispered to us. 'Too many of us will frighten him.'

By this time Kevin had located the source of the food, and after gulping down the second piece, he took a couple of steps in Rich's direction. Rich met Kevin halfway with the third piece, and that was enough to re-establish the bond of trust and friendship between them. Holding out his hand with the remaining pieces of fruit, Kevin bounded over and started helping himself. When he was holding the last one between his two paws, Rich was able to pick him up with minimal resistance and carry him back to my consulting-room table.

'Now . . . where were we?' he enquired jovially.

Relieved that the ordeal was over, I quickly reverted to professional mode and started my examination.

'It looks to me like a simple upper respiratory infection,' I concluded after completing my inspection. 'Mind you, you wouldn't realize it from what's just happened. I fear this little escapade won't have helped it, though, so I think we'd best start him on a course of antibiotics.'

'Right you are. What form will they be in?' he asked, as he and Tim gingerly returned Kevin to his container. 'Are you done with him?'

'Yeah, thanks. Liquid form – you should be able to syringe it into his food.'

'Great, that's what we normally do.'

I calculated the appropriate dose, printed off a label, and went to find the bottle from the carnage-strewn floor in the pharmacy.

'Thanks, Jon. Hopefully this'll do the trick. See you again – though hopefully not *too* soon,' said Rich, as he and Tim carried Kevin out of the room. 'Oh, and Jon?' he added. 'Do us a favour?'

He paused as I wandered back into reception after him.

'What's that?' I asked.

'Get some sleep.'

# Kangaroos: fast facts

*Macropus giganteus*: The eastern grey kangaroo

**Distribution:** Southern and Eastern Australia; Queensland, NSW, Victoria and Tasmania.

**Names:** A male is called a 'buck', a female a 'doe', and the young a 'joey'. A group of kangaroos is called a 'mob'.

**Life span:** 8–12 years.

**Habitat:** Woodlands or forests by day, and grasslands or scrublands by night.

**Diet:** Kangaroos are nocturnal and crepuscular herbivorous grazers, favouring grasses, in particular the young green shoots, which are highest in protein, though they will also eat a range of other plants.

**Gestation:** 36 days, after which the joey takes an incredible journey to migrate into the pouch where it attaches onto a teat and lives for a further 9 months.

**Weight:** A mere 0.8 grams at birth, reaching 42–85 kg as adults.

**Growth:** At 9 months a joey will start to leave the pouch for short periods; at 11 months they leave the pouch completely, but still suckle till 18 months, when they are fully weaned. Females are sexually mature by about 22 months, and males at 25 months.

**Body temperature:** 36.2–37.3 °C.

**Interesting facts:** The eastern grey is the fastest of all kangaroos, able to travel up to 40 mph. Females tend to be permanently pregnant, mating soon after a joey has migrated into the pouch. Although during time of drought or food shortage, males won't produce sperm and females will go into embryonic diapause, in good seasons it is quite possible for a female to have 3 offspring at once, all at different stages: one joey out of the pouch nursing, one in the pouch nursing, and one foetus in arrested development, waiting for the pouch to be vacated. A female is also able to produce two different types of milk simultaneously to meet the requirements of each joey.

**Conservation:** The eastern grey kangaroo is now protected by law in Australia, after a period of prolific hunting when Europeans first settled in Australia. Estimates in 2010 put their population at 11 million across Australia, one of the most numerous of all marsupials, and the IUCN do not consider it to be of concern. In fact in some areas they are so numerous that they need to be culled as part of a population control programme to minimize disease and starvation within these groups. However, many other species within Australia are not as fortunate, with over 1,700 species of animals and plants in Australia threatened with extinction, which is why the work of the Australian Wildlife Conservancy is so vitally important: **www.australianwildlife.org**.

# 18

# ZEBRA

*'I asked the zebra, Are you black with white stripes? Or white with black stripes? And the zebra asked me, Are you good with bad habits? Or are you bad with good habits?'*

Shel Silverstein

'We'll have to use the helicopter.' Cobus's distinctive voice crackled across the two-way radio on the dashboard of my Ford Ranger. 'We'll never catch them now! Let's reconvene at the office for a coffee and I'll call Jacques.'

At a fee of 6,000 rand per hour, a helicopter vastly increased the cost of any capture operation, but with wildlife work there were so many potential pitfalls and complications that if you wanted to have the best chance of success, then realism, practicality and efficiency had to count above expense. Having eyes in the sky simply made sense and had so many advantages, the main one being that the terrain and vegetation in the bush often left huge areas inaccessible by vehicle. Going in on foot could present dangers when working with wildlife animals, and most large mammals never fear an aerial attack, so are often much more approachable from a helicopter. So, as long as it could be afforded, and unless the operation was a simple procedure on the ground, a helicopter had become an indispensable tool for wildlife work.

The objects of our search were the two zebra herds on the farm, but in four hours we had only, and briefly, spotted them a couple of times, before they disappeared into dense bush, never allowing an opportunity to dart them. The decision to call in the helicopter was welcome, eminently sensible, and besides, I fancied a coffee. The crazy and immensely frustrating reality was that on every previous day that week we could have darted all twelve zebras with ease. They were always about, whether at the feeding ground, grazing out in the fields, or at one of the watering holes on the farm. But today, the day we'd set out to catch three of the group, they were, of course, nowhere to be found. Conversely, every other animal on the farm was grazing happily and in full view: there were blesboks, giraffes, wildebeest, impalas, ostriches and hartebeest aplenty . . . but not a single zebra anywhere to be seen. It was almost as if they knew of our plans, and had made themselves scarce.

In Cobus's long experience, however – and he knew a thing or two – it was always the same. No matter how tame the animal, or how easy it usually is to find them, on the day you select for their capture, they instinctively vanish. Changes in behaviour, vehicles, people, noises, feeding regimes – it can be any number of things, but no wild animal will hang around to take a chance.

One of the skills of wildlife capture is therefore to minimize an animal's exposure to the unfamiliar, always approaching in the same vehicle with the same driver, and from the same direction, for example. However, there are times when such a strategy simply isn't possible, and it is then that a proper understanding of different species, and an anticipation of how they'll behave, becomes vital to success. Combined with a bit of talent for the job, this will always give you a fighting chance, and after that it largely comes down to luck.

That morning we had set out early in three vehicles, with the objective of darting and relocating three of the twelve zebras on the 60-hectare farm where we were staying – a very small game reserve, by African standards. The topography was undulating, with several high, barren, rocky peaks, where true grazing and browsing areas were limited. These factors restricted the number of animals the farm could successfully sustain while the type of flora determined the species that it would support.

There were plenty of acacia and mimosa trees to keep the four giraffes well fed, being the only browsers on the farm, but when it came to the grazers, there was more competition. Although different grazing species have slightly varied foraging preferences, they still compete for grasslands. The choice is therefore between having more of a few fauna species, or less of several. The greatest biodiversity an ecosystem can sustain is always preferable to a monoculture, so in order to allow for impalas, wildebeest, blesboks, hartebeest, rheboks and ostriches, as well as the zebras, the calculation was that ten adult zebras were the optimum number for this particular area.

The farm currently had twelve adults and a foal, and three of the mares were heavily pregnant. It had also been an exceptionally dry summer, and the rains still hadn't come, grazing was diminished and the watering holes were dry, which meant water had to be being brought in every week. So, although all the zebras were currently fit and well, they were overstocked, and with three foals imminent, their numbers had to be reduced before the intense competition for food became a welfare issue.

A buyer had meanwhile been found, who wanted one young stallion and two mares, and although the zebra numbers would need to be reduced further when the three foals were born, this would temporarily solve the population problem.

All the animals on the farm had their natural grazing or browsing diet supplemented with lucerne hay every evening. This served several purposes: to accustom the animals to human activity so they were easier to catch; to allow for easy monitoring of their health; and to create an incidentally magical evening spectacle. But as our unsuccessful morning had demonstrated, no matter how used to human activity they had become, they were still wild animals.

Cobus handed me and Laura a coffee each.

'Well, that's wildlife capture for you!' He laughed. 'Hope for the best, plan for the worst. They're so intuitive.'

'I saw them several times,' I said. 'I even tried to go in on foot, but it was almost as though they knew the range of the dart gun and kept themselves just beyond it with a few handy trees and bushes to make any attempted shot impossible.'

'We're always darting within an animal's danger zone – that's the area in which they can perceive a threat. And that's because no dart gun has the accuracy and range to dart outside it. Seventy metres seems to be the key distance, and if you're within that, the animal knows you're there, and with the slightest fright they'll take off. If you can dart them from further away, which we've done a couple of times with a trial system, the animal doesn't react. They treat the dart as a nasty fly bite, give a swish of the tail and then carry on eating. The giraffe we darted dropped under the very tree it was feeding from. It was extraordinary to see.'

As ever, Cobus was a wealth of knowledge, experience and stories, little nuggets of conversation like this were priceless.

'What happened with the new system?' Laura asked.

'Money, politics ... It's a shame. It was a great system, ballistically well designed and thought through, allowing for accurate darting at up to 100 metres. None of this 40 metres and you're pushing your luck!'

'With that system we could be sitting in the bar at the lodge and dart the zebra while they graze,' I said thoughtfully. 'A rum and Coke for me and some Etorphine for the zebra!' We all laughed as we slurped our coffees.

'Where are the students?' Cobus now enquired.

'We left them at the lodge, told them to grab a drink and have a rest,' Laura replied.

'I told Jacques to come at two ... Why don't we have lunch first? It won't take long with the helicopter. Although it will depend on your darting ability,' Cobus added, turning to me with a glint in his eye. 'Do you fancy having a go from the helicopter?'

I nearly spat out my coffee in shock. I had always wanted the experience, but it had never seemed a remote possibility. What with the expense of a helicopter and the expectations of the client, the opportunity had simply never come up. I felt a churlish excitement but then almost immediately felt my heart racing at the fear of failure and of all the things that could possibly go wrong.

Almost as though he could read my mind, Cobus added, 'You've had plenty of experience on the ground. You know what you're doing and we all have to start somewhere. These are my zebras, my darts, my drugs, and Jacques will tell you exactly what to do, and will put you on the animal. It'll be like shooting fish in a barrel. With a good helicopter pilot, and once you get used to it, it can often be easier darting from the helicopter than the ground. I've worked with Jacques for over twenty years and they don't come much better than him.'

His words were reassuring and logically he was absolutely

right. I couldn't wish for a better situation to learn from, and it was as safe and as non-pressurized an environment as I could have wished for . . . but my heart was still pounding. I would be totally exposed: Jacques, Laura, Cobus, fourteen students and most of the capture team would all be relying on me. Everyone would witness any mistake I made, the fear could be paralysing, but this opportunity had presented itself and I was going to grab it with both hands. 'When we give ourselves permission to fail,' I remembered reading somewhere, 'we at the same time give ourselves permission to excel.'

'Thanks, I'd love to do it,' I said now.

Back at the lodge, I was deep in thought as I ate my burger listening to the hive of chatter all around. Rumours were spreading among the students that they might get a ride in the helicopter if there was time after the capture. *Great*, I thought. *Now I'd have a group of disappointed students to deal with on top of everything else if it all went wrong.*

It was stepping into the complete unknown that I always found daunting. I remembered the utter fear of my first bungee jump, and the first time I dived onto a crocodile to restrain it, but the buzz afterwards, and the transformation of having those experiences in my memory bank, had always made the initial fear totally worth enduring. So I knew that whatever happened, in a few hours' time I would be richer for the experience, and that thought added to my motivation.

I was snapped out of my thoughts by the familiar humming sound, and within minutes the helicopter was circling above us, no more than 100 feet up. Seconds later, Jacques landed on the feeding ground in a plume of dust. No matter how many times I had seen this sight before, I always marvelled at it: helicopters truly were the ultimate mode of transport.

The engine cut, the propellers slowed and the dust settled, revealing the R44 helicopter. Taking off his headset and clipping it onto the rack above his head, Jacques opened the door and stepped out, greeting Cobus with a broad grin and firm handshake. Turning to me, Cobus introduced us.

'I thought we'd let Jonathan have a go today,' he said.

'Fine, no problem.'

And with the unspoken understanding that comes from years of working together, they both turned back to the helicopter, removing the four doors and the two jerry cans of extra fuel, placing them by a bush a short distance away.

I headed back to my bakkie to organize myself and gather my equipment. I'd made up a couple of darts that morning and had collected Cobus's, so I had four darts for three zebras. I wasn't too confident that would be enough, but Cobus reassured me, adding that it would be easy to land and make up some more should the need arise. The usual procedure was to make up more darts in the helicopter as required, but this would probably be one step too far for my first outing, and I didn't protest.

With my Dan-Inject CO2 dart gun and container of four darts in hand, I returned to the helicopter where the students had gathered. Borrowing the dart gun from me to demonstrate, Cobus talked through the basic elements of technique, position and safety. Only use the lap strap of the three-point seatbelt so your movement won't be restricted. Your right foot should rest on the skid, so you are halfway out of the helicopter, and your left foot should lock under the pilot's seat to maintain balance. Always point the gun *out* of the helicopter, facing away and down; wait for the pilot's command to get into the shooting position; aim to shoot in front of the helicopter to minimize the effect of the downdraught on the dart . . .

I tried to take it all in, to make a mental note of everything, so that I could play it back to myself as a coaching tool when aboard the helicopter. And then a wave of nausea suddenly engulfed me. What if I accidentally did something stupid and put Jacques's life in danger? He had been flying for over twenty-seven years and never crashed. He alone serviced his helicopters, and knew every nut, bolt and screw. He could control everything about his aircraft – except me. It showed his immense trust in Cobus, I thought, to allow a complete stranger into the helicopter with a dart gun loaded with Etorphine.

Explanations done, Cobus took the students over to the vehicles to get them set up, leaving me with Jacques. I climbed into the helicopter, positioning myself as Cobus had done just moments before. I wasn't quite as tall as him, so with my foot on the skid I was more out of the helicopter than in. I double-checked the seatbelt; it looked secure enough. Having done an external check around the helicopter, Jacques climbed into his seat. He was always punctilious about his checks. Working in a profession where the average life expectancy was six years, I could see why. He motioned to me to put my headset on as he did the same. Suddenly the outside world went quiet.

'Can you hear me?' Jacques's voice sounded as though it was in my head.

'Yeah, fine.'

'All good? Are you happy?'

'Yup, strapped in and set.'

'Great! Just so you know, we can talk freely through this. They can't hear us on the ground, but I can communicate with them on a different frequency. Does that make sense?'

'Got it, thanks.'

'So it's your first time darting from the helicopter? It'll take a bit of getting used to, but I'll talk you through it. We'll go up and find the groups and then I'll work out which one to dart. From there it's all about following them, anticipating their movements and looking at the terrain ahead for the best place to dart them. I'll tell you when to load, when to get ready, when to take the safety off, and then it's over to you.'

'OK, that sounds good. How do you anticipate their movements?'

'All animals have tracks and paths that they use. These are often invisible from the ground, but they are clear as day in the air, so you follow those, but it's also a matter of experience, knowing how different animals move. Flying's the easy part!'

I'd seen these guys in action from the ground and it was always impressive, but I knew I was now about to witness Jacques's skill on a whole other level.

'Oh, one final thing. Make sure you keep that gun well away from the skid. If the dart accidentally hits it, the drug will spray into my face. If that happens I'll be taking you to 5,000 feet, by which time I'll be unconscious, so it'll be your problem!' His laugh had an air of defiance about it, and I knew he wasn't joking.

*Best not hit the skid, then*, I thought, nervously pointing the gun further away outside the helicopter.

'Helicopter to ground crew, do you read, over?'

'Hearing you loud and clear,' came Cobus's slightly crackly reply across the radio.

'OK, let's get this bird in the air!'

Jacques was already flicking switches, and then with a sudden roar, the engine started, the slow revolutions of the propellers quickly picked up, and with a slight jerk we lifted off, hovering momentarily a couple of feet off the ground before we rose into the air, banking away to the right. It was hugely exhilarating. I felt like the ultimate action hero.

Settling at a couple of hundred feet in the air, we headed for the front gate to start a systematic sweep of the farm. Although I knew the terrain fairly well, it now appeared completely alien and unfamiliar, and I quickly lost my bearings.

'There are some of the tracks I was talking about,' Jacques said, pointing out of the helicopter to the right.

He was right: they were as clear as day, well-defined paths through the scrubland, yet barely visible from the ground.

A herd of impalas were the first animals we saw, and then two giraffes browsing at the top branches of a mimosa tree, none of which took any notice of us. Over the rocky terrain on the far side of the farm we found the wildebeest and blesboks. Looking far across to the right, I could see all the students gathered around the bakkies and trailers on the feeding ground, their eyes fixed on us, oblivious to the ostrich that suddenly darted across the road to their left. It was an amazing perspective.

Within minutes we were at the top boundary of the farm – a distance that would have taken over an hour on foot. It was there that we got our first sighting of one of the zebra groups. There were seven animals in all, in thick bush at the top of a rocky hill and completely inaccessible by car. This was clearly one of their secret hiding places.

'We have a visual,' Jacques reported back. 'I'll bring them out into the open for darting. Stand by. Over.'

'Roger that,' Cobus replied.

Looking back towards the feeding ground, I could see a frenzy of activity as they loaded up into the two bakkies in preparation. My heart started to pound. The sightseeing tour was over, and it would soon be over to me.

'I'll bring them down into the open,' he said to me. 'Do you see the second from the back? That's a young stallion, I think we'll go for him first.'

I marvelled at his skill. The vegetation was quite thick, so even from the air they were difficult to see. I could see one that looked quite large so I assumed she was a pregnant female, but as to sexing the rest I was at a complete loss. Flying over them and turning back, Jacques came in low, till he was about 50 feet above them, to direct them down the rocky hill. The proximity of the unfamiliar air attack was enough to set them moving.

'Can you see the path they're following? This isn't the first time they've been up here.' I saw how the path zigzagged from side to side down the rocky embankment. 'You'd never take a shot in this situation.' He slowed the helicopter behind them, all the time watching them and assessing the terrain ahead. 'They're constantly changing direction,' he went on. 'The ideal shot is a path that takes them straight and on an incline so their speed is slowed and you can come in straight behind them. We don't always get that, but we will today. When they come out of the brush they'll turn left and then head off to that bottom field over there.' He pointed at an open expanse of grassland separated by half a dozen large bushes. 'Then I'll bring us back round the other side of them and they'll be heading in single file up the hill – so that will be your shot. You can load a dart now. But keep the safety on.'

'OK, thanks.' It dawned on me that, as we had been flying, he had been carefully studying the terrain, creating a detailed map in his mind of every track and path. He was reading the landscape like I would an Ordnance Survey map, but instead of roads, footpaths and bridal ways, he was seeing impala routes, zebra paths and giraffe tracks. It was a skill I could barely fathom.

Keeping the Dan-Inject well out of the helicopter, I unscrewed the locking mechanism and loaded the dart into the barrel. Screwing the pin back in to seal it, I double-checked the safety was on and then pressurized the chamber. Cobus had said three bars should be right for the distance, so pushing the tap forward I watched the gauge creep up to three. The relatively low pressure meant I'd be darting at a distance of less than 10 metres.

By the time I'd got myself set, the zebras, having followed the exact path Jacques had predicted, were now in the open field. Jacques hung back to let them momentarily settle and regroup.

'Are you ready?' he asked.

'Loaded and pressurized with the safety on.'

'Great. Can you see which one we want? Second from the back on the left-hand side.'

'I've got him.'

'With any luck he'll stay at the back as they round that far bush to head up the hill. Then you can take the safety off. I'll come in low. Then take the shot when you're ready. Don't rush it, but don't hang around. After 50 metres they'll bank off to the left over the hill into scrub.'

With that, he came in low, banking to the right over the large pregnant female who was the last in the group. It was a clever manoeuvre because she took off slightly ahead of the young stallion, which left him at the back as the group headed away from us.

'So it's the one at the back,' he added.

'I see him.'

The zebras followed the exact path Jacques had predicted the first time, and as they turned up the hill past the last bush, they were cantering in single file. Jacques brought the helicopter low in behind the last one till we were no more than 10 metres off the ground. I brought the gun up to my shoulder and found the zebra through the scope. I tried to steady it, fighting my nerves and pounding heart. I clicked off the safety, focused in on the zebra's rump and pulled the trigger.

Nothing happened. I tried to refocus for another shot, but it was too late now. The moment had gone. Jacques pulled up and banked to the left as the zebras broke in the same direction and disappeared into thicker bush. I cursed. I had had the perfect shot but the gun had misfired.

'I don't know what happened,' I said weakly to Jacques, half apologetically and half confused.

'What pressure did you set?' he asked.

'Cobus said three bars so I went with that.'

'Go with four.'

'Oh, really?'

'Yeah, you dropped well short, the dart caught the down-draught.'

'You mean it actually fired? I didn't feel anything or see the dart, so I thought it had misfired.'

'No, no, you fired, it just dropped short.'

I was speechless; I didn't know what to think. It was the strangest sensation. In the hundreds of times I'd previously pulled a trigger, I'd always known whether the weapon had fired, but on this occasion I'd felt nothing. Obviously the heli-copter cut out the sound, but I hadn't seen the dart either. I was absolutely convinced the Dan-Inject had failed to fire, but when I checked the barrel Jacques was right: no dart.

My inexperience had caused me to miss, and that couldn't be helped; it was part of the learning exercise – but I still felt foolish and embarrassed, acutely aware of the limited number of times I could afford to miss. But I had to put it behind me and move on.

Having banked over the thick bushes where the zebras had taken temporary cover, Jacques was now studying the new terrain. I tried to do the same, to see if any of his skills were rubbing off on me, and think through the next plan of attack. Beyond these bushes the ground dropped away, eventually joining one of the vehicle tracks that followed the ridge through the middle of the farm. On the far side of this track the land-scape again opened up into fields, although this time there were acacia trees scattered throughout the open space.

'I'll bring them onto this track and then they'll head for the open field,' Jacques told me. 'But the trees will divide them so they won't be in single file. You'll have to be quick with the shot because I'll be coming in between the trees, so don't get distracted by them. Focus on the one you're going for and stick with it. If you change your mind you'll miss, I guarantee it. There are two in this group that we could take – that young stallion, and there's a young mare that doesn't look pregnant.'

'OK.' I processed everything he said, accepting it all without question. I had no idea how he could identify their age and sex from an aerial view, but I was sure he was right.

Circling over the zebras was enough to encourage them out of their temporary shelter and down onto the track. I reloaded quickly and got myself into position, unsure of how much time I had. Once again the zebras behaved as hoped: splitting around a tree into two groups, three of them sped to the left, and four to the right. When they re-emerged, I had struggled to identify the ones we wanted and was totally confused. Jacques was not: he stuck with the group of four.

'Are you loaded? The back right one is the young mare, I'd go for her. Don't hesitate.'

He dropped in low again, this time with the helicopter slightly banked to the right to avoid one of the taller trees, and I could see our shadow approaching fast from the ground below. This meant that we were drawing in on the zebras at a slightly oblique angle, so I realized my target this time was the thigh and not the rump. I focused through the scope as I took the safety off and without a second thought fired.

This time I could follow the trajectory of the dart, and to my utter frustration and distress, watched, as if in slow motion, it brush the back of her tail and disappear into the grass. I hadn't factored in the different approach and had failed to give enough lead to compensate for her forward movement. I closed my eyes as I rocked back into the seat, instantly re-running the miss through my mind.

'Sorry,' I said feebly.

'Don't worry about it, everyone has to start somewhere. Besides, it was a difficult shot.' His words were kind and comforting, but I couldn't help feeling he must be getting frustrated. I wondered how many attempts I would get before I was gently asked to step down. Damn it, I was sure as hell going to get the next one.

'I think we'll leave this group and find the others,' said Jacques when he'd relayed my miss to Cobus. 'We've chased these guys for a bit, so it's time to give them a break.'

We headed back down towards the main farm entrance and almost instantly saw the other group to the left of us at the lower watering hole. At 200 feet we were no initial threat to them so they paid us no attention. Jacques flew a large circle over the five zebras to assess the topography and the best direction to send them. Although a dozen trees surrounded the watering hole, beyond it lay 200 metres of grassland in every direction. Beyond that to the left were the lodges, and below them the workers' houses, so we would have to direct them back the way we had come.

'There could be two quick shots here,' Jacques noted. 'They'll be in single file along the path leading away from the watering hole – that'll be your first opportunity. Then they'll briefly disappear into the thick bush beyond, but on the other side the ground is very rocky and open and then they'll have a steep ascent up onto the plateau, which will slow them down, allowing you your second shot. Just follow down their back and aim two-thirds of the way down. The speed they'll be moving at will mean you'll hit their rump, but if you're a bit further forward it'll just go into their back muscle.'

'Got it, thanks.' Not only was he focused on his job, he was also aware of what I was doing wrong and coaching me on how to fix it. Everything about this helicopter experience was making me see these guys in a whole new light and to admire a whole new level of skill.

He made another half-circle pass, losing altitude as he did so. The zebras responded for the first time. Two heads came up, one shifting anxiously and another letting out a warning bark.

'OK, so there's a stallion on his own off to the right, two younger ones below the watering hole and then two pregnant mares to the left. We'll go for those two younger ones. Hopefully they'll be at the back.'

'I see them.'

'Good, well load up again. I'll come round and get them moving.'

Dart loaded, four bars of pressure set, I adjusted my position. I had to get this one. As we crested the treetops, the zebras bolted away from us, converging in single file along their familiar path.

'She's at the back.'

'I'm on her.'

Off went the safety. I followed back from her neck through the scope and pulled the trigger. This time I hit, the pink feather of the dart starkly visible against the black and white stripes. It had impacted more on her back than her rump, but it was still a safe shot. The thrill and relief were instantaneous. The impact caused her to slow, check herself and then break off to the right, leaving the group, but Jacques ignored her and continued to follow behind the others.

'Well done! Now reload and get ready for the next shot.' He confirmed the darting with the ground crew and informed them of our pursuit for the second. We were still only 20 feet off the ground as the group disappeared into the thick bush just below us. This time Jacques didn't pull up, and skimming the brush we immediately saw the lead zebra emerge out the other side onto the rocky opening. 'She's second from the back.'

'Thanks.' I was reloading before the instruction came, feeling a pure exhilaration.

And now, for the first time that day, the zebras didn't behave as Jacques had predicted. Instead, the stallion took them off to the left to head for a small opening at the bottom of the rocky enclave that led into a thick wooded area. In hindsight it was probably where they had been hiding when we had started our search thirty minutes before. Jacques adjusted his course. 'Hang on, don't shoot yet . . .'

But it was too late. In my adrenaline-fuelled eagerness, I had already zeroed in on the young mare and pulled the trigger. Changing course, her back dipped as she engaged her hind-quarters to propel her in a new direction, and the dart flew just over her rump.

'Sorry,' I mumbled.

'You can't get too carried away in this game. You need to keep a cool head.' For the first time I sensed annoyance in Jacques's voice. 'We'll go back and find that darted one.' He pulled up and off to the left, turning back towards where we had last seen her. We could see the fully loaded bakkie approaching down the tracks from the feeding ground. I scoured the area looking for the familiar black and white stripes. Jacques spotted her before I did, trotting on the spot under an acacia tree. The drug was already taking effect. Moments later she was down.

The bakkie stopped and everyone disembarked. From 100 feet up, they looked like ants aimlessly wandering through the tall grass. Not being privy to our view, they were clueless as to the zebra's whereabouts, despite our hovering directly above her. Then suddenly she was spotted and the team descended on her like moths to a flame.

'How many darts have you got left?' Jacques asked as he pulled up and away from the now secured zebra.

'I'm out.'

'OK, we'll land and you should probably make up four more.' The statement was polite, but I could sense his frustration.

'Thanks.' I desperately wanted to reply that I'd only need two, but realized it would be my pride speaking so decided not to argue.

Moments later we landed on the feeding ground. As I prepared to remove my headset to disembark, the engine still running and propellers still whirring, I caught Jacques's voice in the headset.

'Don't forget to leave to the front of the helicopter. You want to stay well clear of that back rotor blade.' I was grateful for the reminder. I knew that, of course, but I was so caught up with the darting that I could easily imagine it slipping my mind – a mistake you would only make the once.

I left the helicopter and dashed back to my truck. With a helicopter whirring away behind me, and the group arriving to unload the first zebra in front of me, it was just as well I had plenty of experience of making up these darts. There were enough other pressures and distractions without struggling to remember all the steps involved. Within about ten minutes I had prepared all four darts with the dosage Cobus had suggested, and was heading back to join Jacques in the helicopter, and then we took off again.

'If I can flush them out of here,' I heard him saying in my headphones, 'they'll head up the rocky embankment and onto the upper plain . . . You should have a nice shot on the female and then we'll get the male from the other group. OK?'

'Sure,' I replied. I felt I knew what I was doing this time. If Jacques was right and they headed up the rocky path, it would be a straight-on shot, with no direction change. I would definitely get this one. I felt a surge of excited determination.

Jacques flew deliberately low over the bottom woodland border, turning sharply and banking over the perimeter fence, where we hovered for a moment almost vertical to the ground, a manoeuvre designed to corral the zebras back towards the upper trees near where they had entered.

'Load up. I'll fly low over this area sounding the siren. That should flush them out, so you need to be ready for the shot.'

'Will do.' I didn't need telling twice, and within seconds the dart gun was loaded. At the same time Jacques dropped the helicopter, bringing it in horizontally and low over the trees. The movement gave me the same sensation as a roller-coaster ride, throwing me into my seat. I had to brace myself against the doorframe as my right foot slipped on the skid, but I quickly regained my position, leaning fully out of the helicopter ready for Jacques's instruction. Meanwhile, as we flew over the trees towards the rocky bank, he intermittently sounded the siren, a combination that would have unsettled even the calmest of animals, and sure enough, the group of zebras burst out of hiding 30 feet in front of us.

'She's second from the front,' Jacques said, having instantly assessed and identified them. 'Remember – the same as before. Follow down her back and shoot, I'll come in as they start climbing.'

'Got it.'

Once again, Jacques's prediction proved correct. Ignoring the path to the watering hole they had used earlier, they headed straight for the rocky path and started to climb. I drew the gun into my shoulder, found her head through the scope and followed down her back, aiming left of her spine, tracking past her ribs, and then pulled the trigger. The dart impacted exactly where I had aimed. It was a high shot, maybe a foot in front of her rump, but it hit muscle to the side of the vertebrae and I'd have preferred that than aiming for the rump and missing. I silently congratulated myself; I finally felt I was getting the hang of this.

*Don't get too cocky, boyo*, I told myself. *Two out of five is still pretty poor shooting.* Jacques was immediately on the radio to Cobus, reporting the successful darting. At the same time he pulled up, banking off to the right to encourage the zebras running behind to stick with the front two and continue up onto the flat plain above. Circling behind them, we hovered at a distance to allow them to regroup and settle. Off to our right the bakkie was on the move. Minutes later, the zebra started trotting on the spot as the drug took effect, and her bizarre and unusual behaviour sent the other three zebras fleeing, leaving her on her own. This time the ground crew had spotted her easily and slowly started making their way towards her, ready to get to her as soon as she went down. That was our signal. We left in search of the other group and the last zebra.

This time they were easy to spot; they had not moved far since we left them earlier, having obviously decided that, with the helicopter gone, it was safe to continue grazing on the plain. Our return, however, had sent them running and we found them as they headed back over the brow in the direction of the fields where I had taken my first shot.

'I'll take them back through the thick bush. They'll either head up towards the hiding spot where we first found them or break right and head down towards the fields. Either way they'll be in single file when they come out the other side so that'll be your shot. Load up.'

Now familiar with the routine, I found I had loaded the dart before I had consciously registered what I was doing, my mind playing through the scenario that was about to unfold.

I coached myself through my approach, desperate for another successful shot.

Into the thick brush they went, and with Jacques in pursuit they didn't hang about, emerging out the other side about thirty seconds later. They opted to carry on seeking shelter back where our pursuit had started.

'It looks like he's second from the back. Are you ready? You've got about 100 metres before they head left, and then they'll start heading into the trees again.'

'All set.' I was already in position and as Jacques identified my target I zeroed in on it through the scope. They were moving at a pace, but Jacques was matching them. This area was actually so open and free of trees that he was able to bring the helicopter lower than before, coming in so close behind the last zebra that I had an almost horizontal shot lined up. If I aimed along the animal's back, the angle was so acute the dart might bounce off, so I focused instead on the top of the back leg. I watched a couple of strides to confirm this was a consistent target and squeezed the trigger.

Time had felt suspended, but as the helicopter suddenly pulled up, and the zebra broke left, I realized I had taken the shot at the very last possible moment. But it didn't matter: the dart's pink feather was clearly visible in the middle of the zebra's hamstring.

'Good job! I think you're starting to get the hang of it.'

With my job done, and Jacques's praise ringing in my ears, the pressure was off. I could relax and fully soak up the experience. I felt the same elation I had after my first successful breach calving or first bitch spay as a new graduate, the glorious euphoria of knowing that I had faced down my apprehensions and come out the other side a better vet for it.

# Zebras: fast facts

*Equus quagga*: The plains zebra

**Distribution:** East Africa, from south of Ethiopia down into Botswana and eastern South Africa. It is the most widespread of the 3 zebra species, and the commonest to find in game reserves and zoos. There are 6 sub-species.

**Names:** A male is called a 'stallion', a female is a 'mare', and the young a 'foal'. A group of zebras is called a 'dazzle' or 'zeal'.

**Life span:** 25–30 years.

**Habitat:** Treeless grasslands and savannah woodlands.

**Diet:** Zebras are herbivorous grazers, primarily eating a variety of grasses, but also known to eat shrubs, herbs, twigs, leaves and bark.

**Gestation:** 360–396 days, usually producing a single foal.

**Weight:** About 30 kg at birth, reaching an adult weight of 175–385 kg.

**Growth:** A newborn foal will stand within hours of being born, and starts to eat grass at 1 week, but is not fully weaned until 7–11 months. Young stallions will leave the herd to form a bachelor group when their mother has her next foal, but young mares will stay with the herd. Both sexes reach sexual maturity by about 20 months, but stallions won't be strong enough to breed until about 5 years. They will be fully grown at about 4 years, but only 50 per cent of foals will reach adulthood because of predation, disease or starvation.

**Body temperature:** 37.6–38.6 °C.

**Interesting fact:** Embryological evidence suggests that zebras are black with white stripes, rather than, as was previously thought, white with black stripes. A number of hypotheses have been proposed to explain these markings, whether as camouflage, a visual cue for identifying each other, to deter flies or to help keep them cool. There is evidence to support all of these hypotheses, but the idea that the stripes help to confuse predators by making it more difficult to pick out one particular target in a mass of flickering stripes seems persuasive.

**Conservation:** The plains zebra global population is about 750,000, and as a result the IUCN classifies them as 'near threatened'. Their uniquely attractive skin is the primary reason zebras have been excessively hunted, and habitat loss has also been a contributing factor in population declines. The plains zebra is fortunate in having benefited from numerous of its ranges becoming protected and as such its population remains stable and currently faces no major threat to its population. Sadly, the largest of the three zebra species, the Grévy's zebra, found in Kenya and Ethiopia, is less fortunate: its population has suffered a 75 per cent decline since 1970 due to habitat loss, with an estimated 2,500 Grévy's zebra left in the wild, which is why the IUCN classify them as 'endangered'. See: **www.awf.org/wildlife-conservation/grevys-zebra**.

# 19

# SUGAR GLIDER

*'An animal's eyes have the power to speak a great language.'*

Martin Buber, *I And Thou*.

As a veterinary surgeon there are many surgical procedures we have to perform as part of our job, ranging from removing foreign objects from over-curious dogs to repairing broken bones or removing tumours. Without question, however, the one we perform more frequently than any other, and on more species than any other, is castration.

Over the years I have had to castrate so many animals, of so many species, that it could count as my area of expertize. Hamsters, guinea pigs, rabbits, cats, dogs, sheep, pigs, alpacas, cows, horses and donkeys would just be scratching the surface. Although the end goal of the surgery is the same, the methodology varies depending on the specific anatomy of the species. Failure to acknowledge these differences, and the specific technique required for each, could result in a life-threatening bleed or herniation. So even in a routine surgery, if the species is unusual then its anatomical idiosyncrasies must be understood. Usually these are easy enough to find from an anatomy textbook, but occasionally a curveball comes along and if the relevant information cannot be found, then the best option is to take an overcautious approach.

Each of the pratice's vets had at least one operating day a week, and mine was Wednesday. Scanning the schedule that morning, the procedures seemed fairly routine: two cat spays, a dog castration, a lump removal and a dental. Nothing too troubling ... until, that is, my eyes fell on the last two items on the list: two sugar gliders to castrate. What was a sugar glider again? Until two days previously I hadn't even known they existed.

My Monday evening consulting list had been steady and uneventful until my 6 p.m. appointment: a Miss Toyah, with her pet skunk Sally. Sally had evidently felt that her meal of leftover Sunday roast chicken and vegetables had not been a sufficient feast, so had opportunistically gorged on two bowls of cat's dinner belonging to Socrates and Shakespeare. The result had been spectacularly horrific. In a catalogue of repulsions, Miss Toyah's morning had started with an unpleasant aroma greeting her nostrils; unsure of the source, she followed the wafting odour out of her bedroom and down the stairs, whereupon she stepped in a puddle of Sally's diarrhoea, which spurted up her ankle and squelched between her toes. Attempting not to retch at the intense stench, and to blank the reality of what she had just done, she hopped into the utility room to clean it off, only to find herself standing in a pool of liquid brown skunk ordure, which had also splattered around the bottom of most of the cupboards. The clean-up operation had taken an hour, making her late for work. Sally had been confined to a crate for the day and Miss Toyah had booked a vet appointment for her after work in the hope that a rapid corrective solution could be found.

The consultation progressed normally; Sally was fine in all regards except for her uncontrollable diarrhoea. I advised a temporary dietary adjustment and probiotics that should quickly solve her problem and assumed that concluded the consultation.

'Jon, before I go, can I just ask you about something else?' Miss Toyah asked as I went to get the door for her and Sally.

'Of course.'

'I have two male sugar gliders, they're brothers. I've had them about four months and they've been fine together. But recently they've started fighting quite a lot, so I think I need to get them castrated. Do you think that would help, and is that something you'd be happy to do?'

'If they're young males then they're probably just reaching sexual maturity, in which case castrating them does usually help, yes,' I replied confidently. 'But it'll take several weeks before the hormone levels are reduced so it won't be an instant cure. In terms of castrating them, I'm sure you can appreciate that we don't see many sugar gliders, but I'll read up on their specifics and I'm very happy to do the surgeries.'

'Oh, that would be great. I know that self-mutilation is a big problem with them post surgery, so good pain relief and feeding them on recovery really helps . . . but I don't want to tell you your job.'

'No problem. I'll look into all those things, and if you want them done sooner rather than later I could always do them this Wednesday?'

Miss Toyah gratefully agreed, and after showing her out I quickly googled 'sugar glider' on the office computer. Kind of a cross between a chinchilla and a hamster. Who knew?

I spent my Tuesday evening researching and finding out everything I could about the sugar glider and what I needed to know in order to successfully operate on these two on Wednesday. Self-traumatization was indeed a big issue, as Miss Toyah had said; Buprenorphine was the recommended painkiller of choice; oh, and the male sugar glider had a bifurcated penis. Not that this would have much bearing on my surgery, but it's always good to learn an interesting fact! Armed with all this newly acquired, if moderate, level of knowledge of *Petaurus breviceps*, I felt prepared enough for the procedures that lay ahead.

'Oh my goodness you have got to take a look at the two sugar gilders,' said Julie as she came into the prep room that morning. 'They are so unbelievably cute, with their big eyes and little noses.'

'You've admitted them, then?' I asked.

'Yeah, they were the first on the list to arrive. The owner's brought some food for them, and says we have to feed them as soon as they wake up,' she added, and then, with a slightly puzzled air, 'And she's also brought some pouches to put them in afterwards.'

'Yeah, they're prone to self-traumatizing on recovery so you have to feed them as soon as they wake up to distract them. Being marsupials, the pouches will probably make them feel secure and less interested in their wound.'

'Huh. You seem to know a lot about them, Jon. I can see someone's been doing their homework. I'd never heard of a sugar glider before yesterday.'

'I might have had a bit of a read last night,' I admitted. 'They're actually really interesting. Sugar gliders are nocturnal, which is why they have such large eyes. They literally glide through the air, travelling from branch to branch in search of sugary nectarous food. Hence the name.'

'Huh, cool. So where do they come from, and do many people have them as pets?'

'They originate from Australasia, and they've got quite a fan base in the States as a pet, apparently, but are only just starting to gain some popularity over here, which makes them pretty sought after and quite expensive.'

'Listen to you! You *have* been doing your homework! So what's the plan with the anaesthetic?'

'There are a couple of different protocols that I've found, but given their small size I think it'll be best to just gas them down. I don't particularly fancy trying to give them an intramuscular injection when they're awake, it'll just stress them out.'

'Sounds logical. And what about analgesia?'

'Buprenorphine is best. Non-steroidal anti-inflammatories are debatable, so we'll steer clear of them.'

'OK, glad you know what you're doing. So what order do you want to do the ops in?'

'Let's do the cats first, then the dog, then the lump removal, then the sugar gliders and we'll finish with the dental.'

Two hours later and I was putting the final stitch in a ten-year-old female boxer, from whom I had removed a suspicious-looking lump in her left flank, and the time had come to turn my attention to our two little Antipodean friends.

'Do you want Sean or Shane first?' Julie asked.

Sean and Shane the Australian sugar gliders? Of course, what else could they be called? Especially with Socrates and

Shakespeare the cats and a skunk called Sally. I wondered how many other animals she had. Simon the salamander, perhaps, Seth the saluki. 'I don't mind. Can you tell them apart?'

'Apparently Shane has a larger black stripe on his forehead and a more yellow tinge to his underbelly compared to Sean.'

'Good to know. Well whichever, I honestly don't mind.'

We carried Maisie the boxer back to her kennel where Heather would recover her, and then returned to the prep room to prepare for the first sugar glider. With everything set, Julie disappeared, returning moments later with a small bundle in her hands, which she placed in a small box on the table. A little nose poked out from a green knitted pouch, followed by two beady eyes eagerly searching for something to munch on. I had to admit he was pretty adorable. The box Julie had placed him in was specially designed to anaesthetize any such small animal. Closing the lid on it, I connected up the anaesthetic machine and turned it on, thus delivering a mixture of oxygen and vaporized Isoflurane into the box. After a few minutes the sugar glider was sound asleep. I flushed the box with air before opening it and removed the little fella.

'So this is probably Shane then?' I said, seeing the large black stripe on his forehead.

'Yeah, I think so,' Julie agreed as she connected a small anaesthetic mask to the machine, which we then put over Shane's mouth and nose to maintain anaesthesia throughout the procedure.

Turning Shane over, I got quite the anatomical shock. None of my extensive reading up on sugar gliders had prepared me for quite how large and pendulous their testicles were.

'That's quite the landing gear for these little fliers,' Julie commented.

'Indeed. I understand now why they refer to them as the "pom-pom"!'

'The what?'

'Apparently a sugar glider's testicle sac is referred to as the pom-pom.'

'You serious? I love it. Well, do you remove the pom-pom at the same time as the testicles?'

'I've read about both the normal technique and the scrotal ablation, or de-pom-pomming, but I haven't really decided which I was going to do. I was going to see when I did the surgery.'

'De-pom-pomming? Amazing! Is that the technical term? So, do you want me to clip up the pom-poms and prep him?'

'Let's get him settled in theatre on a heat pad and make sure he's stable. I'll draw up some Buprenorphine and scrub up while you prep him.'

'Sure.'

I calculated the dose – barely a needle full – drew it up and gave it under the skin. Shane didn't flinch.

'He seems nicely asleep,' I said to Julie as she busied herself setting him up on a pile of towels over a heat mat and cocooned in a space blanket.

'That should keep him cosy and warm.'

I started washing my hands as Julie clipped away at the surgical site. It was a delicate procedure which she took great time and care over. So much so, that I'd finished scrubbing up before she had finished, so she briefly broke away to open my sterile kits, which contained hand towels, drapes and surgical instruments. With my sterile gloves on, I started laying out the instruments and sorting through the equipment, and Julie turned her attention back to clipping.

'Oops!' She suddenly exclaimed. 'I don't think I meant to do that. I think I've just de-pom-pommed him!'

It was true. Despite her best attempts at trimming the surgical site, the clippers had caught and in one movement my surgical skills were no longer required.

'Well, I guess that decides what technique I'm going to use!' I studied the wound where moments before the testicles had been. Remarkably, there was virtually no blood. It had been a clean cut.

'I'm sorry, Jon, I feel terrible. Poor little fella,' she added apologetically.

'It appears we have discovered a very efficient way of neutering sugar gliders! If I put one stitch around the vessels, we can glue the skin together and that's the job done.' I placed a clamp on the exposed vessels. 'Can you pass me some 4-0 Vicryl suture.' Moments later the procedure was complete.

'There we go, the most efficient castration in history!'

'I can't believe I did that,' she said, looking at the pendulous anatomy now dangling from the clipper blades. 'Do you think Miss Toyah will want to keep the pom-poms?'

'I can imagine a fashion world that would go crazy for pom-pom earrings, but I don't think the time is quite yet.'

Turning off the anaesthetic vaporizer, we watched and waited for Shane to come round. Happy that the wound all looked fine we popped him in his knitted pouch and armed ourselves with the dried cranberry and apple pieces ready to distract him on his recovery. Minutes later he started stirring. Seemingly no worse off for his ordeal, he immediately picked up the scent of the food. Julie offered him a cranberry, which he grabbed with both front paws and started tucking into ravenously, then turning with equal enthusiasm to my offering.

'Isn't he so *cute* the way he holds his food, bringing it up to his mouth to devour it?'

It was indeed a very adorable sight.

'So what now?'

'If Heather has finished recovering Maisie, she can continue feeding this little fella and we can move on to Sean.'

Adjusting the technique slightly second time around, Sean was successfully and more conventionally castrated using a scalpel blade rather than clippers. He recovered equally well so I was able to discharge Shane and Sean to a delighted Miss Toyah, who also informed us that her week was picking up: Sally was no longer redecorating the downstairs of her house.

'Miss Toyah was very grateful for our efforts,' I reported to Julie as she was packing up the surgical kits we had used that day.

'Oh, I am glad. And how's Sally the skunk?'

'Much better.'

'Sugar gliders and skunks in one week. It doesn't get much weirder than that, Jon.'

'I know, not really what you imagine in a rural veterinary practice. Do you think our de-pom-pomming technique will ever make it into the textbooks?'

# Sugar gliders: fast facts

*Petaurus breviceps*: The sugar glider

**Distribution:** Found throughout the northern and eastern parts of mainland Australia, Tasmania, New Guinea and some Indonesian islands.

**Names:** A male is called a 'sugar bear', a female a 'honey glider', and the young a 'joey'. A group of sugar gliders is called a 'colony'.

**Life span:** 9–12 years.

**Habitat:** Rainforest, or dry forests of eucalyptus or acacia trees. They require a dense mid- and upper-canopy cover to enable them to travel through it. Being nocturnal, they are active and feed at night, sheltering in tree hollows during the day.

**Diet:** Sugar gliders are seasonally adapted omnivores, being insectivorous in the summer and in winter feeding on the sugar gum, sap or nectar that exudes from plants. They are also opportunistic feeders, and will eat small lizards, bird eggs, fungi or native fruits if available.

**Gestation:** 15–17 days, usually giving birth to 2 joeys.

**Weight:** 0.2 grams at birth, reaching an adult weight of about 120 grams.

**Growth:** The joey will migrate to the pouch and latch on to a nipple, where it stays for 60 days. Males can reach sexual maturity as early as 4 months, but females are not sexually mature until about 8 months, neither being fully grown until 2 years.

**Body temperature:** 35.8–36.9 °C.

**Interesting facts:** During cold weather, and when food is scarce, sugar gliders are able to enter a state of torpor as an energy-conserving mechanism, allowing their body temperature to drop as low as 10.4 °C without causing any damage. Torpor is different from hibernation in being a short-term daily cycle lasting anything from 2 to 23 hours. They also possess a membrane between their fore and hind limbs, which allows them to launch themselves from a tree and glide for as far as 50 metres. It has been calculated that for every 1.82 metres they travel horizontally, they drop 1 metre.

**Conservation:** Despite the loss of a lot of their natural habitat in Australia over the last 200 years, sugar gliders have adapted to live in small patches of remnant bush and their numbers have thrived and so they are not considered at risk. The IUCN classes them as being of least concern. However, several of their close relatives such as the Leadbeater's possum and the mahogany glider are endangered due to deforestation. Since 1990 the world has lost over 129 million hectares of forest – an area the size of South Africa. The World Wildlife Fund is working to lobby governments to improve smarter land use to prevent further deforestation between now and 2030. See: **www.wwf.panda.org/about_our_earth/deforestation**.

# 20

# WILDEBEEST

'*Nature is not a place to visit. It is home.*'

Gary Snyder

I was hot, sweaty, hungry and tired, but I couldn't have been happier. I was back in South Africa again. As I surveyed my surroundings on this 3000-hectare game farm, arid scrubland stretched before me in every direction with just the odd acacia tree to add variety. The only signs of human life were our abandoned vehicles and a group of thirty-odd people busying themselves with khaki tarpaulins and wooden posts. Just twenty-four hours previously this area had been untouched land, but now an enormous v-shaped enclosure stretched out from the bed of a large haulage truck to the brow of a small promontory just visible on the horizon over a kilometre away.

The purpose of this temporary construct was to facilitate the mass capture and relocation of about 400 blue wildebeest. Southern Africa had been in drought for over two years and as such the once-abundant vegetation on which the animals depended for grazing was scarce and waterholes were drying up, critically endangering the wildlife on the reserves. A hundred years ago these animals simply would have migrated to find sustenance, but the continent was different now, the human population having grown exponentially to the detriment of its wildlife. In order to protect that wildlife, animals were no longer free to roam but were instead enclosed within large game reserves, which meant they had nowhere to go when drought struck. As their custodians, the reserve had a duty to intervene so we had been asked to move some of the wildebeest off the farm to other locations where the effects of the drought weren't as serious – while praying that the rains would eventually come.

This particular area was a 'big-five' estate and so home to an abundance of species, many of which also needed their numbers reducing, but today's task was the relocating of the blue wildebeest. We had found a new place for only about a quarter of the group, which would mean a repeat of today's complex manoeuvres at a later date. It seemed an inordinate amount of time, effort and manpower for the job involved, but to the capture team and wildlife vets we were working with, this was just another few days at the office; one to load, transport and unload all the kit; another to set up; then probably only a few hours on the actual capture, though that depended on the skill of the helicopter pilot and how far the animals were from this temporary 'boma', as these enclosures were called.

The capture technique was a glorified version of sheepdog trialling – herding the animals using a helicopter and boma instead of a dog and pen. The helicopter would round up the animals, coaxing them into the enclosure before sounding a siren signalling to the team on the ground to pull curtains across the entrance to secure the animals within. The helicopter would continue pushing the herd forwards, funnelling the beasts down towards the truck whilst further ground teams ran behind, drawing curtains across the path in their wake to contain the wildebeest in an ever-diminishing area until they reached the truck and had nowhere else to go but on board. Well, that was the theory, at least!

Deciding on where to position the boma, factoring in access, wind direction and camouflage, was the most crucial step in this complicated procedure. It was not unusual to spend a day setting up the large pen, only then to find the animals were spooked at the entrance and would not cross the threshold. When this occurred the whole set-up had to be dismantled, a new location found and the enclosure reconstructed, so mass capture was (and remains) a huge logistical and time-consuming operation.

It was 9 a.m., the temperature was already in the twenties and there wasn't a cloud in the sky, nor was there any shelter to be found. We, the student and vet team, had already been at work for an hour, assisting the capture team in adding the finishing touches to the boma construction. For us it had been a 5.30 a.m. start, but the capture team were already hard at it when we arrived, having camped overnight – seemingly unperturbed by being on a big-five reserve with predators aplenty. I strolled back to the minibus to grab my water bottle, pondering what creatures surrounded me unseen; black mambas, puff adders, cobras and scorpions for sure but doubtless other creatures besides lay hidden in the brush. Was there a lion crouching, invisible and perfectly disguised, studying my every movement? Experience told me it was already too hot for a hunt and such animals would be in the shade somewhere, sleeping soundly, tails gently swatting away any fly that attempted to trouble them, but the mind is a powerful thing and so I felt a surge of adrenaline pulsing through my veins. I studied every tree I passed, hoping to spot a leopard tucking into an impala carcass – its usual reward from a successful night's hunt.

This was a far cry from my recent stint at Pinewood Studios, where I had been working as the veterinary adviser on the set of a Hollywood blockbuster, giving guidance on how to operate on and take blood from dinosaurs – as if that was something I had learned in vet school! It had been the experience I had gained working out here in South Africa previously that had secured that role for me; with some lateral thinking and extrapolation from my own professional experiences I had felt confident about the advice I was able to give. And who *wouldn't* have taken that gig? The opportunity to see your work translated onto the big screen for potentially millions of viewers across the globe was too great to pass up. It had been surreal but fascinating, working with the director and actors, seeing the manpower and money involved and watching superbly crafted model dinosaurs being brought to life so convincingly by an exceptional team of puppeteers. I had taken every opportunity to understand and involve myself in a world that previously I had known nothing about – and then walked away from it, content that I had made the right career choice; my heart lay in caring for animals and not in movie-making and box-office ticket sales. It had been an incredible experience and I felt privileged to have had it, but it was time to return from the Jurassic period to present-day veterinary work and conservation – and for that, Africa was the front line. I might be the only person to have stitched up a dinosaur, but as I surveyed my surroundings now, miles away from any signs of human habitation, I knew that this was where I belonged.

My thoughts were suddenly interrupted by the all-too-familiar hum of the R44 helicopter appearing as a white speck on the horizon. Moments later it circled above us, its rotor blades creating a cloud of dust into which it landed. Our 'sheepdog' had arrived and the pen was now ready – we just needed to locate the wildebeest.

We congregated on a dirt track for our briefing, giving Bjorn, the leader of the capture team, a canvas on which to illustrate the plan of attack. We were each to be responsible for a curtain within the enclosure, he explained. Our task was simple: to keep out of view until the ground vibrated from the stampeding animals and the helicopter siren could be heard overhead, then, 'run like hell with your curtain and don't stop until you've reached the other side!'

Bjorn looked up at his audience from where he crouched over his dirt diagram, waving the four-inch twig he'd been using as his marker. The plan brought to mind my previous experience of mass capture with eland, which had felt like a military ambush: stealth and silence followed by a surge of adrenaline as the enormous animals galloped past just feet away from where I stood. I had felt I might be trampled at any moment, but then they were past me, the siren sounded and I sprinted as though my life depended on it across the rugged terrain, towards the opposite canvas wall – and safety.

I surveyed the eager faces of the vet students; they had no idea what they were in for – but neither, as it transpired, did I.

'If all goes to plan, it will be as smooth as herding sheep, but if the wind gets under the canvas and they see any escape route then chaos will ensue; there will be no stopping them and we'll never get them near the boma again. If you feel in danger or unsafe then just get out of there,' Bjorn directed. 'Remember, you're all responsible for each other's and your own safety!' he added.

The capacity of each truck was about forty animals, which would mean three runs. I knew from experience that the first one would be the slowest, because it could take some time for helicopter pilot Gerry to locate a herd, which could be anywhere within the estate boundaries. After that, though, the process would be faster. The hope was that our early-morning start would ensure the wildebeest were still congregated around one of the waterholes. In a few hours' time, at the hottest point of the day, they were likely to be elsewhere, seeking the shelter of one of the many dense bushland areas that dotted the farm and moving them then would almost certainly result in some fatalities.

Briefing done, Gerry headed back to his helicopter to commence his search. Moments later the helicopter roared into life, and then it was up and away, disappearing into the pristine blue sky. He had radio communication with us on the ground so would alert us when he located a wildebeest herd, but until then it was the all-too-familiar waiting game.

Bjorn and I turned our attention to trying to hit a bush stump or boulder twenty or thirty metres away with pebbles. It was one of various time-filling games that were a customary part of this sort of work, but I never tired of them; to be out in the African bush again, working with the native wildlife, always gave me a great sense of contentment. It was the complete antithesis of city life, which I had enjoyed as a student but from which I had since fled. Now, any trip for me had to include animals and open spaces.

As the sun approached its highest point, the lack of shelter started to take its toll on us; we were already consuming litres of water and now were forced to retreat to the relative protection of the truck's shade. An hour went by before Gerry's voice crackled across the radio confirming he had located a large herd of well over a hundred wildebeest. They were a couple of miles away by a watering hole but were starting to move off, also seeking shade until later in the day.

Gerry would muster the animals slowly, not wanting them to overheat, so guessed they were about fifteen minutes away;

it was time for us to take to our stations. For this first run, I was to be at the funnel entrance to the boma, in charge of one of the first crucial curtains; once this was closed, the wildebeest would be contained, provided the tarpaulins held firm as barriers. The ultimate goal of loading the animals onto the truck, though, relied on maintaining the herd's forward momentum once within the enclosure, which could be difficult; stressed by their confinement their natural instinct was to circle around and double back on themselves in search of any escape route.

With our destination a kilometre from the truck and Gerry's arrival now imminent, I set off at a brisk pace in the company of Derek, Dumison and Sydney from the capture team. Minutes later we were in position. It was the first time I had seen the entrance to the boma and it was immediately apparent why this hilltop location had been chosen. The direction from which the animals would be approaching meant the vast majority of the enclosure leading down to the truck would be hidden from their view, as would we be thanks to the bushes and trees. The wildebeest would be contained within the boma before they even realized what had happened.

We briefly checked the curtains were drawing smoothly; any snagging could prevent us from being able to close off the entrance, which would hinder our capture efforts.

We were set! In the silence, I was conscious of my own heartbeat. I was by now accustomed to such moments, but never tired of them. While we were surrounded by an expert team of people who had performed these sorts of logistical operations hundreds of times before, we all knew the potential dangers of working with wild animals; catastrophe could be just around the corner.

After a few minutes the hum of the helicopter could be heard, getting ever louder and overpowering the noise of the approaching wildebeest. Uncomfortable as we were, crouched down in our hiding places and being harassed by flies and ants, we remained focused, acutely aware of our responsibility. I felt the ground shake beneath me and suddenly the wildebeest were upon us, the sound of their stampeding hooves deafening, the dust cloud making us cough and splutter – and then they had gone. The helicopter siren broke through the melee – the sprint was on! Disorientated, I used the curtain to guide me as I pulled it across the enclosure while navigating the unforgiving terrain, acutely aware of the implications a fall could have on the capture. But then as I cleared the dust cloud I heard the siren sound again, signalling the animals' progression: they were now in the second zone and the imminent danger of their escape had passed.

My curtain secured, I headed with Derek and Sydney into the boma towards the truck to assist with the loading. The siren sounded twice more before the drone of the helicopter died away; Gerry had landed and the wildebeest had made it through the final curtain. As we jogged from one section to the next, we were joined by others in the team as they too completed their tasks. This capture seemed to have gone smoothly, but until the doors were closed on the truck, there was no room for complacency.

On reaching the final curtain, I heard a commotion coming from the other side, but my fears were calmed when I peered around the tarpaulin to see the animals being herded in a controlled way onto the trailer. Moments later the truck doors slammed shut, safely containing thirty-eight wildebeest. Several of us clambered up onto the truck roof to administer tranquillizers to each animal, injecting them through the roof hatches with a syringe pole. The drug would keep them quiet and relaxed for the journey ahead.

With the animals so subdued, the truck set off with its cargo for the more secure holding bomas a few miles away, where the wildebeest would be housed for a few days before being transported to their final destination under cooler conditions. A second truck took the place of the first in a seamless transition that reflected the routine nature of this whole operation.

After the first muster Gerry had joined the ground crew; despite over twenty-five years as a pilot, he still loved the other aspects of wildlife work and never wanted to miss out on any of the action. But now it was time for him to return to his primary duty. Knowing there were plenty of people on the ground and that I wouldn't be missed, I asked if I could join him in his chopper for the second run.

'Sure, Jono – hop in,' he responded with his typical friendliness.

As I clambered into the R44 and secured my safety belt and headset, I felt an eager sense of anticipation at the thought of experiencing helicopter mass capture in a way I had previously only witnessed from the ground. This second run was sure to be much less time-consuming than the first, Gerry knowing exactly where the herd was located now, so even if the animals had taken shelter from the midday heat they would be easily extracted. Nevertheless, separating one species from a group and then a specific number from a herd requires an intimate knowledge of the animals involved and instinctive piloting skills. Gerry had both in abundance.

Rising quickly into the sky, Gerry banked over the boma and we were soon heading out across the open plain for the watering hole from where the previous group had come. Travelling at speed we could see the perfect shadow of our helicopter moving over the ground a few hundred feet beneath us. Moments later, the watering hole came into view. Frustrated by the earlier disturbance, the wildebeest had returned to the oasis to rejoin the herd of hartebeest they had left behind, and the two species were once again drinking contentedly, but our approach quickly sent them into a frenzy, conscious now of what the helicopter meant. Bolting into the open plain as a mixed group, it was thanks to Gerry's skilful aerial manoeuvres as we descended over them that the herding instinct kicked in, causing a natural separation of the two species. Gerry had expected and so immediately exploited this reaction, coming in low and driving the hartebeest away. Rising up again and banking the chopper around we turned back to the wildebeest, which were now heading roughly in the direction of the boma, but the group was far too big for one truckload so needed to be thinned out. Although Gerry could instinctively tell where to divide the herd to split off the forty required animals, they were galloping so closely together that he was forced to come in low to drive them apart; I could almost reach out and touch them. The speed and altitude at which we were flying should have felt terrifying, but was instead thrilling, thanks to his relaxed demeanour.

With the separation complete, I did a head-count: we had a group of thirty-six; Gerry had been impressively accurate in his estimation. He radioed through to Bjorn and the ground crew our ETA; the herd was already on the move at their own speed so Gerry only intervened when they strayed off course, the sheepdog analogy proving accurate. Slowly and steadily we corralled the animals forwards across the open plain, the boma gradually coming into view as we approached the brow of the hill, its entrance shrouded by bushes and trees, once again justifying the location choice. Despite a wild animal's instinctive sense for danger, the wildebeest were oblivious to the trap into which they were being driven.

After a final push, coaxing the animals into their enclosure, Gerry sounded the siren and curtains appeared seemingly from nowhere, sealing off the entrance. The helicopter continued to drive the group forwards, siren blasts at intervals indicating to the ground crew when to close off the next section. From the air we could see within minutes that the wildebeest had passed the last curtain before the entrance to the truck. Gerry circled the chopper and landed and by the time we reached the vehicle, the animals were safely onboard and simply required tranquillizing.

Two groups successfully contained, we only needed to herd one more today; after the slow start we had made good time.

'Jono, I need you on the suicide curtain for this final run,' Bjorn said to me while Gerry refuelled the chopper.

The suicide curtain was the final barrier at the entrance to the truck. It was aptly named. Situated at the narrowest point of the boma, the animals would stampede past just feet away from the curtain operator (or 'runner', as they are known) before being tightly confined once their escape route had been sealed off behind them. If they moved straight onto the truck then the danger to this person was minimal but if they stalled and started circling or turning back on themselves then the situation would be entirely different. The procedure required the runner's conviction that the curtain would hold firm and the animals would just see a barrier, making a charge unlikely – but being confined in a small space with a panicked herd of wild animals, a sheet of tarpaulin providing the only protection, would test the courage of even the bravest.

'Sure, I'd do that,' I casually replied to Bjorn, fuelled by the adrenalin surge of the morning's activities so far and trusting his professional judgement. If he felt confident having me on the suicide curtain then I felt confident I could do the job.

As Gerry took to the air again, I remained with the ground crew, each of us dispersing to our new stations. Fifty yards from the truck there was a slight slacking in the tarpaulin that provided a shortcut into the boma, allowing us to avoid the hike back to the main entrance or having to go through the truck. Ducking between the steel poles that anchored the sheets in place, I entered the boma and headed back towards the suicide curtain while the rest of the team moved along from the outside of the enclosure to their various posts.

My curtain was closed but not sealed, abandoned after the previous capture when the wildebeest were chased straight through and up the ramp into the track; the ideal scenario. As I reached the curtain I wondered if I would have the same luck, but nevertheless rehearsed what I needed to do to secure it shut and then drew it open again, checking it ran smoothly on its runners. Although I knew the funnelling system was designed to ensure the wildebeest would only make it back as far as the penultimate curtain if I didn't seal mine in time, I was nevertheless nervous.

Happy all my equipment was functioning, I concealed myself behind the crumpled tarpaulin. I had a vivid flashback to childhood days playing hide and seek at my grandparents' house. Just as then, I knew I had to keep quiet and wait. Gerry had already been gone about five minutes and although I was confident in his ability to gather another group quickly from those we had left at the watering hole, my lack of communication with either him or Bjorn meant my first indication of their arrival would be the siren – and there was no knowing whether that would be in ten minutes or two hours.

The waiting allowed my mind to wander, imagining all the potential hazards that surrounded us. That was the downside, but it had its benefits too; it was a rare opportunity to stop and appreciate the nature we were immersed in. As I waited now, I watched a glossy starling dipping into the boma before quickly flying away, finding nothing to scavenge. A small army of ants busied themselves in the dirt, retrieving leaf fragments or twigs ten times their size. A dung beetle, just feet away from me, crawled past, making for one of the piles of droppings left by the previous group.

Still I waited. I tested the smooth-running of the curtain again in a vain attempt to distract myself. I could see a couple of people poised at the next one, not daring to move, expecting the animals' arrival at any moment. Then, with its piercing blast, the siren sounded and the beasts were nearly here! I pressed myself against the tarpaulin wall, huddling behind my curtain, gripping it tightly as I readied myself for the imminent stampede. The siren sounded again and then, moments later, for a third time; the animals were close. My heart raced. I felt the ground start to vibrate and peered out from my cover to see the approaching dust cloud. The siren sounded for a fourth time and the animals galloped past, just feet away from me, the noise deafening, the dirt engulfing. The blurring of tails and heads as the beasts thundered by made it impossible to count their number, but I could see a growing mass of horns as they gathered between the truck and the suicide curtain.

The first few wildebeest had abruptly halted at the truck's ramp; they weren't going to load themselves without encouragement and in a few moments they would start turning back. I needed to close the curtain to contain them, but I had to wait until the last one had passed me. I tentatively peered out from my hiding place; the last few animals were just feet away from crossing the threshold into my zone but had been slowed to a trot by the obstruction ahead of them; my window of opportunity was rapidly closing.

Luckily, the last animal crossed over before the message to retreat had filtered through to the rest of the herd. Seizing my chance I sprinted, pulling the curtain across the enclosure to seal the escape route. Reaching the far side, I secured the canvas with heavy-duty pins. The wildebeest were contained so I had achieved my objective, but turning around to survey the scene there was little comfort to be gained from my triumph; the herd too were aware of the situation. Moving away from the truck towards their path into the enclosure, they were confronted with yet another barrier: me. Sensing a threat, some scraped the ground with their forefeet as though to charge, in the same menacing way they would ward off an attack from a predator. I was suddenly grateful to be facing wildebeest and not buffalo, which would attack without hesitation. Nevertheless, the situation was intimidating. I tried to conceal myself against the canvas, hoping not to alarm them further.

Although giving me a wide birth, as the animals became increasingly agitated by their confinement and desperate to escape, they brushed up against the tarpaulin enclosure walls; if we didn't load them soon then undoubtedly destruction and escape would ensue. I was helpless on my own, but all I could do was wait for backup and in the meantime hope that the intermittent ground-pawing didn't turn into a charge by one of the more confident bulls.

It seemed an eternity before I heard the approach of Bjorn and Sydney at my curtain, though in reality it was only minutes.

'Jono, you there?' Bjorn whispered. 'Have any of them loaded?'

'No, they're just circling, suspicious of the ramp and truck,' I replied.

'I thought as much. Let us in; we've got a tarpaulin we can try to herd them with.'

I felt a huge burden lifted; I was no longer on my own. Tentatively, I unpinned the curtain, careful not to reveal a glimpse of freedom to the wildebeest. Bjorn and Sydney slipped through the narrow gap and moments later had unfurled a large sheet that they spread across the width of the enclosure. The animals reacted with a mixture of fear and aggression, some bunching even closer together, others half-heartedly charging the sheet, catching it with their horns and retreating at the resultant rustling sound.

Bjorn and Sydney took up position at either end of the tarpaulin while I supported it in the middle. Meanwhile, Derek and Dumison had arrived and were now clambering onto either side of the boma wall where it was reinforced. Slowly, with their encouragement, Bjorn, Sydney and I drove the animals forward with the tarpaulin, persuading them onto the truck. It was a huge relief a few minutes later to seal the vehicle doors, finally securing the herd. Job done!

I sat gazing out of the window as we journeyed home. We passed fields of sugar cane, orange groves and banana plantations, fence lines separating them from grazing antelope and zebras, and a small congress of baboons crossing the empty road ahead.

It had been an exhilarating day in the African bush – just another in a fun and varied career to date, and a long way from the dreams of an ambitious six-year-old. It was pretty hard to believe. What adventures lay ahead? With that thought I closed my eyes and drifted off to sleep.

# Wildebeest: fast facts

*Connochaetes taurinus*: The blue wildebeest

**Distribution:** Southern and eastern Africa. There are 5 subspecies.

**Names:** A male is called a 'bull', a female is a 'cow', and the young a 'calf'. A group of wildebeest is called a 'confusion'.

**Life span:** 20 years.

**Habitat:** Short-grass plains on the edge of bush-covered acacia savannahs, migrating to coincide with annual rainfall and grass-growing patterns.

**Diet:** Wildebeest are herbivorous grazers, primarily eating short grasses.

**Gestation:** 257 days, usually producing a single calf.

**Weight:** 20 kg at birth, reaching 260–290 kg as adults.

**Growth:** A newborn calf will stand within 15 minutes of being born and is capable of keeping up with the herd after a few days. They are weaned at about 4 months, but remain with their mother for the first year, at which point males will leave the herd to form a bachelor group. Females reach sexual maturity at about 2 years old and males between 3–4 years of age. Between 4–5 years of age the males will establish their own territory.

**Body temperature:** 38–39.2 °C.

**Facts:** They can reach speeds of up to 50 mph, making them one of the top ten fastest land animals. Calves are born within 2–3 weeks of the rainy season, which allows the lush grasses to provide nutritional support for a cow to feed her calf.

**Conservation:** In the Bible, humanity is given 'dominion over the fish of the sea, and over the birds of the heavens, and over every living thing that moves on the earth' (Genesis 1: 28). The *Oxford English Dictionary* defines 'dominion' as an authority to rule. But with that authority comes a responsibility. We all inherently crave leadership that is principled rather than exploitative, and the same should apply to humanity's relationship with nature.

The seventeenth-century poet John Donne famously claimed that 'No man is an island, entire of itself; every man is a piece of the continent, a part of the main. If a clod be washed away by the sea, Europe is the less, as well as if a promontory were, as well as if a manor of thy friend's or of thine own were: any man's death diminishes me, because I am involved in mankind, and therefore never send to know for whom the bell tolls; it tolls for thee.'

Maybe 'man' should be replaced with 'species' in this quotation, for when a species becomes extinct, life on earth as a whole, including humanity, is the worse off for it. An estimated 200 species are going extinct every single day, a rate that is a hundred times faster than what might be considered normal. John Donne's mourning bell should be ringing round the clock. In the last forty years the number of wild animals on the planet has halved. The majority of these species disappear unnoticed by most of the world, but you just have to consider the popularity of nature or wildlife documentaries, or of zoos and nature reserves, to realize how entwined humanity is with the natural world. The organization United for Wildlife has set out to unite the world's leading wildlife charities under a common purpose to create a global movement for change (see **www.unitedforwildlife.org**). What world do we want to leave to our children and our children's children? We each have a duty and a responsibility in caring for the natural world and we can each do something positive to conserve it. So what will you do?

# ACKNOWLEDGEMENTS

have already quoted John Donne's famous statement, 'No man is an island, entire of itself', and never is that more true than with this book. I have been incredibly privileged in the support, encouragement and help I have had in writing it, from friends, family and colleagues.

In truth I have felt for many years that I would one day like to write a book documenting some of the amazing experiences I have been fortunate enough to have, but I always envisaged that it would be many years away. It was thanks to the huge encouragement of Rachel Mills and her team at Furniss Lawton, and Clare Drysdale, Kate Ballard and their team at Allen and Unwin, that this dream could be realized at all, let alone on such an accelerated time frame.

But if it hadn't been for the support, help and inspiration I have received throughout my career to date, I would never have had any stories to tell and so these groups need to be mentioned. There are few bonds stronger than those made while enduring the highs and lows of a six-year veterinary course together; I want to thank those friends who did the journey with me and for their continued friendship and wisdom. Some of the most cherished memories of my career to date come from my first job at Charter Veterinary Group in North Devon, a wonderful team of people who helped grow my passion and love for the profession. Larkmead Veterinary Group in Oxfordshire was a wonderfully helpful work environment too. The team at Dragon Veterinary Centre, Cheltenham must deserve a special mention for being so incredibly supportive, encouraging and accommodating in allowing me the time to write. Clients also have been a great source of encouragement in their words of motivation or the enthusiasm with which they have spurred me on. The team at Wildlife Vets in South Africa have annually welcomed me with open arms, showing, teaching and allowing me to experience so much. My annual trips to South Africa truly are the fulfilment of a childhood dream. The team at Haifu Medical Technology, Chongqing, China, have been incredibly helpful and generous in supporting my VetLIFU work, in their incredible hospitality and in arranging my time at Chongqing Zoo. The team at Chongqing Zoo were incredibly welcoming and hospitable during my time with them.

These thanks so far have been professionally based – to colleagues, many of whom I now consider close friends – but wider thanks must go to a countless number of other friends, who have been so wonderfully supportive, encouraging, helpful, dependable and wise advisers. To name some would be to omit others, but I can't begin to express my gratitude to you all.

Most importantly I have to thank my wonderful family. My parents, who never doubted my desire and passion to pursue a career in veterinary medicine and who have been supportive, wise and encouraging, every step of the way. My three brothers, who demonstrate the very definition of brotherly love in their care, kindness, help, encouragement, affirmation and the fun and laughter we share. My sisters-in-law, who bring out the best in my brothers and too have been so incredibly supportive. My wider family, including my late grandparents and Laura's family, have all played a huge, influential and supportive role. My beautiful and wonderful wife Laura; my best friend, travelling companion, wise counsellor, challenger and promoter, who drives me to be the best person I can be and to be a fellow advocate of the animal kingdom for which we both share the same passion.

Finally, I want to thank God for his 'indescribable gift'. The greatest adventure in life is discovering your talents and using them to the glory of God. Thank you.

Jonathan Cranston
July 2018